Networking

BY EXAMPLE

A Division of Macmillan USA
201 West 103rd Street, Indianapolis, Indiana 46290

Barry Press

Marcia Press

Networking by Example

International Standard Book Number: 0-7897-2356-5

Library of Congress Catalog Card Number: 00-100688

Printed in the United States of America

First Printing: May 2000

02   01   00   4   3   2   1

Trademarks

Warning and Disclaimer

Publisher
Paul Boger

Acquisitions Editor
Gretchen Ganser

Development Editor
Maureen A. McDaniel

Technical Editor
Matt Keller

Managing Editor
Matt Purcell

Project Editor
Pamela Woolf

Copy Editor
Michael Dietsch

Indexer
Sheila Schroeder

Proofreader
Megan Wade

Team Coordinator
Cindy Teeters

Interior Designer
Karen Ruggles

Cover Designer
Duane Rader

Copywriter
Eric Borgert

Editorial Assistant
Angela Boley

Production
Ayanna Lacey

Mark Walchle

Contents at a Glance

Table of Contents

About the Authors

Barry Press has designed leading-edge computer hardware, software, and networks for over 25 years, including a unique cable television modem, campus-wide ATM networks, a desktop computer capable of analyzing adverse drug interactions, and an artificial intelligence planning system. He has programmed for Microsoft Windows since version 1.0 and has taught as an adjunct professor of computer science at the University of Southern California. He is the author of *PC Upgrade and Repair Bible* (now in the 3rd Edition) and *Teach Yourself PCs*.

Marcia Press worked in public accounting as a tax CPA for what was then one of the Big Eight, moving later to her own practice. She handles the administrative part of the work for the Press computer books—the tracking, calls, follow-ups, and research—and does the sanity checks on their initial drafts.

Dedication

Networking by Example is dedicated to the patient, inventive researchers and developers who persevered in creating the networking technology we now take for granted well before anyone even thought of personal computers. We all owe a big debt to people like Vinton Cerf, David Clark, Steve Crocker, Robert Kahn, Leonard Kleinrock, J.C.R. Licklider, Robert Metcalfe, Paul Mockapetris, Jon Postel, Lawrence Roberts, and many, many others.

And, of course, Al Gore.

Acknowledgments

We gratefully acknowledge the assistance of the following people and companies in the development of this book:

3Com Corporation, Actiontec Electronics, Advanced Micro Devices Incorporated, George Alfs, Belkin Components, Bill Bruggemeier, Brett Combs, Compaq Corporation, Compatible Systems Incorporated, Delphine Sofware International, Evan Deneris, Michael Dietsch, Drew Dutton, Eastman Kodak Company, ESC Technologies, Fluke Corporation, Mickey Fuller, Gretchen Ganser, Gathering of Developers Incorporated, Glen Garcia, Holly Hagerman, Layne Heiney, Hewlett-Packard Company, id Software, Intel Corporation, Ipswitch Incorporated, Matt Keller, Julie Kuntz, Lexmark International Incorporated, Peggy Lohmann, Lovdahl Consulting Incorporated, Macsense Connectivity, Maureen McDaniel, Lori Mezoff, Microsoft Corporation, Network Appliance, John Nishikawa, Susan Opp, James Peters, Tara Poole, Drew Prairie, Katy Press, Jen Press, Jan Rasmussen, Maureen Robinson, Mandie Rowell, Joe Runde, Shandwick International, Sheila Schroeder, Sharon Sulse, Symantec Corporation, Terminal Reality, Sam Tingey, Adam Trunkey, TSI Communications, Manny Vara, Matt Wagner, Mike Wilson, Megan Wade, and Pamela Woolf.

We shot all the photographs in this book not credited to others with Kodak DC265 and DC290 digital cameras. When we started writing computer books, digital cameras weren't capable of publication-quality results. The tremendous advances in technology delivered by these cameras have completely eliminated the need to shoot film at all in our books, with no loss of quality in the published results. These are just amazing cameras.

Thanks to all of you.

Introduction

Networking by Example is a beginning-level guide to networks. You'll learn the latest technologies through clear explanations and concrete real-world examples. The book covers general networking concepts, connectivity, updating existing networks, and making the right decisions for new networks.

Coverage in *Networking by Example* focuses on what you need to know, both theory and practice, to work with networks in small businesses, homes, and home offices. You'll learn what networks can do for you, what the different kinds of networks are, how to choose your network technology and install the hardware, how to set up (and tame) the software, and how to use your network to enhance what your computers can do. You'll apply examples to improve how your network ties to the Internet, find bottlenecks and trouble spots in your network, and boost the performance you get.

By the time you're finished with *Networking by Example*, your network will be your ally. You'll be able to connect two or more computers with a local area network, connect that network to the Internet, set up and access services on the network, and share resources across the network. You'll also be able to troubleshoot problems in small networks and to identify and address bottlenecks limiting network performance.

Who Should Read This Book

We've written *Networking by Example* for people with little to no experience with computer networks, and with limited experience with computers themselves. If you can successfully frame a problem, learn concepts, and adapt directions to specific situations, you'll do fine. If you're a complete novice with computers, though, the first book you read should probably be one of these introductory computer titles:

- **The Unofficial Guide to PCs** by Lee Hudspeth, Dan Butler, and T. J. Lee (Que Corporation, ISBN 0-7897-1797-2, published July 1999)

- **The Complete Idiot's Guide to PCs, Seventh Edition** by Joe Kraynak (Que Corporation, ISBN 0-7897-2135-X, published October 1999)

You'll be working with computer hardware to build and enhance your network. You might not have to open up your computer, but even if you do you'll learn in this book that the operations involved are simple and straightforward, carried out with common tools. We've provided an overview of what's inside a computer in Chapter 6, "Picking and Installing Your LAN Adapters," including cases, power supplies, disks, and the electronics. For many people, Chapter 6 will be all the hardware instruction you need.

You can get as deep into the hardware as you want—you'll even learn how to make your own network cables in this book—but if you'd prefer the buy-it-and-snap-things-together approach, that's possible too.

The popularity of introductory computer book titles notwithstanding, we think people who read this book are likely to be perfectly capable and quite possibly highly skilled in other areas. What we expect you lack is specific knowledge, not basic intelligence. Our goal is to give you the instruction you need.

What's in *Networking by Example*

In some respects, we've written *Networking by Example* to be read from front to back. That's not to say you can't jump into the middle to get answers to specific questions—you can—but rather that we've organized the book so that the information you need to understand concepts anywhere in the book should always be available in some of the earlier chapters. That way, should you choose to read the book front to back, the concepts build on one another in a logical way.

Networking by Example consists of five parts:

- **Part I: Network Basics (Chapters 1–3).** This part covers the reasons you'd want to have a network, including the things a network can do for you, the different kinds of networks that exist, and the ways software works in networks.

- **Part II: Building Your Network (Chapters 4–6).** Networks are all about connecting computers together, so you'll need some additional hardware besides the computers themselves. Here, you'll learn how to choose, assemble, install, and configure your network hardware.

- **Part III: Setting Up Your Network Software (Chapters 7–10).** Hardware is what connects computers together, but software is what makes everything work. You'll learn in this part what the software components are in your network, where to get them, how to set them up, and how to configure each one.

- **Part IV: Using Your Network (Chapters 11–13).** Getting your network built and running is only the first step, even though it's likely to seem the hardest. After your network is complete, you'll learn how to exploit your network to save you time and money, and to make possible things you couldn't previously do.

- **Part V: Getting the Most From Your Network (Chapters 14–17).** Networks are no different from computers—after you've lived with one for a while, you might find you've outgrown what you have and need to speed it up, and might run into problems. In this part, you'll learn how to set up your network for high-speed Internet access, how to find slow spots in your network, how to redesign your network to eliminate the bottlenecks, and how to troubleshoot problems.

Throughout the book you'll find examples illustrating concepts and lessons. The examples in Part I show you how you might apply networks to specific situations; the examples in Parts II–V show you step-by-step how to accomplish specific tasks.

What's Required of Your Computer

The most humble computer—laptop or desktop—can benefit from being connected to a network, but the job of setting up your network will be easier if your computers were built within the past three or four years and run reasonably current operating systems. It's easier to add the hardware you need to connect a computer to the network if your computer supports PCI or USB (look in Chapter 6 for explanations of what those are).

Our experience is that the easiest systems to set up and configure networking software are those running Windows 95 or 98, followed in order of increasing complexity by Windows NT 4 and Windows 2000, and Linux. We expect readers of this book to run any or all of those operating systems, so we've included information and lessons covering how to work with all of them.

Although Linux can run acceptably on computers with an Intel 486 processor and limited memory, we suggest you use computers of at least the performance of an Intel Pentium running at 133MHz, having at least 32MB of memory, and having several hundred megabytes of free disk space after all your usual software is installed. Windows NT and 2000 have yet more aggressive hardware requirements; your best choice overall is for networked computers to have a faster processor and more memory than the minimum required to run the operating system and your application programs.

We're vitally interested in your experiences with this book and your suggestions for making it better. Your feedback to the Macmillan Web site at http://www.mcp.com will get to us.

Barry and Marcia Press
February 28, 2000

Part I

Network Basics

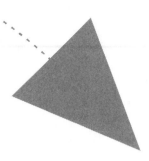

Why Have a Network?

In this chapter you will learn

- How networks extend what you can do with computers
- To build networks based on ideas you already understand

A simple network need be nothing more than two computers connected together so they can exchange information. Figure 1.1 shows the idea; when you build your network, you'll do little more than connect the computers you have to a special wire.

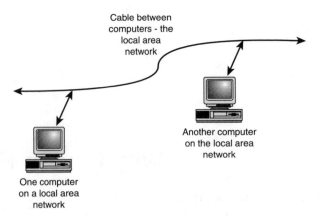

Cable between computers - the local area network

Another computer on the local area network

One computer on a local area network

Figure 1.1: *A network is simply computers connected by wires.*

You'll use some new cards, called *network adapters*, inside the computers, and you might use some other boxes along the wire, but the essence of a network is computers connected by wires. The connected computers can be in the same room, but can equally be in different buildings, different cities, or different countries. The U.S. National Aeronautics and Space Administration (NASA) has even used computer networks to communicate between computers on Earth and those on distant spacecraft.

As straightforward as this view of networks is, we expect to convince you by the time you finish reading this book that interconnected—or networked—computers are far more powerful than ones that stand alone and to show you how easy it is to tap into that power.

One of the first people credited with really understanding that a computer network itself has value beyond that of the individual computers was Bob Metcalfe, the inventor of the Ethernet local area network (LAN) technology and co-founder of the highly successful 3Com Corporation, who said:

> The power of the network increases exponentially by the number of computers connected to it. Therefore, every computer added to the network both uses it as a resource while adding resources in a spiral of increasing value and choice.

Metcalfe put three important ideas into that statement. First, he recognized that the power of a network grows rapidly as you add computers. You don't get twice the power when you double the number of computers; you get much more than that. Second, he realized that what computers add to networks are resources—processing power, storage, communications, information, and more. Those resources can be available to anyone on the network. Third, he pointed out that any given computer can both add resources to the network and access resources on other computers.

When you add your computer to a network, you both gain power and deliver increased power to the other users.

Figure 1.2 illustrates some of what Metcalfe said. If you focus on the computer in the middle, you'll see that it accesses information coming from the computer on the left and storage from the computer on the right. Less apparent is that the computer in the middle also provides services to the network, delivering information on what customers want and permitting fax access to those customers. Every computer in the network both gains by accessing other computers and serves by providing benefits to other computers.

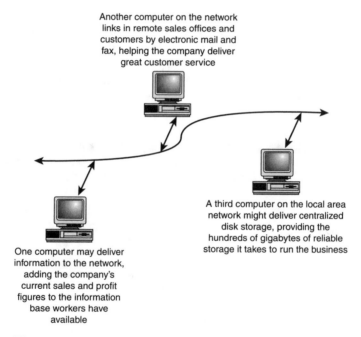

Figure 1.2: Network computers deliver and receive services.

With his three ideas, Metcalfe predicted today's office networks and the globe-spanning Internet, both of which so many people now rely on. Metcalfe was a little short on specifics, though; in practice, there's a wide variety of things local area networks will let you do, including file sharing, printer sharing, Internet access sharing, remote faxing, simplified backup, accessing shared equipment, and collaboration.

No matter how grand or complex Metcalfe's view of networks sounds, don't be intimidated by any of what networks do. The underpinnings of networks, like computers, are highly technical, but the scientists, engineers, and companies that make the network products you'll use strive to ensure that the complexity is hidden. Nothing you'll find in this book is any more complex than the basic things you do now with your computer; it's just different. Each of the network capabilities we describe in the following pages should convince you that this statement is true, because each one is, for all its power, no more than an extension of something you already do with your computer.

File Sharing

Every permanent bit of information you keep in your computer is stored in a file. No matter whether the information is a program or data, it resides in a file.

Just like in an office, where files are kept in filing cabinets at night when the lights are off, computer files reside on disks when the power is off. Figure 1.3 shows some of the files you'll find on a typical machine running Windows 98 Second Edition. Files all have names; filenames on Windows machines ending with .exe are programs, whereas most other files are data.

Figure 1.3: *Files on disk in Windows 98.*

Figure 1.3 shows files, whereas Figure 1.4 shows the files stored on the disks in the machine. The computer used for the figure has two floppy disks, three hard disks, and two CD-ROM drives, but its total storage is only a little over 4GB. You can see that by adding the Total Size figures for the local disks (C:, D:, and E:). If you total the Free Space numbers, you'll see there's only 2.9GB of local storage free.

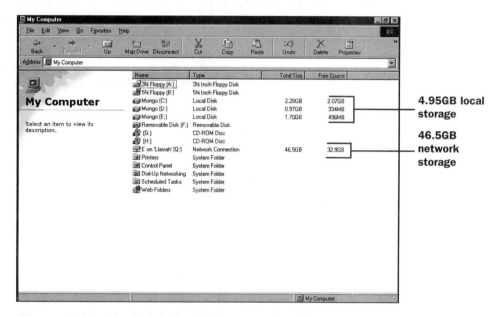

Figure 1.4: Disks in Windows 98.

Look a little farther down the figure, though, and you'll see why there's no need to worry about the machine running out of storage: It's connected over a LAN to a disk capable of holding a whopping 46.5GB! The LAN you build can do the same thing, connecting your computers to as much storage as you want.

As a user on the machine shown in the figure, you don't need to care where on the network all that extra storage is, just that it's there. Everything you can do on a local drive you can do on a network drive—copy, move, open, print, and delete. You can put both programs and data on the network drive. If your network's fast enough (you'll learn how to boost speeds in Chapter 16, "Enhancing Your Network"), you won't even see a difference in performance.

Better yet, if you have more than one computer connecting into the network drive, all the people connecting to it see the same files. That's much better than distributing copies of files to everyone who needs access, because if everyone used copies of the files (even if they contain the same data), they would find it more difficult to share work. We'll explain that more in the section "Collaboration" later in this chapter.

Network file access is easy to set up, too. Linux users will have to work harder than Windows users (who can share disks and files on a network in no more than a handful of mouse clicks). Whichever operating system you use, though, all the software you need comes right in the operating system package.

Printer Sharing

A general rule you'll learn in this book is that you can make anything on one computer accessible from other ones. Printers are a great example of how that works.

If you have several machines without a network, you have three options for what to do when you want to print:

- Buy a printer for every machine you have
- Physically move a printer from one machine to the next when it's time to print
- Put files on disks and carry the data to the machine with the printer

None of these is a good answer at all. Buying a lot of printers is expensive; moving printers often is a good way to damage the printers or computers; and moving files on disk requires either that the files are small (so they all fit on floppy disk) or that every computer have a high-capacity removable disk.

A better answer is what we've shown in Figure 1.5, where we've used the Windows Explorer to look at the Printers folder on the same computer we discussed earlier. The figure shows two printers: a Hewlett-Packard (HP) DeskJet 970C inkjet printer, and an HP LaserJet 6L laser printer.

What makes Figure 1.5 interesting is that neither printer is attached to the local machine; both are at remote locations across a LAN. One is attached to the network through a second computer, whereas the other is attached through a specialized print server box.

No matter whether you're in an office or at home, networked printer access is the right answer when you have more than one computer. You can put printers where they're most used, and yet access them from anywhere. There's no problem with lost or damaged cables from moving printers, no problem finding a place to put the printer when you move it, and no problem of discovering the software you need isn't installed on the other machine when you go to transfer a file by disk.

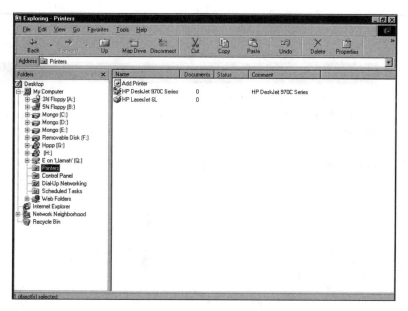

Figure 1.5: *Windows 98 printers.*

Because the total number of printers can be fewer, you can afford to get better equipment when you use shared printers. That's what we did in Figure 1.5 by connecting a faster black-and-white laser plus a color inkjet. If each computer gets its own printer, you're pretty much forced to get a general-purpose unit everywhere. If you can share printers, though, you can have a mix, choosing among black-and-white laser printers, general-purpose inkjets, high-quality color lasers, and photo-quality color. Your printer budget might not be high enough that you can afford all those kinds, and you may not need them all. The point is that, when you network printers, you gain options. You're not constrained by artificial limits on what devices are connected where.

Setting up a shared printer is a little more complex than setting up file sharing, but not much. The only complication is that you have to install the printer software on every machine that will use the shared printer. That's no harder than if you installed the printer locally on each machine, so you can be confident you can do everything that's required. You'll learn how to set up shared printers in Chapter 11, "Sharing Printers and Fax."

Printers do have two characteristics that make them more complicated to network than disks: They can run out of paper and ink and can at times experience paper jams. Most home and small-office printers are designed to be used with a direct connection to one computer, so their software often doesn't support remote notification that there's a problem. More expensive printers designed for great network support include the software you need to watch for problems from a remote, networked computer, saving you a trip over to the printer to check its status.

Internet Access Sharing

As powerful and wonderful as the Internet is, connecting to the Internet can be hard with even one computer. You have to set up an account with an Internet service provider (ISP), put a modem in your computer, connect your modem to a phone line, dial the ISP, and make all the software connect. Figure 1.6 shows all those steps, all of which are required before you can actually communicate with computers out on the Internet.

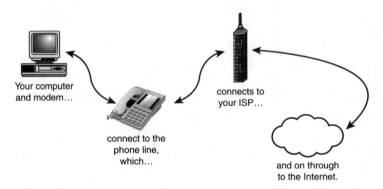

Figure 1.6: *Single computer Internet connection.*

You have two options for making two or more computers connect through to the Internet at the same time. One option is to have two (or more) modems, phone lines, and ISP accounts. That adds costs every month and increases costs every time you add a computer. The other option, shown in Figure 1.7, is to use your local area network to connect multiple computers through the one with the modem and phone line connection. All your computers can still get to the Internet, but they share the modem and connection.

You need a little extra software on the computer with the modem to let the LAN computers connect through to the Internet. We'll show you in Chapter 12, "Sharing an Internet Connection," that you can get the necessary software free with Linux or Windows 98 Second Edition, or you can get it inexpensively for use with Windows 95 or the original version of Windows 98.

After you do the necessary setup, everything else is painless and automatic. When any of the computers want access to the Internet, the messages go to the modem computer, the modem dials and connects if necessary, and the messages flow on to the ISP and the Internet. Return messages retrace the same path, back through the modem computer and out on the LAN to their destination. There are a lot of computers in the path, but they're mostly invisible.

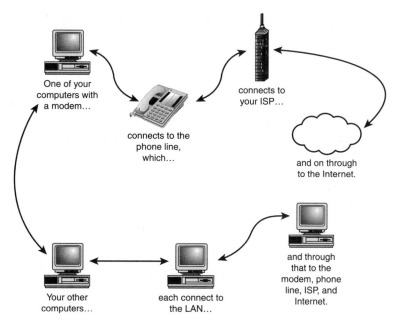

One of your computers with a modem...

connects to the phone line, which...

connects to your ISP...

and on through to the Internet.

and through that to the modem, phone line, ISP, and Internet.

Your other computers...

each connect to the LAN...

Figure 1.7: *Multiple computer Internet connection.*

You'll see that last point in action throughout this book, and it's the underlying source of the power in networks. When you network computers together, it rarely matters (and is rarely apparent) how many computers are between you and the computer you want to talk to. The network itself hides all the necessary connections, much as the U.S. Postal Service or Federal Express hides all the separate truck and airplane journeys required to ship a package from one place to another.

Collaboration

There are things you can do with a network that are (at best) hard to do without one, all of which you can describe as communication or collaboration between people. For example, computer networks let you do the following:

- **Plan and schedule meetings.** We've all fumbled around trying to find appointment or meeting times that fit everyone's schedule—you just can't solve the problem without access to each person's calendar. Using calendar software that collaborates with other people's computers across the network, you can find out what the common open times are. You still might choose to call the meeting when some of the participants have a conflict, but you'll do so knowing that in advance.

- **Cooperate on projects.** Working with other people requires not only a plan for dividing up the effort, but also a way to coordinate while you're working and a means to combine the separate efforts when you're finished. Even if the work itself happens outside your computer (such as painting houses or landscaping parks), keeping the work plan in shared files on a network where everyone can check and update the status makes the coordination job easier. If the work itself is on the computers too, such as different chapters of a book being written by different authors, shared access lets everyone check results as the work progresses and makes it easier to combine the individual products into a whole one.

Figure 1.8 shows how easy sharing files can be in practice. We've shown the draft version of this chapter opened in Windows WordPad; you can tell it's a file shared across the network by examining the File, Open dialog box. The file resides on another computer ("llamah"), accessible from the computer in the screen shot through a shared network drive. Used this way, everyone can access the same file, ensuring changes and comments are visible to everyone working on the file.

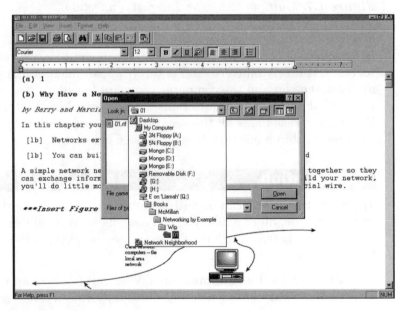

Figure 1.8: *Opening a shared file.*

- **Talk over telephone or videoconference.** Computer and telephone networks have far more in common than you might expect. You can see how much they have in common, for example, when you consider that (for most people) your computer makes a voice telephone call to connect to the Internet. The similarities work both ways—not only can the voice network carry computer data, data networks can carry live voice and video conversations. Using commonly available software and hardware, you can converse across your LAN with people in the next building or across the Internet with people across the globe.

- **Compete against your friends.** Chances are you've already played some of the amazing games computers make possible. Most computer games let you play against a computer opponent; the most interesting ones let you play the game against a human one. Whether you're playing Hearts, Backgammon, or the latest space combat simulator, computers provide rich simulated environments for games including Las Vegas casinos, fantasy worlds, children's books brought to life, and gritty combat zones, none of which you'll find quite so realistically portrayed in a board game. What computers don't do as well is play as your opponent—computers tend to be less inventive than people and tend to repeat moves and strategies. Play that same computer game against a live, human opponent across a network, though, and you're in for a deeper, more varied challenge. Play that same person on a network across a room, so you can see and scream at each other, and you're in for an intense free-for-all in which—as it should—the competition becomes the focus, not the computer.

Despite the many new network applications being invented, communicating, working, and playing with other people remains the number one reason people use computer networks, with electronic mail being the number one application. What might surprise you is that this has been true since the advent in the early 1970s of the systems that eventually became today's Internet. Not the World Wide Web, not electronic commerce, but electronic mail—arguably creating a revival of the old tradition of actually writing letters.

The computers you'll use on networks not only implement many of the well-known forms of communication, but they also enhance them. Letters became electronic mail, gaining rapid delivery and painless copying for multiple destinations in the process, along with repetition of the original message in replies to preserve context. Party-line telephones became text-based chat rooms, allowing wide-ranging connections and (for better or worse) faceless, anonymous presence. Public bulletin boards became "newsgroups," accessible worldwide and searchable for any content using freely available tools.

None of those enhancements were immediately obvious; they're the ideas of people who used the networks and invented new and better ideas. You'll do the same thing—when you start to *use* your network, versus *toy* with it, the way you use your computers will change.

Fax Sharing

Many people who've only used self-contained, standalone fax machines never think about how similar they are to computers. If you see only a fax machine, you see a place where your transmissions go in, a place where received pages come out, a place for blank paper, and a telephone line connection.

If you've thought about each of the individual functions in a fax machine— for example, if you've used a computer as a fax or considered how each of the fax functions could be done by a computer—you see something different when you look at a fax machine. Instead of an opaque box, you see a machine that combines a scanner, printer, and modem with some processing to control it all (see Figure 1.9). When you put pages into the scanner and process them, you convert the page to image data in the computer; the printer can reconstruct a printed page from the image data. What turns the assembly of scanner, printer, modem, and computer into a fax machine is software that can take image data, send it down the modem and telephone line, receive it on another computer, and dispatch the received image data to the printer on the distant machine.

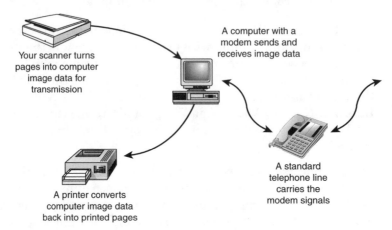

A computer with a modem sends and receives image data

Your scanner turns pages into computer image data for transmission

A printer converts computer image data back into printed pages

A standard telephone line carries the modem signals

Figure 1.9: *Fax machine functions by computer.*

You're not constrained to use a scanner to fax by computer; you can get software that makes the fax functions appear as a printer to other programs you run. With that software, you can print to the "fax machine" from any application on your computer and have the printed copy show up on a distant fax machine anywhere on Earth.

Because you can print to the fax software, you can set your network up so the "fax printer" is accessible across your local area network. Figure 1.10 shows the idea—the second computer we added to the drawing (on the left) is configured to connect to a fax printer located on the computer in the center of the drawing.

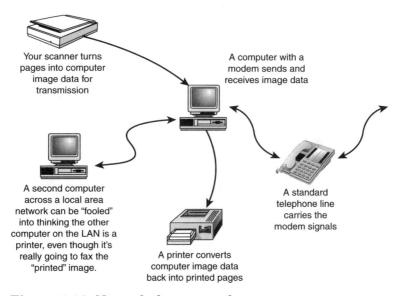

Your scanner turns pages into computer image data for transmission

A computer with a modem sends and receives image data

A second computer across a local area network can be "fooled" into thinking the other computer on the LAN is a printer, even though it's really going to fax the "printed" image.

A printer converts computer image data back into printed pages

A standard telephone line carries the modem signals

Figure 1.10: Networked computer fax access.

With a network fax setup, you can sit at any computer on the LAN, no matter where it is, print to the fax software, and have a fax transmitted. The machine you're using doesn't need a fax modem and doesn't need a telephone connection. All you need is a network connection and the right software.

Backup with Shared Tape Drives

The reason you fax across a network is because one machine on your network has to have a fax modem and software. Fax isn't the only service you can put on your network requiring specialized equipment or capabilities. For example, one of the most neglected operations on computers worldwide is backup—making a copy of the data on your disks you can use to recover from a crashed computer or a destroyed file. People neglect doing backups because, without the right equipment, they're tedious and time-consuming.

The key idea for backups is to create an *exact* duplicate of *all* the important files and store that copy in a safe place. It's unreliable to try and decide which files are important and really awkward to discover later that you goofed, so we recommend backing up *everything*.

When you decide to do backups, the problem you have to solve is to find a way to copy gigabytes of data onto a removable medium in a reasonable amount of time. Casual computer users might need to back up a few gigabytes, but businesses might have to back up *terabytes* (thousands of gigabytes). Backing up all our computers, for example, requires writing out substantially more than 200GB.

One of the best ways to do backups is to write the data out to tape. Even relatively inexpensive tape drives can hold 2–4GB on a single tape and write data at a rate of tens of megabytes per minute. More expensive drives are bigger and faster.

The problems with tape, if you have a lot of computers and a lot of data, are that the operation can take a lot of time and putting a tape drive on each machine can get expensive. (For example, if you're paying $200 per drive for each of 10 machines, you're out $2000 just for tape drives before you even buy the tapes themselves.)

Your network will rescue you from this problem, too, because it will let you share a single tape drive among all the machines you have. The key to sharing a tape drive is that a backup is a copy of the *files* on your computer, and the network lets you share, move, or copy files from one machine to another.

Figure 1.11 shows how a network backup works. Suppose, for example, that you want to back up all the files on the left-hand computer to the tape drive connected to the right-hand computer. All you have to do is, from the computer on the right, share the disk of the computer on the left. You now have access to all the files on that disk, so when you run your backup software you can write them all out to the tape drive.

By sharing disks and writing files to tape, you eliminate the need to buy a drive for each computer. Much as sharing printers might make it possible to have more types of (or better) printers, sharing a tape drive might let you buy a faster, higher-capacity drive that will shorten backup times and reduce the number of times you have to change tapes.

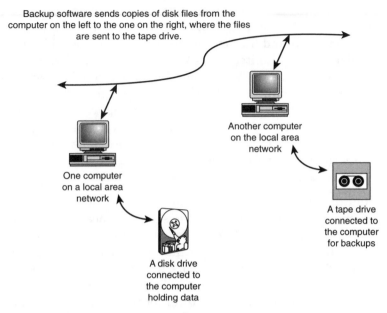

Backup software sends copies of disk files from the computer on the left to the one on the right, where the files are sent to the tape drive.

Another computer on the local area network

One computer on a local area network

A tape drive connected to the computer for backups

A disk drive connected to the computer holding data

Figure 1.11: *Networked backup.*

Sharing CDR or Zip/Jaz Drives and Moving Files

So far, we've presented networks as a way to share resources over distance. File sharing lets you get at remote disks, printer sharing accesses remote printers, and backing up files over a network shares remote tape drive.

Another way to think about networks, though, is as a way to move information rather than things. File sharing moves data rather than disks (you could physically transport the disk), and so on. We mention this other viewpoint because sometimes moving information *is* the problem you have to solve; you might have a report or presentation in one place but need to work on it in another. If you have that problem, you can do one of two things:

- **Physically move the data.** If you don't have a network, writing your files onto disk and carrying the disk from place to place could be your only option. (Picture people carrying disks from place to place and you'll see why this approach is commonly called *sneakernet*.)

- **Ship the data electronically across your network.** Using file sharing, email, or file transfer, you can simply copy files from one computer to another elsewhere on the network.

The first way to move copies of your data, writing the files to removable disk, worked fairly well years ago when most people's work on computers was only text and file sizes were small. People would commonly write files to floppy disk—limited to 1.44MB in most cases—and carry the files with them. Even today, newer removable disk technology such as writable CD-ROM (holding 650MB) or the Iomega Zip and Jaz drives (holding 200MB and 1GB, respectively) has kept up with increased file sizes driven by more capable software and widespread use of graphics. It takes a relatively long time to write a recordable CD-ROM, though, and although essentially every computer can read a CD-ROM, the Zip, Jaz, and similar drives are nowhere near universally available.

Your network creates an alternative to carrying disks around, one not bound by arbitrary limits on file size, distance between computers, or availability of specialized disk hardware. You simply send the file from one computer to the other and you're finished. The time to transfer files across a network depends on the network speed, so you can expect transfer times to be shorter on the higher-speed local area nets than over the Internet. Nevertheless, even over the Internet file-transfer times are likely to be less than if you have to write a disk and mail it to a distant city.

Summary

Even though the technology and programs you'll use with your network are nearly the same as the ones you use on a standalone computer, the results are not. The power to reach out from your computer to other machines isn't just an addition to what you already have, it's a distinct and more powerful way of using computers. Not more difficult, just different.

Think of this example to illustrate how compelling your network will eventually become. Both our children have used computers and networks for as long as they can remember. If we have network problems, both of them walk away as if the computer itself broke, because without the network their computers seem useless. Constrained to the capabilities of a standalone computer, they can't do what they want.

You'll come to feel the same way.

What's Next

Before you start building your network, you need to learn about the kinds of networks. In the next chapter, we'll help you to understand the different kinds of networks.

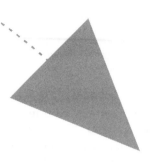

Kinds of Networks

In this chapter you will learn

- How networks differ relative to distance, technology, and software

- How to design your network to combine those factors to meet your needs

Just as different vehicles—cars, trucks, or buses—meet different requirements and serve different purposes, so do different kinds of networks. We'll show you in this chapter that the key differences among networks are the distance they span physically, the technology and hardware they use to make connections, and the software they use to transfer information. We'll also show you that you can choose characteristics in each of these categories to build the network that best meets your needs.

There's one other key characteristic of networks—the number of people directly connected to the network. We didn't call out that characteristic in the list earlier because it transcends all our categories. The number of directly connected people is affected by the distance spanned (because you have to come within reach to make a connection), by the network technology (because the data rate on the network can limit how many people can be supported effectively and some technologies inherently limit the number of connections), and by the software (because some network software supports large numbers of people better than others). We'll look at the connectivity each network option provides as we cover the details.

Once again, though, remember that for many applications, setting up a network is straightforward. If you have a small local area network (LAN), you'll undoubtedly use a technology called Ethernet, carrying signals over wires similar to telephone cable. If you're setting up a home network, you'll either use the same Ethernet technology as in an office, or you'll use Ethernet technology carried literally over the telephone wires you already have. Both networks will likely connect to the Internet over standard telephone lines—a metropolitan area technology—or some newer, faster telephone technology.

The rest of the network applications, such as wireless connections that allow you to roam around or the high-speed, globe-spanning connections that bind the Internet together, are relatively specialized, meaning you normally don't have to worry about how to set them up, or (like the Internet backbone) they are taken care of by others with the necessary skill and training. We'll cover those kinds of networks in this chapter, but keep in mind that you can set up and use large, powerful networks without ever having to confront anything but the basic technologies.

Distance

The first way we'll categorize networks is by the distance they span. People commonly use three categories: local area networks (LANs), metropolitan area networks (MANs), and wide area networks (WANs). The underlying technology overlaps among the three network categories; because the technology is what typically determines the maximum span of a network, there's overlap among the categories. LANs and MANs both use wireless links, MANs and WANs both use telephone trunks, and all three use fiber-optic lines.

Local Area Networks

LANs are the smallest networks, ranging from a few feet to a few miles. With the exception of otherwise standalone computers that dial up to the Internet, all networked computers connect to LANs.

Although LANs are limited to a span of a few miles, with most being well under that, LAN technologies are available to connect from a few to thousands of computers to a single LAN. The cost of the technology you'll need goes up when you connect a lot of computers, because the total transmission capacity you need goes up, but (as we'll show you in Chapter 16, "Enhancing Your Network") you can build a very large, high-performance LAN without having to do anything too exotic.

TOPOLOGY

Figure 2.1 shows the defining characteristic of nearly all local area networks, which is that when one computer transmits, all the other computers on the LAN can receive the transmission. This characteristic is called *broadcasting*. Most LANs use a single cable connected to all the computers on the LAN to carry signals, and require that only one computer transmit at a time.

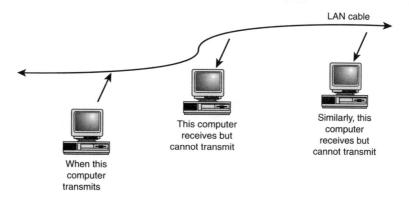

LAN cable

This computer
receives but
cannot transmit

Similarly, this
computer
receives but
cannot transmit

When this
computer
transmits

Figure 2.1: *One computer transmits at a time on shared media.*

If you think of the shared cable as one of the old-time telephone party lines, for example, you can see where the need for only one computer to talk at a time comes from. On a party line, and on a LAN, if two people (or computers) try to talk at once, what they say will mix together and be unintelligible.

People on a party line know to wait and listen for silence before starting to talk. Computers on LANs based on Ethernet use the same technique, only it's called *Carrier Sense Multiple Access / Collision Detect (CSMA / CD)*. The fancy name is simply computer jargon meaning "don't send when another computer is already sending (carrier sense), and check what you sent to see whether some other computer accidentally mangled it (collision detect)." You'll see in Chapter 15, "Evaluating Network Performance," that too great a load on a LAN increases the number of collisions and reduces performance.

Older networks in some businesses use a different approach to preventing collisions called *token passing*. LANs based on token passing are typically called *token rings*. Figure 2.2 shows how a token-ring network differs from Ethernet. Instead of being connected to a cable with no loops, computers on a token ring connect to a cable that makes exactly one loop past all the computers. Instead of listening for silence, computers on the ring transmit only when they hold a special message called the token.

The connection pattern of the cable among the computers determines the topology of the network. Ethernet LANs are required to have no loops in the cable, whereas token-ring LANs must have precisely one loop. In Chapter 4, "Picking Your LAN Cable Technology and Speed," we'll show you how that difference makes Ethernet easier to install and maintain.

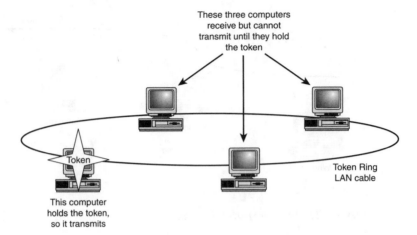

These three computers
receive but cannot
transmit until they hold
the token

Token

Token Ring
LAN cable

This computer
holds the token,
so it transmits

Figure 2.2: *Only the computer with the token transmits.*

DATA RATE

Networks are also characterized by the data rates they support. Network data transmission speeds are measured in bits per second, but most connections are fast enough that bigger units are used, as shown in Table 2.1.

Table 2.1: Transmission Data Rate Units

Abbreviation	Definition
Kbps	kilobits (1,000) per second
Mbps	megabits (1,000,000) per second
Gbps	gigabits (1,000,000,000) per second

Note that there's a difference between Kbps and KBps in that the latter means kilo*bytes* per second, so writing 10KBps means 80Kbps.

For a given data rate, the farther you send the data, the more expensive the data transmission equipment. For example, it's very easy and inexpensive to send data at 10Mbps across a LAN, but quite expensive to send the same data at 10Mbps across a city or country. LAN data rates are, therefore, usually higher than MAN or WAN data rates. Common LAN data rates are 1Mbps, 10Mbps, 100Mbps, and 1Gbps.

These data rates, 1Mbps to 1Gbps, are the *signaling* rates, which are the rates at which bits actually flow onto and off of the LAN cable. The net data rate you see moving files or messages across the LAN will be lower because of the time needed to see if the cable is free and to recover from collisions. In many cases, you can achieve a net rate that's 80% of the signaling rate. Table 2.2 uses the 80% figure to show the maximum net data rate you can expect for each of the common signaling rates.

Table 2.2: Net Data Rates

Signaling Rate	Maximum Net Data Rate
1Mbps	800Kbps or 100KBps
10Mbps	8Mbps or 1MBps
100Mbps	80Mbps or 10MBps
1Gbps	800Mbps or 100MBps

The actual maximum net data rate you'll achieve is strongly affected by the speed of the computers you have, the number of computers you have, and the distribution of traffic among those computers. The highest performance will be between two fast computers sending long messages; the lowest will be among many slow computers all sending very short messages.

TYPICAL TECHNOLOGIES

There's seemingly more short-range ways to connect computers than you can imagine, but they all end up using cables, radio (wireless), or fiber-optic transmission. By far the most prevalent are wired connections; wireless and fiber-optic setups tend to be more expensive and difficult to install.

The most common wired technology uses twisted pairs of copper wires bundled together in an outer sheath, much like common telephone cable. The connectors are similar to modular telephone jacks too, only larger. Figure 2.3 shows the rear panel of a typical network device using these connectors. The connectors you see in the figure labeled (from right to left) 1 through 8 are the network cable ports. Cables snap into the connectors exactly like telephone cables snap into wall jacks.

Figure 2.3: *Wired LAN technology using telephone connectors.*

Individual cable runs using the most common LAN technology are limited to 100 meters (including the cables from the computer to the wall), and don't work well when you need to walk around with the networked computer. When you need to roam around or to make longer connections, you'll turn to wireless technologies. (Fiber optics works for increased distances, too.) Figure 2.4 shows typical long-range wireless equipment. The vertical assembly at the left and the ridged plate on the top right are antennas; the box at the bottom right houses the radio electronics.

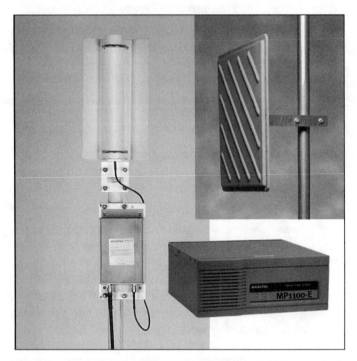

Figure 2.4: *Long-range wireless LAN technology (photos courtesy Solectec).*

You can extend a LAN several miles using either wireless or fiber-optic equipment. Wireless approaches can be affected by weather and buildings blocking the line of sight between antennas; fiber-optic cables have to be strung between the points on the network, which can be a problem if you don't own all the property in between or if there are intervening geographical obstructions such as cliffs, canyons, or rivers.

PROVIDERS AND PARTNERS

If you're using the common wired LAN technology, equipment from essentially all vendors works together, because the standards for wired Ethernets are very well defined. Eliminating vendor interoperability as an issue lets you concentrate on secondary factors when you pick equipment, such as reliability, price, availability, and features. You'll learn more about what to look for in Chapter 6, "Picking and Installing Your LAN Adapters," when we discuss choosing equipment manufacturers.

The standards for wireless and fiber-optic LAN equipment aren't as well defined, so you're better off getting all your equipment from the same manufacturer if you're using one of these technologies. The equipment is harder to work with and install, too, so you might want to consider enlisting a local company as your partner for installation, support, and maintenance.

Despite the increased installation complexity, fiber optics is an effective way to extend the reach of LANs. Using simple fiber-optic adapters, you can extend the reach of your LAN out to nearly two miles without the expense of MAN or WAN equipment.

KEY DESIGN CONSIDERATIONS

Surprisingly enough, the most important consideration when you're deciding how to build your LAN is time. You're likely to put the LAN cabling in walls, which makes it expensive to change after it's in. You can expect to live with the decisions you make now for a long time, so you'll want to make sure you think far enough ahead to put in adequate wiring. There's no shortage of companies now going through expensive upgrades, ripping out old wiring that's perfectly serviceable except that it can't support today's faster rates.

We'll cover this issue more in Chapter 4; overall though, you're pretty safe if you choose what's called *Category 5 unshielded twisted-pair* (or Cat-5) or better wiring.

Metropolitan Area Networks

Of the three categories of network (LAN, MAN, and WAN), you're least likely to have heard of MANs. Some sources don't recognize the MAN as a distinct category, lumping what we're calling MANs in with WANs. We've separated MANs out in this book because there are times when you need to span distances greater than LANs can handle, but don't need to span distances so great that you have to tie in to the complexities of WANs.

TOPOLOGY

The key difference between LANs and both MANs and WANs is the use of shared media in LANs, enabling many computers to attach to the same wire. MANs and WANs don't work that way. Instead, they typically use point-to-point connections with one computer at each end of the link (see Figure 2.5). The computers at the ends of the MAN link are also connected to LANs; through those computers, messages from computers anywhere on one LAN can be sent to computers anywhere on the other LAN in the figure.

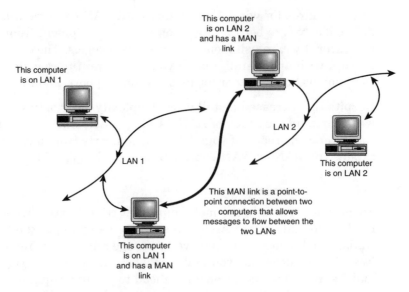

Figure 2.5: A MAN interconnecting two LANs.

People want their networks to be reliable, much as they expect telephone service to always work. Because of that, the computers connecting MAN or WAN links to LANs are rarely PCs or other computers people use. Instead, they're often specialized computers called *routers,* dedicated to communications work. Even if you don't have a router yourself, you use routers all the time when you connect to the Internet through your ISP.

DATA RATE

MANs use all sorts of different data rates, depending on the technology you're willing to pay for. Table 2.3 shows the range of data rates you can expect for common MAN technologies.

Table 2.3: Typical MAN Data Rates

Technology	Range of Data Rates
Telephone Company	10Kbps to 622Mbps
Fiber Optics	10Mbps to 100Mbps
Wireless	100Kbps to 50Mbps

TYPICAL TECHNOLOGIES

In addition to the telephone company technologies we'll discuss under WANs, there are fiber-optic and wireless MAN technologies you'll want to know about. The key distinction between these technologies and the WAN technologies is that, with a MAN, it's practical to consider implementing a private network.

For example, consider a MAN built by the school district in the city of Evanston, Wyoming. The costs to connect the telephone and data network systems at the schools in the district were relatively high in the mid-1990s, so the district analyzed the options it had for linking the schools with fiber optics. Figure 2.6 shows the general idea of what it did. By obtaining rights of way on telephone poles throughout the city, the school district was able to route cables with multiple fibers between the schools. Communications equipment far less expensive than required to meet telephone company interface standards terminated the fibers at each school, connecting the fibers to their LANs, private telephone switches, and other equipment. In the process, the school district reduced its communication costs and increased the speed at which it could transfer data between campuses.

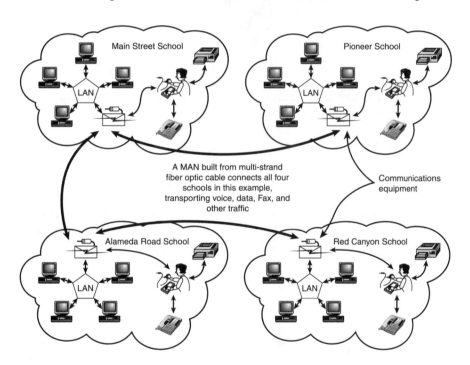

Figure 2.6: *A MAN interconnecting multiple sites for voice and data.*

Figure 2.7 is a typical example of hardware you could use to link two LANs together, a Belkin Model F5D134 Fiber Optic Transceiver. You connect your LAN to one side of the transceiver and a pair of fiber-optic cables to the other. Fibers are one-way connections, so you need a pair for two-way traffic. With a few hundred dollars worth of equipment, you can link sites over a mile apart at 10Mbps.

Figure 2.7: *Twisted-pair to fiber-optic transceiver (photo courtesy Belkin Components).*

You can also use wireless equipment related to what we showed in Figure 2.4 to construct a MAN link. Figure 2.8 shows the difference between the equipment in Figure 2.4 and what you'd use for a MAN. The left-hand diagram shows equipment suitable for a LAN. The antenna radiates in all directions, so computers are unrestricted in where they can move, but the range of the signal is shorter. The right-hand diagram shows a directional antenna, which focuses the signal and permits longer range or higher data rate. Only the computer in the antenna beam can connect to the network, though—the other three computers in the picture are disconnected from the network.

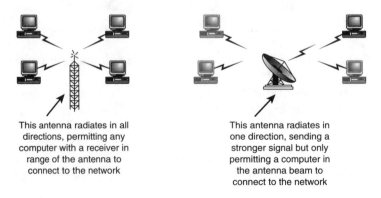

This antenna radiates in all directions, permitting any computer with a receiver in range of the antenna to connect to the network

This antenna radiates in one direction, sending a stronger signal but only permitting a computer in the antenna beam to connect to the network

Figure 2.8: *Wireless antenna patterns.*

PROVIDERS AND PARTNERS

We stated earlier that MANs can often use less expensive equipment than you'll need for WANs. One reason that's true is because, unlike the situation for WANs and LANs, manufacturers of MAN equipment tend to use their own proprietary standards. You shouldn't expect equipment from different vendors to interoperate.

Proprietary equipment locks you in to the equipment manufacturer for service and upgrades unless you're going to replace the entire MAN. Different manufacturers have varying track records for how long and how well they support their products, so if you'll be spending a significant amount of money, ask the manufacturer how long it'll guarantee support of the models you're buying, and ask for reference customers you can talk to about their service and support.

KEY DESIGN CONSIDERATIONS

The overriding design question for a MAN is determining how you'll get the connection from one end of each link to the other. If you lease a telephone line from a public or private communications company, physical routing of the cables becomes the company's problem. You don't have right-of-way problems if you use wireless equipment, but you'll have to be concerned about range; line-of-sight obstructions from buildings, trees, and hills; and reduced signal strength during rain and snow storms. Ask the company selling or installing the equipment how it's compensated for these effects. Better yet, get a written performance guarantee that covers those conditions.

Wide Area Networks

Everyone who connects to the Internet uses a WAN connection somewhere. The connection might be at the Internet service provider (ISP) or off a private LAN. Either way, user computers rarely connect directly to WANs; there's almost always an intervening LAN, and often a dial-up MAN connection, too.

Beyond their ability to span the globe, the dominating characteristic of WANs is that they all are built on a vast set of standards to which all connecting equipment must comply. The degree to which WANs incorporate standards, and the requirement that all connecting equipment meet those standards, both stem from the high cost of building WANs. The only way to cover the costs of stringing fiber-optic cable across countries and oceans, or of launching satellites and building the necessary Earth stations, is to share those costs among many network users. Because the networks are shared, all users have to follow the standards defining the network operation so everyone's traffic can be carried without interference.

In short, you have to play by the rules when it's not your own private network.

TOPOLOGY

WANs use point-to-point physical connections, just like most MANs, but with a twist. WAN technology usually derives from systems built by and for the telephone companies, which means WAN links are *trunks*—physical connections that carry many distinct data streams (see Figure 2.9). A device called a multiplexer combines the independent traffic from all the users sharing a fiber into a composite signal that can be broken apart at the other end of the fiber. Many individual fibers, wrapped by a sheath into a bundle, form a cable.

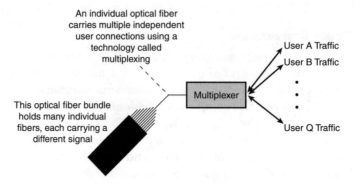

Figure 2.9: Trunking in WAN links.

An example of a multiplexer used in telephone company operations is the device that combines 24 separate phone calls into one high-rate signal that's then fed down a trunk called a *T1* circuit. You can't hear the other 23 calls in the T1 circuit when you're talking on the telephone, because your call is kept separate by the multiplexer.

DATA RATE

Let's digress a little from data networks to continue our example of the T1 circuit telephone companies use to send 24 individual calls down one set of wires. One telephone call requires a 64Kbps data rate. Multiplexing 24 calls together creates an aggregate data rate of over 1.5Mbps, which is the speed of the T1 line.

Economically, aggregating slower signals into faster ones is very nice for the telephone companies, because they can take the same wires that would normally carry a mere 64KBps, upgrade the electronics at both ends, and carry 1.5MBps. Because laying cables is the major expense in a WAN, not the electronics, boosting the speed while retaining the ability to dole out individual, slower lines to customers is a perfect approach. In practice, the telephone companies have trunks that run at 1.5Mbps, 45Mbps, 155Mbps, 622Mbps, 2.4Gbps, and faster. All of them can be multiplexed down to the slower trunk rates, such as a 45Mbps T3 line being multiplexed down to T1 or individual 64Kbps connections.

Returning to data networks, the telephone companies can provide you as much of their trunk connections as you're willing to pay for. Your communications computers feed data into the trunk through electronics called *Channel Service Units/Data Service Units (CSU/DSUs)*, which, for all the long name, are simply boxes that connect to the telephone company wires on one side and your equipment on the other.

Satellite links are also common for very long-range WAN links. A typical satellite link transmits tens of megabits per second; some are faster. The link connects two satellite Earth stations, which in turn connect to LANs, MANs, or other WAN links (see Figure 2.10).

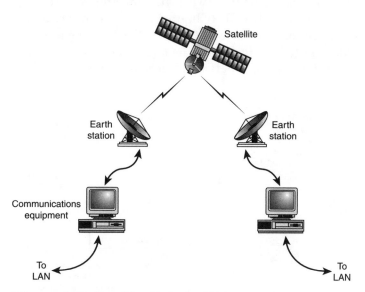

Figure 2.10: *Satellite links in WANs.*

TYPICAL TECHNOLOGIES

You'll find copper wires and fiber optics in essentially all WAN links you encounter, along with satellite radio links. WAN links using radio waves directly between two terrestrial sites are common, but you're not likely to receive a radio interface directly from the service provider.

The most common copper wire–based technologies are the T1 and T3 lines, running at 1.5Mbps and 45Mbps, respectively. Digital Subscriber Line (DSL) signals are eating away at the market for T1 service, because DSL is much less expensive. DSL availability is sparse, and service is often unavailable in what the telephone company claims are covered areas because there are limitations on the distance that DSL service can cover. DSL might also be unavailable on specific lines because of limitations on equipment in the line between you and the remote telephone company equipment.

There's no real correspondence between the telephone company standard line rates and the common LAN rates. You'll use specialized communications computers (called *routers*) to interface your LAN to the WAN connection; part of the work the router does is to select out the LAN traffic destined for the WAN and to match the otherwise dissimilar LAN and telephone company rates.

Figure 2.11 shows the most common hookup between your LAN and a T1 or T3 line. The equipment between the line and your router, although commonly called a CSU/DSU (Channel Service Unit/Data Service Unit), is really two separate devices. One, the CSU, is like a modem—it converts digital data to the signals on the telephone company line. The other, the DSU, matches signals between the router and the CSU.

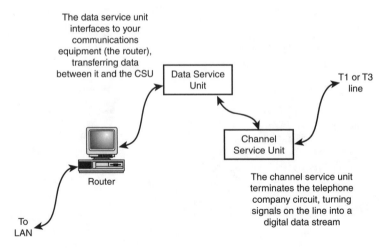

Figure 2.11: LAN connection to T1 and T3 lines.

Fiber-optic WAN circuits aren't terribly different in that they run at standard rates, have equipment analogous to CSU/DSUs to interface your computers to the line, and use multiplexing to combine independent data streams.

The individual terms and technologies are different, though. The most common WAN fiber-optic technology is SONET (Synchronous Optical Network). The most common SONET speeds at the customer interface are OC-3c (155MBps) and OC-12 (622Mbps), although even OC-192 (nearly 10Gbps) exists and is in use.

There are two common multiplexer technologies running on SONET. One is ATM, or Asynchronous Transfer Mode; the other is Frame Relay. Using either ATM or Frame Relay, you can install a line much faster than you need (for example, OC-3c SONET at 155Mbps) and pay for and use only what you need. When you need more bandwidth, you just renegotiate with the service provider. You don't have to remove the old line and install a new one until you run out of capacity. Even then, if you installed fiber, you might be able to just upgrade your electronics and continue using the same fiber.

PROVIDERS AND PARTNERS

A surprising number of companies own global cable and fiber-optic networks, including AT&T, the Baby Bell companies, Sprint, MCI, Cable and Wireless, and a number of others. Many service resellers base their networks on lines provided by these primary providers; examples include UUNET, Concentric, Electric Lightwave, and Qwest. Most of the time you won't need to contract directly with WAN providers; if you do, such as to provide very high-speed access for a LAN, consider having feeds from two or more so if one has network problems, you'll still be able to operate using service from the others.

KEY DESIGN CONSIDERATIONS

Because the telecommunications standards pretty much level the technical playing field, you'll pick a WAN provider and design your WAN access based on the rates you'll pay, the performance you'll get, and the reliability of the service you'll get. You'll want to investigate those characteristics when picking an Internet service provider too; generally you'll find that the ISP can't be any better than the underlying WAN service they use.

Technology and Wiring

The second common network categorization is by the transmission technology and the type of wiring used.

The network you'll build is likely to be a LAN, so that's what we'll focus on in this book. The first thing you'll do is plan and build your network. We'll start with the simplest possible network, a two-computer hookup using a simple cable, to explain the concepts. After we've presented the basic ideas and terminology, we'll move on to the most common network technology, Ethernet, and the less common telephone lines and wireless networks.

The key characteristics we'll examine are computer interface, connectors, couplers, and tools; distances supported; data rates; reliability; and cost.

Direct Cable Connection

The simplest network is one made up of two connected computers. The simplest connection between two computers is a cable that joins serial ports from the two computers together, a technique we'll call *direct cable connection*. There are other, more complex ways to connect two computers together; this approach is simple in that it uses hardware already part of the computers, requiring only an inexpensive, readily available cable.

COMPUTER INTERFACE, COUPLERS, CONNECTORS, AND TOOLS

Figure 2.12 shows the wiring for a direct cable connection using serial ports. On either computer, the serial port converts bytes to individual bits and sends them out the transmitter. The signal for each bit travels across the cable to the receiver, which forwards it to the receive side of the serial port for conversion back to bytes.

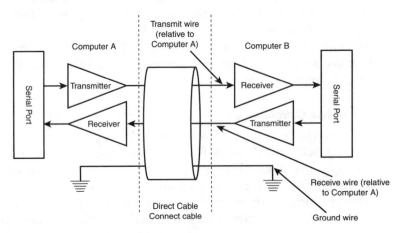

Figure 2.12: *Direct cable connect wiring.*

We've described the wiring of this network connection because, by knowing the wiring and signaling, you can understand the limitations of this technology.

The presence of distinct wires for transmit and receive signals makes it possible for the two computers to transmit simultaneously, which is called *full-duplex* operation. Other network technologies (such as some versions of Ethernet we'll describe in just a few pages) use the same wire for both transmit and receive, so only one computer can talk at a time. (As you might expect, single-wire systems use *half-duplex* operation.)

Figure 2.12 shows all the parts you need to make a direct cable connection, but in practice you might not be able to easily get a cable that connects the transmit lines on one computer to the receive lines on the other. In that case, you'll use a coupler called a *null modem* that swaps the signals, converting a transmit-transmit and receive-receive connection to a pair of transmit-receive lines. You'll learn how to build a null modem cable in Chapter 4.

Serial-port direct cable connections use standard serial-port connectors, which are most often the 9-pin D connector you see in Figure 2.13. Key elements of the figure include the outer shell, which protects the pins, the pins themselves, and the threaded studs for retention screws that you'll find on the mating connector.

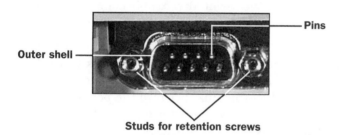

Figure 2.13: *Standard serial port connector.*

Serial-port connectors used to have 25 pins, most of which were unused. The newer 9-pin version eliminates most of the unused pins; signals in the connector—in addition to transmit, receive, and ground—include "handshaking" signals used to tell the transmitting computer when to start or stop sending based on how busy the receiver is.

You can't plug 9- and 25-pin connectors together directly, but you can convert 9- and 25-pin connectors using adapters readily available at stores such as Radio Shack and CompUSA, or on the Internet from sites such as Cables N Mor (http://cablesnmor.com).

DISTANCE

Another key characteristic of the serial-port direct cable connection is the seemingly innocuous ground wire. Every electrical circuit requires two wires; for computer signals, the two wires are the signal wire (transmit and receive, here) and ground. The transmit and receive signals share the same ground wire in a direct connect cable, which makes the signals vulnerable to noise and other problems. The noise increases for longer cables, eventually causing errors in the received data. The maximum usable cable length has to be less than the length at which data errors become noticeable.

The maximum cable length you can use reliably depends on the quality of the wire and the data rate you send over the wire. Higher-quality wire is built to resist the intrusion of noise and to degrade the signal less over long distances. Faster data rates give less time to each bit as it travels on the wire, so a noise pulse is more likely to corrupt the signal for the entire duration of the bit.

The noise vulnerabilities of direct cable network connections are such that you'd not want to run the cable more than 10–50 feet.

DATA RATES

Aside from the fact that it's difficult to connect more than two computers together, the weakest points of the serial direct cable connection approach are that it's slow and it presents a major load on your computer's processor.

The serial port chips in essentially all computers are limited to 115Kbps, about a tenth of what even the slowest of the other network technologies deliver. Keep in mind that rate is *bits per second*. You divide by 10 rather than 8 to get bytes per second on this link, because the port itself adds an extra bit at the start and stop of every character as part of transmission across the wire, so the port delivers only 11.5KBps.

The serial port chip has another problem—it requires attention from the processor every few characters. The chip *interrupts* the processor when it needs help, a process not unlike what happens when you're interrupted. The processor saves all its work, figures out what's going on, handles the request, and goes back to what it was doing. Because those interruptions happen at least several thousand times per second, the processor gets much less work done.

RELIABILITY

Direct cable connections are as reliable as your computer itself if you set them up correctly using good cables, because there are no electronics required to establish the network beyond what's already in your computer.

COST

The software you need comes with Windows, so the only cost you'll incur to set up a direct cable connect network is the cable itself. The cable you'll need is often sold as a *laplink* cable (named after the program that first made intercomputer serial data transfers common). You can get an eight-foot cable for $10 on the Internet (try http://cablesnmor.com).

EXAMPLE 2.1   WIRE A DIRECT CABLE CONNECT NETWORK

The most common, and best, application of a direct cable connect network is to tie a laptop computer to a desktop machine so you can move files back and forth. Follow these steps to get the parts you need and install the cable:

1. Look at the back of your laptop to verify you have an available serial port and to see what style of serial port connector the computer uses. Figure 2.14 shows the multitude of connectors on the back of a typical laptop computer. If you look at the leftmost connector, you'll see it's a 9-pin serial connector like that in Figure 2.13.

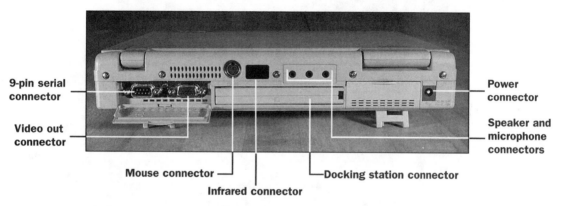

Figure 2.14: *Serial port connector on a laptop computer.*

Look carefully at the connector just to the right of the serial port (labeled video out connector in Figure 2.14). That connector has a similar size and shape, but has 15 sockets rather than nine pins. Be careful not to confuse the two.

2. Look at Figure 2.15, which shows the connectors on the back of a typical desktop computer. There are two serial-port connectors on this computer, about halfway down on the right. Because this computer has an internal modem and a separate mouse port, it's likely that both serial ports are available. Computers with external modems, or with older-style mice, can use one or both serial ports. You have to have a free serial port for a serial direct cable connect network.

3. Find a supplier and order the cable. Figure 2.16 shows a typical laplink cable. What's unique about the cable in the figure is that, in addition to having the wiring setup to connect to two computers, it has connectors for both 9- and 25-pin serial ports. The figure shows a total of four connectors—the two at the front are one end of the cable, whereas the two at the upper left are the other end. You only use one of each pair of connectors.

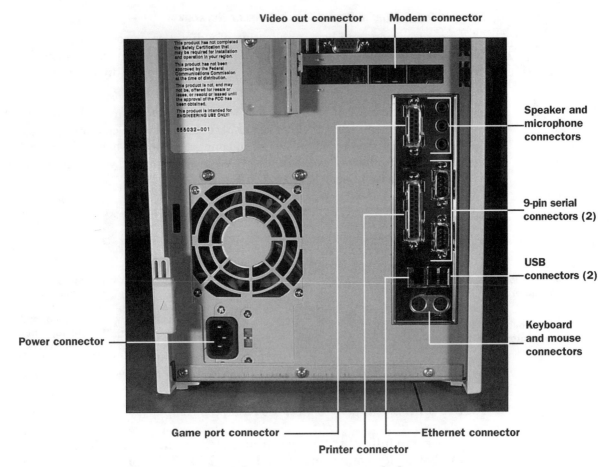

Figure 2.15: Serial port connectors on a desktop computer.

You can order a cable like the one in Figure 2.16 from Cables N Mor. Connect your computer to the Internet, and go to http:// cablesnmor.com. Use the search box to look up laplink. The product list resulting from your search should include a dual serial laplink cable—click that and you'll get to the page for part number P22312, which is an eight-foot version of the cable. Finish up the order and wait for delivery.

Alternatively, you can order a cable direct from Belkin at (800) 223-5546. Part number F3X171-10 is a 10-foot cable similar to what you see in Figure 2.16, whereas numbers F3B207-06 and F3B207-10 are 6- and 10-foot cables, respectively, with only 9-pin connectors at the ends.

4. After the cable arrives, there's nothing to finishing up the connection—just plug a connector from one end of the cable into one computer, and a connector from the other end into the other computer. You don't even

need to power down the computers first to connect and disconnect from serial ports, even though you *must* power down when you're changing printer, video, mouse, or keyboard connections.

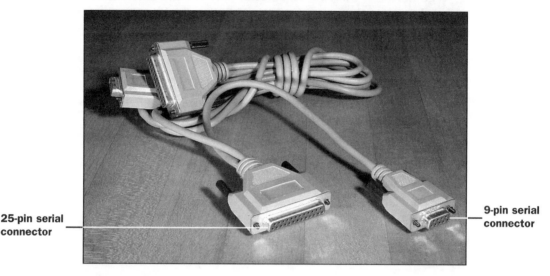

25-pin serial
connector

9-pin serial
connector

Figure 2.16: Laplink cable.

The serial direct cable connect network has all the pieces you'll find in any network setup and is very inexpensive, but it's slow and (unless you have lots of available serial ports) doesn't handle more than a few computers.

Ethernet

A more capable networking technology, the one used in nearly all computers connected to LANs, is Ethernet. You'll pay somewhat more to build an Ethernet LAN, although not much more if you're only connecting two computers, and you'll get far better performance over much longer distances.

You'll learn more about the details and construction of Ethernet cables in Chapter 4.

COMPUTER INTERFACE, COUPLERS, CONNECTORS, AND TOOLS

Two distinct Ethernet cabling schemes are used today. One uses coaxial cable, similar to the cable you use for television signals, whereas the other uses cable much like the familiar telephone twisted pairs. You won't want to actually use television or telephone cable, because their specifications aren't quite right for Ethernet—get cable designed for networks instead.

Figure 2.17 shows the wiring to attach one computer to an Ethernet based on coaxial cable. The cable itself is a signal wire surrounded by an insulator, which is in turn surrounded by a shield. The signal wire and shield together form the two-wire signal path for the entire network. The shield is analogous to the ground wire in the direct cable connect wiring; the transmitter and receiver in the computer connect to both the signal wire and the shield.

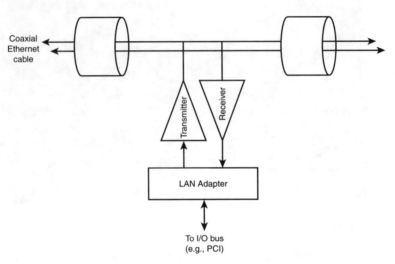

Figure 2.17: *Coaxial-cable Ethernet wiring.*

No matter which Ethernet technology you choose, you'll need what's called a *network adapter*, which is a card you put in your computer to interface between the computer and the network. The network adapter serves the same purpose as the serial port we talked about earlier but is much more tailored to the requirements of high-speed networks. The transmitter and receiver you see in Figure 2.17 are themselves on the same circuit card as the rest of the LAN adapter.

When a computer transmits on the coaxial cable, the resulting signal propagates both left and right, so it's heard by every other computer along the cable (including the transmitting computer). There's only one signal wire, so only one computer can transmit at a time (what you learned earlier to call half-duplex operation). When two computers transmit at once, a *collision* results, garbling the messages from both computers. Because the computers are listening while they send, they can detect the collision and retransmit a little later.

Figure 2.18 shows what Ethernet coaxial cable, called 10Base-2 wiring according to the IEEE standards, looks like. The coaxial cable itself, with what's called a BNC connector on the end, is on the left in the figure. You can't just connect the cable to the back of your computer, though; you need the other parts shown in the figure. The device in the middle is called a terminator; the one on the right is a tee connector.

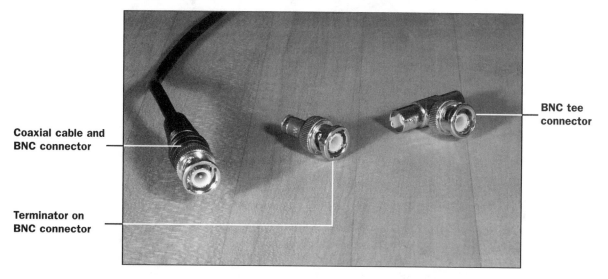

BNC tee
connector

Coaxial cable and
BNC connector

Terminator on
BNC connector

Figure 2.18: Coaxial cable and connectors.

EXAMPLE 2.2   WIRE A COMPUTER INTO A 10BASE-2 NETWORK

The steps to hook computers together with coaxial-cable wiring are quite straightforward. We're assuming here that you already have a 10Base-2 network adapter card installed in each computer; if not, you'll learn how to do that in Chapter 6. Follow these steps:

1. You'll need a tee connector (T connector) for each computer you're connecting to the network, along with a cable to go between each pair of computers. Figure 2.19 shows a typical setup for three computers, for which you need three tees (or Ts; either way is correct), two cables, and two terminators. You always connect the computers in a line, so you need two terminators no matter how many computers you hook up. Get cable, tees, and terminators intended for 10Base-2 networks. If you don't, you're likely to create noise on the network cable, possibly so much that the network will fail to operate.

2. Install a tee connector on the back of each network adapter card. The tee connectors slide on easily, with pins on the adapter-card connectors sliding into grooves on the tees. When the tee slides on all the way, turn the sleeve surrounding the adapter connector a quarter turn until it clicks, letting you know it's firmly attached. You should not have to force anything to make secure connections.

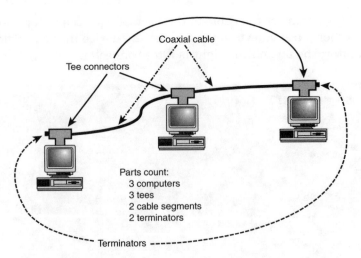

Figure 2.19: Counting parts for a 10Base-2 network.

3. Run the coaxial cable between the computers, attaching the connectors on the cable to the tees on the back of the computers. Turn the connector sleeves until they click on just like you did to attach the tees to the adapters.

4. After you've connected all the cables, you should have an open connection on the tees at the farthest ends of the cable. Put a terminator on each, and your network wiring is complete.

10Base-2 is the only network technology you'll find any more that uses terminators. You must not leave the terminators off the ends of the cable, though, because if you do the network is likely not to work, and (worse yet) might fail only intermittently. The problem is that signals aren't everywhere on the cable at once, even though they travel along the cable very quickly. When a signal hits an unterminated end of the cable, it reflects just like light in a mirror. If that happens, the reflected signal corrupts subsequent signals traveling down the wire, corrupting messages and making the network inoperative. Don't forget the terminators.

You can make your own 10Base-2 cables, buying bulk wire and screw-on or crimp-on BNC connectors. If you're experienced in stripping wire and attaching connectors for television coaxial cable, 10Base-2 should be no problem at all.

Although all the early Ethernets used coaxial cable, most LANs today use telephone-type wiring in what's called a 10Base-T or 100Base-T network. Figure 2.20 shows how the wiring works using two pairs of wires to each computer. One pair of wires goes to each transmitter and receiver, so there's no shared ground wire. The two pairs from each computer go to a port for that computer on the hub, where any transmitted signal is repeated out on the lines to the receivers.

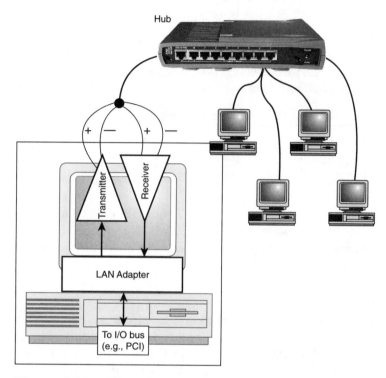

Figure 2.20: *10Base-T and 100Base-T Ethernet wiring.*

It's possible for two computers to send messages at the same time on any Ethernet. If that happens on the network in Figure 2.20, the hub detects the collision but passes the corrupted signals on to all the receivers. Most hubs report the collision by lighting an LED on the front of the hub.

You can get hubs with varying numbers of ports. The smallest ones are generally four ports; larger ones typically come with eight, 12, or 24 ports. You can connect hubs together using either special cables or a special port on one of the two connected hubs. All the hubs you connect that way act as one large hub. As you increase the number of ports (and therefore the overall network traffic on the hubs), you increase the likelihood of a collision. If your network gets so loaded that you're seeing frequent collisions, you'll want to upgrade to a higher-performance network using the examples in Chapter 16.

If you only have two 10Base-T or 100Base-T computers to network together, you can omit the hub and directly connect the two together with an inexpensive cable. You'll learn how to do that in Chapter 5, "Installing Your LAN Wiring."

You can use any of several kinds of wire building a twisted-pair Ethernet, as we've shown in Table 2.4. In the table, UTP stands for *Unshielded Twisted Pair*; whereas STP stands for *Shielded Twisted Pair*. STP wire degrades signals less over distances than UTP but is more expensive.

Table 2.4: Twisted-Pair Ethernet Wiring

Wire Type	Range of Data Rates
Category 3 UTP	10Mbps
Category 5 UTP	10–100Mbps
Category 5 STP	10–1000Mbps

Ethernets running at 1Gbps ("Gigabit Ethernet") do exist, as we've noted in Table 2.4 in the entry for Category 5 STP cable. Gigabit Ethernet is really designed for fiber-optic cables; you can only run very short cables using copper cable.

DISTANCE

IEEE (Institute of Electrical and Electronics Engineers) specification 802.3 defines 10Base-T networks, and includes the limitation that a cable can be no more than 100 meters (328 feet) long. That length includes the distance from the hub to the wall, up and down walls, and from walls to computers, so the linear distance between the computer and the hub is likely to be less.

The standard for 100Base-T networks is IEEE 802.3u. The maximum distance is also 100 meters.

10Base-2 networks can run up to 185 meters (607 feet).

You can extend a 10Base-T or 100Base-T network by connecting hubs together at a distance. You can connect up to four hubs together, so the absolute maximum cable distance would be 500 meters. Rather than extend the network with hubs, though, you'd want to use media converters (refer back to Figure 2.7) so you can take advantage of the distances over one mile (1,600 meters) possible with fiber-optic cable.

DATA RATES

Ethernets typically run at either 10Mbps or 100Mbps. You'll only get 10Mbps over coaxial cable; you can run either 10Mbps or 100Mbps over twisted-pair. You'll see up to about 8Mbps and 80Mbps, respectively, maximum net data rate.

Both 10Mbps and 100Mbps technologies are very common, so it's as important to understand how to mix the two rates as to pick the specific data rate you'll run. You'll find three types of devices:

- **10Base-T only.** Older and less expensive devices run only at 10Mbps. You can interconnect some 100Mbps devices with the older ones, but the faster devices will be constrained to run at the 10Mbps limit

- **100Base-T only.** Some of the early 100Mbps devices can only run at the faster rate. If you have any of those, be careful to connect them only to other 100MBps devices; connections to 10Mbps units won't work.

- **Mixed 10/100Base-T.** Most 100Mbps devices now being built can automatically sense the speed capability of the device at the other end of the cable, and run at either 10 or 100Mbps. The autosense devices will always pick the faster rate, if possible.

Unless you're on a rock-bottom budget, we recommend getting 10/100Base-T devices. As you use your network for more sophisticated purposes, you'll find your bandwidth requirements going up. If you've bought 100Mbps-capable equipment and cable everywhere you can afford it, you'll have less to replace when you want the added performance.

EXAMPLE

EXAMPLE 2.3   CHOOSE A COMBINATION OF 10BASE-T AND 100BASE-T EQUIPMENT

Example 2.3 shows you how you might make budget choices and still make upgrades easy. Follow these steps:

1. Count how many computers you'll be networking. If there are only two, use 100Base-T network adapter cards in both and use a *crossover cable* to connect them. You can skip the remaining steps (see Chapter 5 for how to make a crossover cable).

2. If you're networking three or more computers, you'll need a hub. For high-quality boards, there's little cost difference between 10Base-T and 100Base-T network adapters, so unless you're pushing down cost to the exclusion of all other factors, use 100Base-T network adapters.

3. If your budget permits an extra few hundred dollars cost, use a 10/100Base-T autosense hub. Otherwise, use one capable of only 10Mbps operation.

4. In all cases, use Category 5 UTP wire (there might not be any benefit from shielded twisted-pair and, if you don't get the shield connected properly, STP can actually degrade signals).

RELIABILITY

Twisted-pair Ethernet is more reliable than coaxial cable and overall is the most reliable LAN technology in use.

The key disadvantage of 10Base-2 (coaxial cable) Ethernet is that any problem along the cable is likely to take out the entire network, making troubleshooting difficult. Combined with a greater chance of individual failure (we've seen terminators broken by whacking them against the wall when pulling cable, tees broken by pushing computers too far back against the wall, cables pulled out of connectors, and other problems with 10Base-2), 10Base-2 Ethernets are less reliable and harder to live with.

Twisted-pair Ethernet has few or none of the problems of 10Base-2. A problem on a cable only takes out the computer the cable is connected to, making troubleshooting much simpler. The connectors are rugged and stay out of harm's way while plugged in. LEDs at either end of the cables, called *link lights*, help you troubleshoot because they go dark when there's a connection problem on the corresponding wire.

COST

As with a serial direct cable connect network, the software you need for an Ethernet network comes with Windows and, because Ethernet is very widespread, with Linux. The costs you'll incur to set up an Ethernet network are for the network adapters, cables, and hub. A number of computers are sold with built-in 10Base-T or 100Base-T Ethernet adapters, reducing the cost to complete the network.

Looking again at the Cables N Mor Web site, we found Category 5 cables from $2.50 for a three-foot cable to $30 for a 100-foot cable. We found a four-port 100Base-T (also called Fast Ethernet) hub made by 3Com for $88.95 on the Internet; we found a similar Intel product for $83.95. We also found 10Base-T network kits including network adapters, cables, and a hub in the same price range.

EXAMPLE 2.4   PLANNING AND COMPLETING AN ETHERNET INSTALLATION

There's no one application Ethernet does best, so here you get an overview of what you'll do to get your Ethernet network up and running. You'll start by planning what you need. Follow these steps:

1. Start by understanding what you expect to do with your network. You learned the basics of what you can do in Chapter 1, "Why Have a Network?"; you'll learn the details in Chapters 3, "Understanding and Evaluating Network Services," 11, "Sharing Printers and Fax," 12, "Sharing an Internet Connection," and 13, "Collaboration and Multiplayer LAN Games."

2. Identify the computers you'll have on your LAN, including ones you don't have yet but anticipate adding, and draw a map of where they are. Taking into account the walls and ceilings that you can use to hide cables, decide how many hubs you'll need and where you'll put the hubs. Remember that you're limited to 100-meter runs, including the patch cords from wall jacks to the hub and to the computer.

3. Count up the parts and supplies you'll need, including LAN adapters for your computers, cable, RJ-45 connectors if you're going to make your own cables, a connector crimping tool, and hubs. Depending on how you're going to run the wiring, you'll need wall plates and jacks, and might need conduit. (You'll learn about how to run LAN wires in Chapter 5.) Whether you make your own cables depends on the cable length and whether you're using conduit; if you're making relatively long runs or pulling wire through conduit, it's probably easier to put in the wire and install the connectors yourself.

4. Install the wiring, LAN adapters, and hubs.

5. Connect all the computers.

6. Configure your networking software. (You'll learn how to do that in Chapters 8, "Configuring Your System Software," and 9, "Sharing Fixed Drives and Setting Access Controls.")

Telephone Lines

There's another network use for home or business telephone wires besides calling your ISP: You can use your existing telephone wiring to interconnect the computers on your LAN. No pulling new wires through walls, no cutting holes, and a LAN drop most anywhere you'd want it.

COMPUTER INTERFACE, COUPLERS, CONNECTORS, AND TOOLS

The technology behind using your telephone lines for your LAN is similar to that used for high-speed DSL (Digital Subscriber Line) connections between you and an ISP. You can still use your telephone lines for voice calls while the LAN is in operation for exactly the same reason you can use the same line for voice and DSL. Figure 2.21 shows how the technology works: The telephone line network adapters use frequencies much higher than voice telephone calls. Because the voice and network services use disjointed parts of the frequency spectrum, and because there's a gap between the two that permits unwanted frequencies to be filtered out, your network operates without effect on normal voice service.

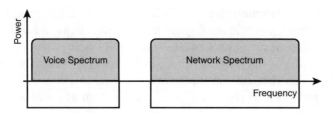

Figure 2.21: *Sharing spectrum to transport network data.*

Physically, telephone line networking technology plugs together and works like twisted-pair Ethernet in most respects. There's a network adapter card in each computer, with the functions shown in Figure 2.22. As with other Ethernet-style LANs, a transmitter and receiver connect to the LAN wiring. A pair of standard RJ-11 modular telephone jacks on the network adapter connect to the wall jack and provide line access for the telephone that would normally be plugged into the wall, although a local telephone is not required.

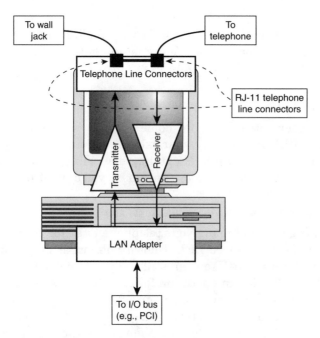

Figure 2.22: *Telephone line network computer interface.*

Telephone lines use two wires in homes and many small businesses, so the telephone line LAN operates half-duplex like a coaxial-cable Ethernet. Unlike the straight-line connections required for coaxial-cable Ethernet, though, telephone wires in the walls can connect almost randomly to jacks and computers (see Figure 2.23). You don't need a hub, either—the telephone wiring serves to connect all the computers on your LAN.

DISTANCE

Telephone line networks are normally rated for a maximum number of computers (typically 25, although performance is likely to suffer with that many computers active), not a maximum wiring distance. The technology is designed for use within homes and small businesses, however, so it's reasonable to expect that the maximum distance is limited to a single building.

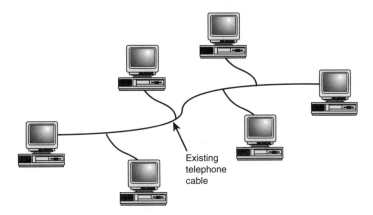

Existing telephone cable

Figure 2.23: Telephone wiring network connections.

DATA RATES

You can choose one of two data rates for telephone line network equipment—1Mbps or 10Mbps. You'll want to make sure all the equipment you get is the same, so that 10Mbps equipment isn't forced to slow down to a 1Mbps rate. The 1Mbps equipment is suitable for sharing Internet connections, printer sharing, and casual file transfers between machines; you'll want the newer 10Mbps technology for larger numbers of computers or if you're regularly sharing files among different computers.

RELIABILITY

You can expect telephone line networks to be more reliable than coaxial-cable Ethernets, but probably not as reliable as 10Base-T or 100Base-T systems. The use of standard RJ-11 modular jacks and wiring, rather than coaxial cable, tees, and terminators, means there are fewer things to go wrong, and fewer exposed parts to bang around. Telephone wiring is sometimes of poor quality or carelessly installed in buildings, though, which could lead to intermittent connections, which are difficult to troubleshoot. Telephone line networks lack hubs, too, which reduces cost and eliminates the need for all cables to go to a central place, but also eliminates the isolation of a failed computer the hub provides.

You'll have to live with a few restrictions to have a telephone line network operate properly. You can't use the system with a private branch exchange (PBX) telephone switch in an office, and can't use phone line surge suppressors on telephone lines connected to network adapters.

COST

Telephone line networks are remarkably inexpensive. You can get kits with two adapters and software for around $100. You can buy additional network adapters for around $50 as you need them. The adapters typically come with a patch cord to run from the computer to the wall jack, but any standard, inexpensive modular telephone cord will do.

Better yet, because telephone networks run on the existing telephone lines, there might well be no cost to install the network wiring.

Many companies offer telephone line network adapters and kits; if you ensure you get products compatible with the Home Phoneline Network Alliance (HPNA) standards, you can even buy products from multiple vendors with the expectation that the hardware will all work together. The software for telephone networking is less standardized, but you'll learn in Chapter 8 how to use Windows to solve that problem.

EXAMPLE

EXAMPLE 2.5   SHARING INTERNET ACCESS WITH A TELEPHONE-LINE NETWORK AND WINDOWS 98 SECOND EDITION

It's not accidental that telephone-line networks are defined by the Home Phoneline Network Alliance standards; the limit of 25 computers quickly excludes medium-to-larger businesses, making the likely sites for the technology homes, home business, and very small offices.

So far, the most attractive application for home application of telephone line networks has been shared Internet access. You saw what shared Internet access can do in Chapter 1 (look back to Figure 1.7, for example). We'll cover the details in Chapter 12, but there are only a few steps to go through using Windows 98 Second Edition to set up shared Internet access:

1. Purchase a telephone-line network adapter for each computer to be on the LAN. The computer with the shared modem requires telephone-line connections to both the modem and the network adapter. You don't have to use the same telephone line for the modem as for the network adapter.

2. Install an adapter in the computer with the shared modem. (The computer should previously have been configured for Internet access.) Power up the computer and install the software for the adapter.

3. Install Internet Connection Sharing (ICS) from Windows 98 Second Edition. When you configure ICS during the install, set the telephone-line network adapter as the network interface and the modem as the shared Internet modem.

4. Install an adapter in each computer to be on the LAN, and install the software for the adapter.

5. Installation should be complete; the computers should automatically see each other and should automatically have access through the modem to the Internet.

Wireless

The last common LAN technology is wireless, using infrared light or radio waves instead of wires or fiber optics to transport the network signals. You'll be limited to data rates in the 1–11Mbps range, but without wires you'll find it easier to accommodate mobile users and to put computers where wires are difficult to place.

COMPUTER INTERFACE, COUPLERS, CONNECTORS, AND TOOLS

After years of proprietary systems, wireless networks are converging to follow the IEEE 802.11 standard, which specifies half-duplex network operation using the same CSMA/CD technique we described for Ethernet LANs.

There are several options in the IEEE 802.11 standard, so you'll have to be careful when buying hardware to ensure that all of what you buy uses the same option (see Table 2.5).

Table 2.5: Wireless 802.11 Network Options

Technology	Modulation	Data Rates
Radio	Frequency Hop	1Mbps
	Direct-sequence	1, 2, 5.5, and 11Mbps
Infrared	Pulse Positioning	1 and 2Mbps

The Modulation column in Table 2.5 refers to the mechanism used to convert data from your computer to signals capable of wireless transmission. Both frequency hopping and direct sequence are types of *spread spectrum* modulation, which is a technique for spreading a signal out over a wide frequency range, both to permit multiple transmitters to operate at the same time and to help improve the system's noise resistance.

Even though frequency-hopping and direct-sequence modulation both use radio technology, the two modulations are absolutely incompatible. You won't be able to receive a frequency-hopped signal with a direct-sequence network adapter, and vice versa.

Faster wireless network adapters should be able to interoperate with slower ones using the same modulation. Check with the manufacturer to be sure.

There are two topologies you'll find in IEEE 802.11 wireless networks: ad hoc connections and *star-connected* configurations using an *access point* (see Figure 2.24). The ad hoc organization works well for all-wireless setups (and costs less); the access point organization is better when you want to use the wireless network as an extension of a wired LAN.

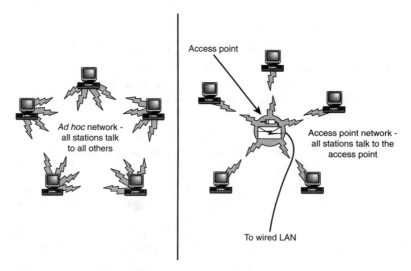

Figure 2.24: *Wireless network topologies.*

Some wireless LAN vendors also offer a third topology in which two stations operate in a point-to-point mode using directional antennas. You'd use point-to-point stations as a wireless bridge between two wired LANs when you can't run a wired connection.

DISTANCE

Infrared wireless LANs, which are intended for indoor use, are limited to operation over relatively short distances (a paper from IBM, for example, describes operation in a 30×30–foot room).

Radio-based IEEE 802.11 LANs work over longer ranges and are capable of outdoors operation. The distance you'll get depends on the data rate you run (slower rates go farther) and what's in the way of the signals, such as walls or trees and shrubbery. In general, you can expect ranges of 500–1,400 feet. Some manufacturers offer "range extender" products for longer range requirements.

DATA RATES

You want to consider range and data rate together when laying out your wireless LAN. Because the frequency band used by the IEEE 802.11 standard has strict and relatively low radiated power limits, you'll get longer ranges at lower rates and higher rates at shorter ranges. If you're in a relatively close-range office environment with clear lines of sight between stations, you can expect to use the highest rates. If you're in a large warehouse with metal shelving and supports to bounce signals around, you might need to limit your LAN to the lowest rates to get reliable transmission over the entire area.

Separate from the raw transmission rate, the achieved performance of your network will be affected by the visibility that stations in the network have to other stations. If you use an ad hoc network and some stations are hidden from other stations by blockage, you might incur a 40% performance hit. Networks using access points require visibility only from the station to the access point and so aren't vulnerable to that problem.

RELIABILITY

Both radio-based versions of the 802.11 specification transmit in the unlicensed 2.4GHz band in the United States and Canada. The 2.4GHz band is reserved for industrial, scientific, and medical (ISM) purposes, meaning there's a wide variety of devices besides wireless LANs in the band. The other two ISM bands are at 900MHz and 5.6GHz.

Until recently, the 2.4GHz band was relatively quiet, especially in comparison to the 900MHz band, which has a lot of traffic for wireless telephones. Some of the most recent systems using the 2.4GHz band include newer wireless telephones and the Bluetooth cable-replacement system targeted at computers, telephones, stereos, and other applications. All in all, the 2.4GHz band is becoming noisier, which means that some locations will be less reliable for wireless radio LANs running near maximum distance than others.

Cost

Wireless LANs can be significantly more expensive than their wired
Ethernet equivalents, so you'll want to use them only when one or more of
their unique features—mobility and elimination of the need to run wires—
are important. We've seen IEEE 802.11 radio wireless stations priced from
$70–600 per port. If you need an access point, you'll be adding from
$1,000–2,000 cost to the network per access point.

Using a Wireless Network

Suppose you run a warehouse in which different forklift crews store incoming items and retrieve outgoing ones. If you run a busy operation, your
forklift operators might need help finding items on shelves. If you tie the
forklifts into your computer systems with a wireless LAN, the operators can
both tell the computers where new material has been stored and find out
from the computers where to go to fill an order.

Or, suppose you live in a building with lath- and plaster-covered cinder-
block walls. Drilling through the walls and setting boxes for LAN connections could be difficult or impossible. If, instead, you tie your computers
together with a wireless LAN, you can be networked with no reconstruction
whatsoever.

Summary

You've learned in this chapter that network technologies vary depending on
the distance the network spans, and that even for local area networks there
are several common implementation technologies you might use. Each technology has its own unique characteristics you'll want to think through
when you design your installation.

What's Next

In the next chapter, you'll start to learn about the role software plays in
networks and see some of the details of how software makes your network
tick.

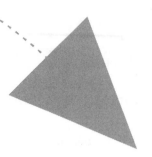

Understanding and Evaluating Network Services

In this chapter you will learn

- The role of your computer's operating system and software in your network

- How operating systems and software create network services

We believe that you'll do more and have more confidence working with your network if you know what's going on rather than viewing it as an unknown black box. We've known a surprising number of very capable people who, for lack of understanding, used their computers from scripted lists of commands, not knowing what each command did, but believing they'd get what they want after they finished the incantation. When what they did worked, they went on to the next task; when what they did failed, they'd either sit there puzzled or look for help. Without understanding why their computers did what they did, these people were helpless.

Although you should know a fair number of things about computers and networks to be effective, none of them are really all that complex when looked at individually. Both your computer and your network comprise many simple elements, though, so if you try to understand them as an undivided whole you're facing a large, difficult problem.

You'll learn in this chapter what the key elements of the software on your computer are—both software that runs the machine and software that runs the network. If you've been around computer people much you'll probably realize you've heard many of the terms we'll introduce you to. Taking each one as a distinct part of the whole, you'll understand more of what you've heard.

Operating Systems

Let's start dissecting the software in your computer near the bottom, with what's called the *operating system*. Once more, that's just fancy jargon, this time to identify a particular set of software.

Everything your computer does is directed by software, because software is just a sequence of instructions for the hardware to carry out. As a child, you learned basic things as sequences of simple instructions. Later, you learned to do and understand more complex things as sequences layered onto those previously learned capabilities. In the same way, your computer layers programs (software) one on top of another to carry out the functions you're interested in.

Figure 3.1 shows the typical layering of the software running on a networked computer. At the bottom of the stack you see the computer hardware itself, such as the processor, memory, disks, and other components. Hardware itself sometimes has software embedded in it, such as the Basic Input/Output System (BIOS) software that starts the computer when you turn on the power. The operating system overlaps the hardware layer some, because it contains specialized programs called *device drivers* that let the operating system issue commands to the hardware. Without the right device driver, the operating system can't make hardware work.

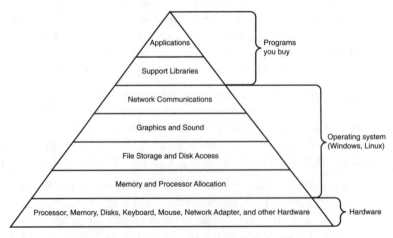

Figure 3.1: *Different programs layered one on another make your computer work.*

The four layers shown above the hardware and below the applications are one view of what's in the operating system. You know the operating system as Windows (or, for some, Linux); in reality, there are lots of different components in the operating system. Some operating system components (such as simple word processors) are themselves really applications packaged with the operating system; the components we've labeled *operating system* are the ones responsible for allocating and controlling the resources in the computer.

Memory and Processor Allocation

Everything your computer does happens because a program issues a sequence of instructions to the processor. Programs must reside in memory (often called *random access memory*, or *RAM*) to run. Each program needs its own private memory area, because if two programs were to unintentionally share the same memory they'd interfere with each other and crash.

When you start a program running, the operating system allocates some memory to hold the program, assigns it uniquely to that program, loads the image of the program from the disk, and assigns the processor to execute the instructions in the program. When the program finishes, the operating system sets the processor to another task and frees up the RAM once used by the program you ran, making it available in the future for other programs to use.

EXAMPLE

Example 3.1   Starting a Program Running

Aside from the work involved in maintaining the graphical interface you use to interact with the computer, Windows and Linux do a surprising amount of work behind the scenes when you start a program running:

1. In Windows, for instance, use the command Start, Run, type notepad in the dialog box, and click OK.

2. The first thing Windows does when you click OK is to look at the notepad.exe file on disk to find out how much memory it needs to run.

3. After Windows examines the file and calculates the required memory size, it alters its internal tables to allocate a block of memory and show that memory as owned by a running copy of notepad.exe.

4. Windows then reads the contents of the notepad.exe file into the freshly allocated memory block and identifies the location of the first instruction of the program.

5. Finally, Windows adds the ready-to-run setup for notepad.exe to the schedule of tasks the processor is to execute. When the time comes, the processor picks up the first instruction in the program and starts working.

File Storage and Disk Access

You know files as information stored on disk. To the operating system, a file is a sequence of characters (bytes) created by a program and stored on the disk that's associated with a particular name—the filename.

The operating system does a lot of work to make files be the simple, straightforward objects you use. It allocates space on the disk as programs write data to files, makes sure a given space on the disk can only be used by one file, makes sure only authorized people can access the file, grows or shrinks the file as programs request, and frees the file space when the file is deleted.

As much as that is, there's more to files than that list, because the operations we listed only include the functions involved in maintaining a *file system*, which is a collection of files. In addition, the operating system has to arrange to get file and file directory information onto and off of the disk drive itself, which involves keeping track of exactly what spot on the disk holds what information plus reading and writing to the disk. Those read and write operations eventually turn into commands carried out by the device driver for the disk.

EXAMPLE

Example 3.2   Reading a File from Disk

Example 3.2 describes how the operating system, device driver, and disk drive cooperate to read a file for an application program. Follow these steps:

1. Reading data from a file starts when a particular program asks for access to the file. The operating system responds by looking for the file in the file directory (called *folders* in Windows). If the file exists, the operating system notes where its file system information is stored and returns information about the file to the program.

2. After the program knows the file is accessible, it asks the operating system for data from the file.

3. The operating system receives the data request and, using the information in the directory, goes and finds the disk location of the first chunk of data for the file.

4. The disk device driver uses the address of the start of the file to command the disk drive to read data, storing the result of the read into memory.

5. After the read to memory completes, the operating system returns to the program with an indication that the memory holds the requested information.

Graphics and Sound

The low-level work of drawing images on screen and playing sounds through the speakers also falls to the operating system so that, as with files, applications can use high-level functions abstracted away from the complexities and peculiarities of the hardware.

Network Communications

Although applications communicating over networks can be quite simple, the low-level work to reliably send and receive messages is difficult. That work is handled by the operating system in both Windows and Linux to ensure the international networking standards are followed and to ensure that more than one program can use the network at once.

Network communications are hard because you can't know the exact time when the computers at the other end of the network connection are going to respond, and because things go wrong in networks. Messages can be lost or garbled, computers that should be visible might be turned off or unreachable, and the software at either end of the connection might not work correctly.

Networks send and receive messages using standard, formalized agreements to counter these reliability problems. The agreements for how to send and receive messages are called *protocols*; the operating system software components implementing the protocols are called *protocol stacks*.

Protocol Stacks

The robustness and standardization of the protocols on the Internet that you'll see in the next paragraphs might lead you to conclude that the development of network protocols has been straightforward and guided by consensus among network developers. Nothing could be farther from the truth, and in practice there is no one set of protocols that's best for all purposes. In this section, you'll learn about several of the most common protocols—ones you can put on your networked computer today—and learn why you'd pick one over another.

Internet

The most widely used protocols in the world are the ones underlying everything on the Internet. Those protocols are *Transmission Control Protocol / Internet Protocol (TCP/IP)*. The Internet Protocol (IP) transports messages across the Internet through the many computers and routers that make up the network. IP doesn't guarantee reliability, so programs can use the Transmission Control Protocol (TCP) to ensure messages sent across a net with IP make it to their destination.

Many protocols have been designed and built on top of TCP/IP to implement network services including file sharing, file transfer, printing, Web access, real-time chatting, and others. You'll learn about these TCP/IP-based service protocols later in this chapter in the section "Services."

TCP/IP has two important strengths not found in other network protocols: It's defined and standardized by an open, public standards group (the Internet Engineering Task Force, or IETF), and it's capable of spanning the largest networks known:

- **Open, public standard.** Changes and additions to TCP/IP can be proposed by anyone and are reviewed through a process defined by the IETF. The breadth of ideas and depth of review that result from that process have ensured TCP/IP has grown with the latest network technologies and have lead to TCP/IP support being mandatory for market success of new networking products.

- **Routable across large networks.** Large LANs, many MANs, and all WANs require specialized communications computers called routers to direct network messages across multiple communications links to their destination. TCP/IP is designed to be routable across the global Internet. As you'll see in the next two sections, other protocols are either not routable, which means messages using those protocols can't leave relatively small LANs or can only route across a large LAN.

The three most common networked operating system environments are Microsoft Windows, Novell NetWare, and UNIX/Linux. All three have protocols native to the operating system and, as you'll learn in the last part of this section, all can run in a mixed protocol environment.

One of the disadvantages of TCP/IP, a consequence of its ability to scale to very large networks, is that it requires each computer to be assigned a unique network address (a number) and on many LANs that assignment must be done by hand. Automatic mechanisms such as the Dynamic Host Configuration Protocol (DHCP) are available to do network address assignment, but many LANs don't take advantage of them.

Another disadvantage of TCP/IP, a consequence of its use as the protocol set for the Internet, is that it opens computers connected to the Internet up to attack by people wanting to pass viruses, steal files, or otherwise invade your property.

Microsoft

Microsoft added networking to Windows well before adding support for TCP/IP, introducing a new protocol called both NetBEUI and SMB (Server

Message Block). NetBEUI is the more common name, whereas the SMB name is used commonly in the UNIX/Linux community.

One key design goal for NetBEUI was clearly simplicity of use. Networks built on NetBEUI require no network address assignments—it's all completely automatic—and provide named computer identification. The protocol inherently supports sharing files and printers. Figure 3.2 shows NetBEUI operating on a LAN—all the computers on the LAN, each with a unique name, are visible in the right pane of Windows Explorer. Even though network messages operate using network addresses, which are numbers and not names, the only configuration we had to do was to assign the names. You can see from Figure 3.2 that NetBEUI automatically takes care of the rest of the details—the address numbers aren't even visible in the figure.

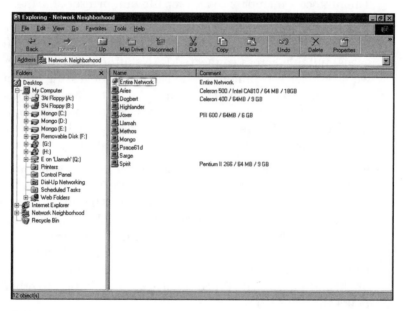

Figure 3.2: *NetBEUI automatically assigns network addresses to names.*

Both Windows 9x and Windows NT/2000 support NetBEUI, so running the protocol on a network of Windows machines is simple and straightforward: You simply install network cards, load the Windows networking software, set up access permissions, and you're finished. You'll learn how to do that in detail in Chapters 8, "Configuring Your System Software," and 9, "Sharing Fixed Drives and Setting Access Controls."

The major disadvantage of NetBEUI is that it's strictly a local area network protocol. Routers do not forward messages using the NetBEUI protocol, and because routers are what connect LANs together, you can't forward

NetBEUI traffic from one LAN to another. NetBEUI is an appropriate choice for the home or a small office where the LAN is isolated. If you'll be connecting the computers on the LAN to the Internet, though, you'll have to add TCP/IP too.

Novell

About the same time Microsoft was developing NetBEUI, Novell developed its NetWare products based on the IPX (Internetwork Packet Exchange) and SPX (Sequenced Packet Exchange) protocols. Although different in detail, IPX fills the same role as IP, whereas SPX fills the same role as TCP.

NetWare doesn't require address assignment; like NetBEUI, it's capable of fully automatic addressing and matching of computer names to addresses. The protocols include services for file and printer sharing.

The IPX/SPX protocols add the concept of a network number to the simpler assigned addresses used by NetBEUI, which makes IPX/SPX network messages routable across connected LANs after you've made the proper network number assignments. The NetWare addressing scheme isn't as robust as the one in TCP/IP, which is part of why the Novell protocols did not migrate out from corporate LANs to become the technology underlying the Internet. IPX/SPX networks are still widely used, although newer Novell products target TCP/IP and Internet compatibility.

With one exception, the transition Novell has made from IPX/SPX to TCP/IP suggests you're better off choosing TCP/IP (or NetBEUI, depending on your requirements) for a new network. That one exception is multiplayer games across a LAN. For years now, multiplayer games have used IPX to communicate between computers on a LAN—whereas TCP/IP support is now almost universal in games, the transition only occurred within the past few years. If you have older games you still want to play on your LAN, you might need to install IPX/SPX software in addition to other protocols to make the games run.

UNIX and Linux

UNIX is an operating system widely used on Internet servers and engineering workstations. There are many variants of UNIX, including Linux (free, developed by programmers worldwide), FreeBSD (also free, but developed by a relatively small group of programmers), Solaris and SunOS (commercial products developed by Sun Microsystems), AIX (a commercial product of IBM), HP-UX (a commercial product of Hewlett-Packard), and others. The UNIX operating system is the environment in which most TCP/IP development has been done. In practice, most UNIX/Linux systems have only TCP/IP installed. SMB support is widely available, but you have to manually install the software on most systems, and configuring the computers to make SMB work can be difficult. You'll learn how to make SMB work on Linux in Chapter 8.

UNIX and Linux depend on TCP/IP for much of their operation, so if you plan to have UNIX or Linux on your LAN, you'll want to plan on using the TCP/IP protocols.

Mixed Protocol Networks

It's very common to run multiple protocols on a LAN. Prior to the release of the most recent versions of Windows (Windows 98 Second Edition and Windows 2000) in which Microsoft significantly improved support for operation on networks, mixed protocols were the only way to make Windows and UNIX computers coexist easily unless you bought additional software.

The choice of what protocols to run wasn't always easy. Windows 3.1 and earlier versions weren't designed to support more than one protocol, although they could be tricked into it with great pain. Windows 3.11 attempted to solve some of those problems, but was only successful in limited ways. Windows NT 3.51 had problems too. If you're going to run Windows-based computers on your network, you should plan on running nothing older than Windows 95 or Windows NT 4.0; you should update Windows 95 with the available service packs and update Windows NT 4.0 at least through service pack 4. (A *service pack* is Microsoft jargon for a set of patches to the operating system designed to fix problems—bugs—and, in some cases, add new features. Patches can add new bugs as well as fix old ones, but these Windows 95 and NT service packs are worth having. Service pack 6 was current at the time we wrote this chapter; our statement that you should have at least service pack 4 is based solely on the networking aspects of the patch. Many people choose to keep their computers absolutely current to make sure they have the latest bug fixes and security patches.)

If you're running the initial version of Windows 98, you'll want to get the service pack that delivers the bug fixes that were part of Windows 98 Second Edition.

One reason you might want to run multiple protocols is to improve the security of computers connected to the Internet. If you load both NetBEUI and TCP/IP, you can isolate file sharing to NetBEUI and still have Internet access through TCP/IP. That combination improves the security of your files because NetBEUI is incapable of reaching out to the Internet.

Services

Unless you're a computer scientist, simply passing messages between computers is pointless unless you can get some useful work done. The capabilities offered by one computer to others on a network are called services. Computers using a service are called clients, which is where the term *client/server computing* comes from. A given computer can be both a server and a client, depending on what work is being done where.

File Sharing and Transfer

Figure 3.3 shows one of the most common LAN services, sharing a disk drive or CD-ROM on a server with clients elsewhere on the LAN. The figure shows disk storage available on the left-most computer being accessible from the other two computers on the LAN. Relative to accessing that shared disk, the machine on the left is the server, whereas those in the center and on the right are clients.

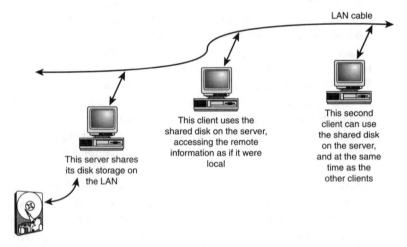

LAN cable

This client uses the shared disk on the server, accessing the remote information as if it were local

This server shares its disk storage on the LAN

This second client can use the shared disk on the server, and at the same time as the other clients

Figure 3.3: *Client/server computing separates the computer doing the work from the one delivering the results.*

EXAMPLE

Example 3.3   Planning a File Server

There are a lot of advantages to dedicating specific computers on your LAN as file servers. Done properly, a dedicated file server isn't anyone's personal computer and doesn't run applications. Instead, it's in some out-of-the-way place, readily accessible only from the LAN:

1. Decide how much storage you need now in the file server, and how much you're likely to need through its useful life. If your network's fast enough and you take care to make sure it's reliable, you can keep data files and software installations on the server disks. Doing that can relieve the pressure to constantly add more disk storage to the machines on people's desktops.

2. If you're sharing software installations off a file server, you'll need at least as much storage as all your programs need, plus reserve. It's not that hard to end up with gigabytes of programs (surprised?).

3. If you're keeping data files on the server too, the disk space you need can grow astronomically. Video and music files—quaintly called multimedia—can easily be tens of megabytes each. Photographs from digital cameras can require half a megabyte or more; scanned photographs from film cameras can be even larger. Even games can be huge. A 400MB game is common; the game Baldur's Gate occupies a whopping 2.5GB.

4. As cheap as disks are today—a Seagate 28GB disk already sells for under $220, with prices always coming down—it's both easy and a good idea to have far more disk storage than you ever think you'll need. We don't recommend planning a dedicated file server with less than 25GB of disk.

5. Investigate how many CD-ROM titles you regularly use. Not all CD-ROM titles permit sharing the disk across a network, but for those that do, having a shared CD-ROM drive (or multiple-disk CD-ROM changer) in the file server can help leave the CD-ROM drives in people's individual computers free for more specialized uses.

You won't necessarily save money on software by sharing installations through a file server. Licensing terms vary from one software company to another, but in general you shouldn't expect to be able to buy one copy of a program and use it freely on lots of computers. Be sure to read the program license to find out what you can and cannot do.

Although the arrangement in Figure 3.3 (with the role of client and server kept distinct) is very common, many people choose to set up small LANs so that each computer both shares its disks and accesses disks on other computers. Mixing client and server roles like that is called *peer-to-peer networking*. Figure 3.4 shows the difference—the computers sharing their disks out to the LAN aren't dedicated file servers; they're the computers on people's desks. The same computers that access remote files as clients share disk storage as servers to other computers.

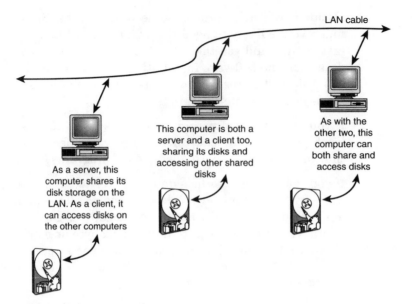

LAN cable

This computer is both a server and a client too, sharing its disks and accessing other shared disks

As with the other two, this computer can both share and access disks

As a server, this computer shares its disk storage on the LAN. As a client, it can access disks on the other computers

Figure 3.4: *A peer-to-peer LAN has computers acting as both client and server.*

You can implement both client/server and peer-to-peer file sharing with any of the three protocol families you learned about earlier. Peer-to-peer sharing is most common with the Microsoft NetBEUI protocols, but it works with IPX/SPX and TCP/IP too. NetBEUI and IPX/SPX provide the additional specialized protocols for file sharing along with the basic transport protocols. There's a distinct file-sharing protocol called NFS (Network File System) you add to TCP/IP.

You can also transfer files between machines without being able to access the remote disk itself. That capability is inherent in UNIX-like systems, using a protocol called FTP (File Transfer Protocol).

Printer Sharing

Pause for a minute to look again at Figure 3.1 in the context of what you just learned about file sharing. What the network did to implement file sharing was to layer on top of other capabilities of the operating system, extending access to those capabilities out onto the network.

That last statement, "layer on top of other capabilities of the operating system, extending access to those capabilities out onto the network," is in one sense the essence of what networks do. Anything a computer can do can be extended across a network for other computers to use.

With that in mind, you can see how networks let you share printers. Figure 3.5 shows what happens: The operating system includes printer device drivers, which embody capabilities that can be extended over the network. Applications normally use printer device drivers to send data to locally attached printers; when the printer is remote and shared over the LAN, the device driver accesses the network to transport the print data to the remote print server computer.

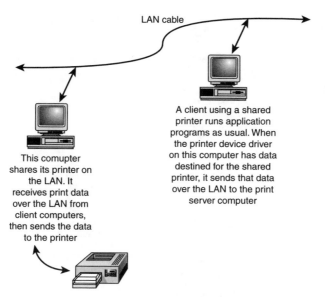

LAN cable

A client using a shared printer runs application programs as usual. When the printer device driver on this computer has data destined for the shared printer, it sends that data over the LAN to the print server computer

This comuputer shares its printer on the LAN. It receives print data over the LAN from client computers, then sends the data to the printer

Figure 3.5: *Printer sharing uses the client / server relationship.*

NetBEUI and IPX/SPX include print sharing in the protocols; TCP/IP has additional, task-specific protocols implemented by programs called lpr, lpq, and lpd.

Internet Access and Services

You probably know that you can connect your computer to the Internet over a modem, and you saw earlier that specialized communications computers called *routers* can connect an entire LAN to the Internet. No matter which way you connect—directly through a modem or indirectly across a LAN—you use the TCP/IP protocols to carry your message. In both cases, software in the computer or router connected to the modem wraps one additional protocol, PPP (Point-to-Point Protocol), around your messages for transport across the telephone line.

Figure 3.6 shows where PPP is used when you access the Internet. Your Internet service provider's equipment removes PPP from around your messages as soon as they arrive; PPP serves only to help transmit the messages through the modem and across the telephone line. PPP is a very simple protocol, serving mainly to help the communications equipment identify where one message ends and another begins.

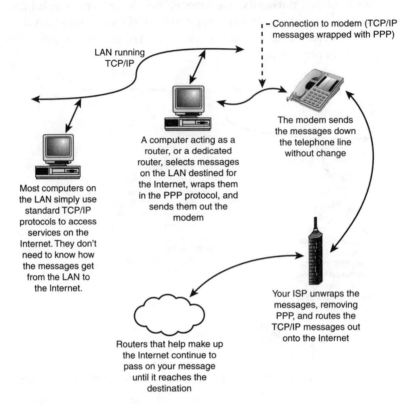

Figure 3.6: The PPP protocol wraps your TCP/IP messages for transport across the telephone line.

If you're accessing the Internet from across a LAN, as illustrated in Figure 3.6, no additional protocols are needed to carry your messages besides TCP/IP and PPP. The computer-addressing mechanisms that the IP protocol implements exist just to do the work of carrying your messages through routers and as far as they need to go to get to the destination computer.

Specific services you use on the Internet each typically have their own implementing protocols. You learned about FTP earlier; the next sections cover many of the other TCP/IP-based Internet protocols you'll use.

Domain Name Service (DNS)

The people who developed the Internet technology realized early on in their work that nobody wanted to refer to computers by numeric addresses.

When hooked to the Internet, your computer can send messages to the computer at the address 208.218.3.1, but you aren't likely to care until we tell you that address belongs to the computer named disney.com.

Like everything else on a network, the service that translates computer names you use into addresses that computers use has a protocol—Domain Name Service (DNS)—associated with it. When your computer has to decode a name you've given it, it uses the DNS protocol to ask a domain name server (which is typically another computer at your ISP) for the translation.

INTERNET CONTROL MESSAGE PROTOCOL (ICMP)

The routers that make up the Internet have ways to communicate with each other and discover characteristics of the parts of the network they connect to. ICMP is one of the protocols providing those services. You can use ICMP to find out if a remote computer is alive and responding using the ping program, which reports how long it takes for ICMP messages to reach the remote computer and return to you. You'll learn in Chapter 17, "Troubleshooting Network Problems," that ping is one of the most important network diagnostic tools you have.

HYPERTEXT TRANSFER PROTOCOL (HTTP)

The World Wide Web is, second only to email, the most popular application on the Internet. The Web works on a client/server model like most other network applications (see Figure 3.7). The client/server operation is similar in concept to what you learned earlier for file sharing: The client computer makes a request to the server using a service-specific protocol, receiving information back from the server in response to the request. For the World Wide Web, the protocol between client and server is the Hypertext Transfer Protocol.

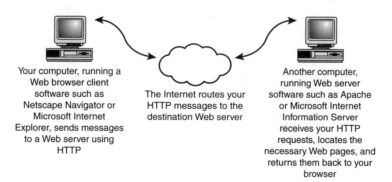

Your computer, running a Web browser client software such as Netscape Navigator or Microsoft Internet Explorer, sends messages to a Web server using HTTP

The Internet routes your HTTP messages to the destination Web server

Another computer, running Web server software such as Apache or Microsoft Internet Information Server receives your HTTP requests, locates the necessary Web pages, and returns them back to your browser

Figure 3.7: The Hypertext Transfer Protocol underlies the World Wide Web.

Your Web browser is capable of implementing other protocols, including FTP, which is why you see http or ftp at the start of a complete Web address.

EXAMPLE

Example 3.4   Using Protocols in Web Addresses

Example 3.4 shows how the prefix in a Web address specifies the protocol being used. Follow these steps:

1. Connect to the Internet, start a Web browser (we've used Microsoft Internet Explorer), and enter the URL (uniform resource locator) http://www.linux-mandrake.com. When the page comes up, you'll see the default Web page for the Web site supporting the Mandrake distribution of the Linux operating system (see Figure 3.8).

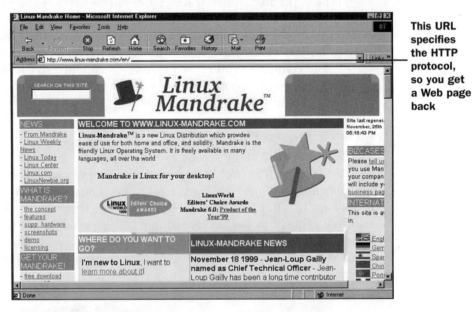

This URL specifies the HTTP protocol, so you get a Web page back

Figure 3.8: An HTTP URL accesses Web pages.

2. Edit the URL slightly, changing http:// to be ftp:// and press Enter. You've left the server computer address the same doing that, but changed the protocol you use to access the server. Because of that, the results of the new request come back as in Figure 3.9—instead of receiving a Web page back, you get back a listing of the directories on the FTP server.

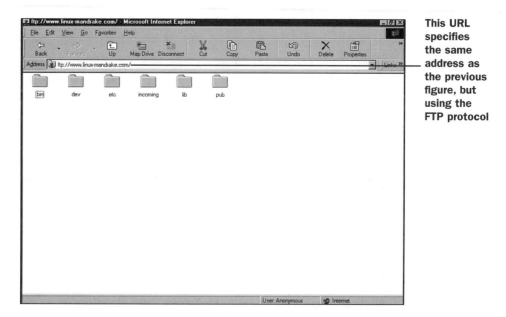

This URL specifies the same address as the previous figure, but using the FTP protocol

Figure 3.9: An FTP URL accesses directories and files at the same address.

SIMPLE MAIL TRANSFER PROTOCOL (SMTP)

Email is, at its core, simply text messages sent in a particular way from one computer to another. Newer email client programs extend the simple text-based messages to hold a wide variety of data formats, but the underlying transport remains text.

Computers transport email using the standard client/server relationship and the Simple Mail Transfer Protocol (SMTP). SMTP serves to identify who's sending the mail, the ultimate destination, the subject, and a variety of other items. Your email client puts that information in a standard set of *header* lines that precede the message information itself and then sends the package to an email server. The email client takes responsibility for correctly forming the email header.

If you've used email for more than a few weeks, though, you've probably received more than a few unsolicited commercial emails, more commonly known as *spam*. Spammers almost always forge the contents of the header lines to try and avoid being identified, using spamming tools that permit the insertion of bogus information into the protocol header.

There are many other protocols on the Internet, including one for global bulletin boards (Network News Transfer Protocol, NNTP), real time chat rooms (Internet Relay Chat, IRC), time of day reporting (Network Time Protocol, NTP), and others. All of them operate on the client/server model, encapsulating the specific functions needed to extend a service across the network.

You're likely to find the same Internet protocols on an intranet, which is essentially a mini-Internet with access restricted to within a corporation or other community. By adopting the rich, robust set of Internet protocols, intranets provide a way for companies and organizations to share information and work internally without having to develop their own unique software and protocol sets.

Summary

You've learned in this chapter that operating systems work in support of applications, providing common services those programs can use. Software developers commonly call the combination of hardware and operating system services a *development platform*, which is simply more jargon naming the complete set of resources the application program has to work with.

Networks extend access to the services and resources in the development platform using agreements for how to send and receive messages called protocols. There's typically a unique protocol for each service or resource being shared across the network. The three major protocol families are NetBEUI, IPX/SPX, and TCP/IP. Of the three, TCP/IP is the most common because it's the protocol set underlying the Internet.

There are other services besides the ones we've described. Some are public standards, such as ones for videoconferencing, whereas some are proprietary to one or another company. Every service has an underlying protocol; to get the service on your LAN requires that you identify computers that will work as the server or the client and install the necessary application plus protocol software.

What's Next

Now that you've developed a sense of what networks can do and how they work, it's time to start building your LAN. You'll begin that process in the next chapter, where you'll learn how to choose the LAN cable technology and speed that's right for you.

Building Your Network

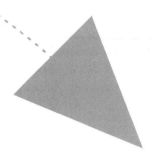

Picking Your LAN Cable Technology and Speed

In this chapter you will learn

- How to estimate the data rate your network needs to support what you do

- How to choose the network technology that best meets your requirements

- Techniques for building network cables

You're going to start learning how to build a LAN in this chapter. The first topic you'll read about is how to decide how fast a network you need; after that you'll see how to pick a specific LAN technology and how to build or buy network cables.

Probably the most neglected part of building LANs, at least among those who haven't experienced the pain of maintaining a poorly built network, is the cabling. LAN cables are just wire and plain-looking connectors, so it's easy to overlook the fact that the quality of the cable and of its installation will determine whether your LAN is dependable or not.

No matter what cable you pick, there are two concerns you need to think about: The first is the type and quality of cable you use; the second is the where and how you install the cable. This chapter covers choosing a specific cabling technology and making sure you have the cables you need; Chapter 5, "Installing Your LAN Wiring," covers how to install the cable.

Unless you're a practiced, trained electronics assembly technician, making cables is a tedious, error-prone job best left to factories with the right machines to do the job well. You're almost always better off buying a good quality premade cable than collecting the parts and building one yourself. You might not save any money making cables yourself, either.

Despite that, there are three specific cases in which we do recommend making your own network cables:

- When you're installing cables in walls

- When you need short patch cables you can't buy commercially

- When you don't have a commercial source for premade cables

Network cables are the only cables we recommend you make yourself (don't bother making cables for inside your computer, for instance), and even then these are the only times it's likely to be worthwhile. We'll show you how.

Determining Your LAN Requirements

There are three performance characteristics of a LAN you're likely to care about:

- The rate at which you can move data across the LAN

- The latency between when you send a message and when it's received

- The chances there will be a collision when a computer sends a message that requires a retransmission

Calculating Your LAN Data Rate Requirement

You learned in Chapter 2, "Kinds of Networks," that your LAN is likely to run at 1, 2, 10, or 100Mbps. Table 4.1 summarizes the network technologies you can use at each of those data rates.

Table 4.1: LAN Data Rates and Technology

Data Rate Kbps	Data Rate KBps	Net KBps	Technology Choices
115.2	11.52	10	Serial Direct Cable Connection
1,000	125	100	Telephone Line Network (HPNA standards), IEEE 802.11 Wireless LAN
2,000	250	200	IEEE 802.11 Wireless LAN
10,000	1,250	1,000	10Base-2, 10Base-T, 10Base-FL Ethernet Telephone Line Network (HPNA standards), IEEE 802.11 Wireless LAN, USB Direct cable Connection
100,000	12,500	10,000	100Base-T Ethernet

The 10Mbps (10,000Kbps in the table) categorization for USB and wireless is only approximate but is close enough for planning network speeds. There are two rate columns in Table 4.1; one expressed in the usual Mbps, and the other expressed in MBps. You convert from Mbps to MBps by dividing by 8 (because there are eight bits in a byte) for everything but the serial direct cable connection. Convert bits to bytes for the serial cable technology by dividing by 10 to account for the two bits the serial port hardware adds to every byte transmitted.

There's a third column in Table 4.1 too, one that uses the 80% maximum LAN throughput rule of thumb to suggest the actual maximum sustained data rate you'll see on a LAN using each technology.

The other information you need to decide the LAN data rate you want is the size of the blocks of information you'll transfer across your LAN and the rates that information is available for transfer across network (fast for disks, slow for modems). Table 4.2 shows some of the possibilities for how much information you're likely to transfer.

Table 4.2: Data Transfer Sizes by Type of Data

File Size Range (KB)	Kind of Data
1–100	Text and email
10–2,000	Graphics
1,000–5,000	Sound
5,000–10,000	Video
1,000–100,000	Combined text, graphics, sound, and video
1,000–3,000,000	Software installations

Using the information in the two tables, you can estimate how long data transfers of each type are likely to take using the different LAN technologies. Example 4.1 explains how to do the calculations.

EXAMPLE

Example 4.1 Calculating LAN Data Transfer Times

Suppose you regularly work with large data files—perhaps documents containing text and photographs. From Table 4.2 you'd estimate file sizes in the range of 100KB–100MB.

If you're considering 10Base-T Ethernet, Table 4.1 shows you that you can calculate using a 10Mbps data rate, and suggests you'll get a maximum of 1MBps transferred across a network.

If you divide the data size estimate by the data rate estimate, you'll see that the transfer is likely to take 0.1–100 seconds if there's no other activity on the LAN at the time.

The calculation in this example applies if you're sharing files across the LAN, and perhaps (depending on the speed of your computer and the complexity of the document) if you're printing to a shared LAN printer. The rates in Table 4.1 could be irrelevant if the data transfer is information coming off the Internet, because your modem speed is probably slower than your network. Table 4.3 shows the maximum data rates you're likely to achieve using the common Internet access technologies.

Table 4.3: Typical Maximum Internet Access Data Rates

Data Rate (Kbps)	Outgoing	Internet Access Technology Incoming
33.6	33.6	Analog modem (V.34 specification)
53	33.6	56Kbps digital modem (V.90 specification)
64	64	Single-channel ISDN (Integrated Services Digital Network)
128	128	Dual-channel ISDN
7,168	1,088	RADSL (Rate Adaptive Digital Subscriber Line), a common version of ADSL
10,000	2,000	Cable modem

You're likely to see lower rates than in Table 4.3 because your telephone lines or cable network might not support the maximum rate or because you've chosen a limited rate to reduce cost. Your immediate conclusion from Table 4.3 should be that, unless you have an ADSL or cable modem Internet connection, the speed your LAN runs at is irrelevant for information coming in over the modem.

After you've identified all the information you need using Tables 4.1, 4.2, and 4.3, use Example 4.1 to calculate data transfer times typical of how you expect to use your network. Example 4.2 shows a typical case.

Example 4.2   Characterizing Network Performance

EXAMPLE

The most common small LAN applications are file sharing, printer sharing, and Internet access sharing. Suppose you're planning a home LAN you expect to use primarily for printer sharing and Internet access sharing.

Looking at Table 4.1, you see that you can get HPNA LAN equipment running at 1 and 10Mbps. The 10Mbps technology is newer, but it's likely to be a little more expensive.

Table 4.2 suggests you could see network transfers to the shared printer of up to 100MB. You know the biggest projects you've seen on your home computers have been photographs and school reports with files as big as a few megabytes, so you scale back the 100MB number to 10MB.

The modem you'll be sharing for Internet access uses the V.90 modem standard. Table 4.3 shows you that you're only going to see maximum data rates of 53Kbps, so you discount the Internet traffic as a factor in sizing your network data rate.

Using the approach in Example 4.1, you calculate that (if the network is the limiting factor and not the computers or the printer), 10MB print jobs would take 100 or 10 seconds on the 1Mbps and 10Mbps technology, respectively. Based on that analysis, you conclude that either technology would work in your situation, and decide to base the choice on relative cost and to go with the faster 10Mbps version if the cost is too close to matter to you.

Understanding Latency and Jitter in Your LAN

Most of the time the only LAN performance characteristic you're going to care about is the data rate, which determines the time it takes to get something done. You learned to analyze your data rate requirements in the last section. If you're doing something like talking in a network videoconference or playing multiplayer games across your LAN, though, you'll also care about how long it takes for individual messages to move across the LAN, and about how variable those times are. Those two measurements are called *latency* and *jitter*.

The reason latency and jitter are the important performance measures for videoconferencing and multiplayer gaming is that those applications depend on an uninterrupted flow of messages to keep the processing on the computers running smoothly. Delay or drop messages in those applications and it's likely that the software will pause noticeably. Pauses are irritating in video, can make audio unintelligible, and can cost you the match in multiplayer gaming.

Latency and jitter originate inside your computers, as shown in Figure 4.1. Each block in the two computers is a processing step that has a minimum time delay. The delay a specific message encounters in each step is variable and most often depends on what's happening at that instant of time on the LAN infrastructure (even though the cable and hub themselves have a relatively constant transit time).

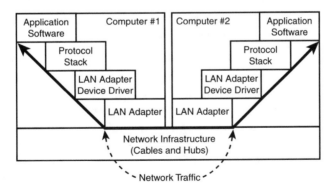

Figure 4.1: *Sources of network latency and jitter.*

Each processing step has its own function and its own unique reasons for introducing latency and jitter:

- **LAN Adapter.** The interaction between the LAN adapter and the network infrastructure is the original source of latency and jitter beyond the minimums, because the LAN adapter is required to wait until there is no interfering traffic on the cable before it transmits a message. If there's no traffic on the network the wait will be the minimum possible; if there's very heavy traffic, the wait can be relatively long.

Because it's possible for two computers to believe the cable is clear and start transmitting a message at the same time, collisions can occur, corrupting both messages and requiring both to be retransmitted. The loss of the transmitted messages introduces delays in getting the messages to their destinations, increasing latency. LAN adapters in Ethernet networks are required to wait a random time before attempting to retransmit, which increases jitter.

- **LAN Adapter Device Driver.** The device driver is responsible for controlling the operation of the LAN adapter, giving it messages to send, accepting received messages, and monitoring the adapter for problems. Drivers from different manufacturers use different techniques to decide it's possible to hand off or receive messages, and to find out about problems, differences that cause variations in transit time that add to latency and jitter.

- **Protocol Stack.** Even with the best efforts of the LAN adapter and the device driver, messages can get lost on networks. When they do, the first line of defense responding to the problem will be the protocol stack implementing TCP/IP, SPX/IPX, or NetBEUI. Messages can be lost without notification, though, so protocol stacks have to wait for a timeout period before declaring the message lost. The timeout periods are very long compared to normal latencies, introducing a lot of delay and one of the major sources of jitter.

- **Application Software.** How the application software handles lost or delayed messages ultimately determines how stringent the latency and jitter requirements on your network will be. Applications insensitive to latency and jitter typically send enough data in every message that dropped messages might cause a skip in what you perceive but won't stall the receiving program. More data has to be transmitted in each message to meet that requirement, though, increasing the traffic on the LAN. More sensitive applications actually wait for the receiver to send back a confirmation that each message has arrived. Those applications generate less traffic but can stall completely when a collision causes a message to be dropped.

Ultimately, the source of abnormal latency and jitter on a LAN is collisions on the cable or in the hub. You can reduce the probability of collisions by increasing the network data rate, which reduces the time each message takes to transit the network and increases the percentage of free time. For a given traffic load, networks running at 100Mbps will have lower latency and jitter than ones at 10Mbps, which in turn will display lower latency and jitter than 1Mbps networks. If videoconferencing or fast-action multi-player games are important applications on your network, you'll want to favor the higher-speed technologies.

Collisions are also the reason why you're unlikely to be able to use more than about 80% of the transmission data rate on LAN and might get far less. Simulations and traffic analysis show that when there are too many collisions, the computers end up spending all their time retransmitting lost messages and no useful work gets done.

Direct Cable Connection

After you pick a network technology and speed, you'll want to start laying out the components you need to build the network. Don't turn first to the electronics; start with the cabling and take the time to get it right. The time you invest in well-built, reliable cabling will be returned to you many times over in time you save by not having to troubleshoot the network.

You're better off buying premade cables for serial direct cable connection networks. We're going to show you how to make one in this section so you'll understand what's involved and what can go wrong. (Another reason to make a serial direct cable connection cable is that if you slow the data rate to 9.6Kbps or less, serial cables made with good quality wire can run a surprisingly long distance. Although it's well beyond specifications, we've run serial connections a few hundred feet. In a pinch, a slow connection might be a lot better than no connection.)

Table 4.4 shows the parts and equipment you'll need to make the cable.

Table 4.4: Serial Direct Cable Connect Cable Parts and Tools

Quantity	Item
2	9- or 25-pin female D-subminiature connectors.
2	Backshells for connectors.
1 length	8-conductor cable. Category 3 or 5 unshielded twisted-pair Ethernet cable works fine.
1	Wire stripper.
1	Needle-nose pliers.
1	Low wattage soldering iron.
	60/40 tin/lead rosin core solder. Do not use acid core solder for any electrical application.
	Small bench or table vise.
	Steel wool (use to keep soldering iron tip clean).
	Magnifying glass with stand (optional).

Figure 4.2 shows you what the connectors, backshells, and cable look like. Specific appearances will vary, but the general shape and style of the connectors will not.

Figure 4.2: *Serial direct cable connect cable parts.*

You need one more thing before you start building the cable: a wiring diagram so you'll know how to route the wires to the pins on the connectors. We'll show wiring diagrams in this book as drawings showing signals connected to pins, along with a drawing of the connector to show how the pins are numbered.

Figure 4.3 shows the pinouts for the D-subminiature connectors you'll use to make the serial direct cable connect cable. The drawings represent the connectors when you're looking from the side that plugs into the computer. Be careful about pin numbering; if you look at the connector from the side where the wires connect instead, you'll end up numbering the pins backward and the cable won't work.

Figure 4.3: *D-subminiature connector pinouts.*

Figure 4.4 shows the wiring for a serial direct cable connect cable for 25-pin connectors. Look at the diagram carefully, because the signals go to different pins on the left and right sides of the drawing.

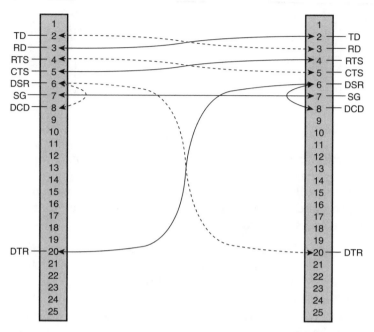

Figure 4.4: *Serial direct cable connect cable wiring for 25-pin connectors.*

Table 4.5 explains what each signal in Figure 4.4 is. If you compare the signal functions in Table 4.5 with the wiring in Figure 4.4, you'll see that related signals are crossed over and connected to each other. For example, the transmitted data on one computer becomes the received data on the other. Figure 4.4 also shows the DSR and DCD signals connected together within the same connector; that's the only pair of signals connected together within one connector.

Table 4.5: Serial Port Signals

Signal Name	Purpose
TD	Transmitted data
RD	Received data
RTS	Request to send
CTS	Clear to send
DSR	Data set ready
SG	Signal ground
DCD	Data carrier detect
DTR	Data terminal ready

Figure 4.5 shows the equivalent wiring diagram for 9-pin connectors. All the same signals are present, but the pin assignments are different.

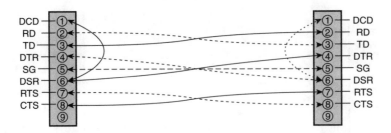

Figure 4.5: *Serial direct cable connect cable wiring for 9-pin connectors.*

You can build a serial direct cable connect cable with a 9-pin connector on one end and a 25-pin connector on the other—just match up the signal names and wire accordingly.

After you collect the parts and tools and determine what signals to connect where, you have to assign signals to colors of wire in the cable. We chose to use Category 5 unshielded twisted-pair Ethernet cable to make these serial direct cable connect cables because it has acceptable electrical characteristics and is readily available. Table 4.6 shows one way you could use the colors in the Category 5 cable to carry the serial port signals.

Table 4.6: Serial-Port Signal Assignments to Category 5 Wire Colors

Signal Name	Purpose	Left Wire Color	Right Wire Color
TD	Transmitted data	Orange	Blue
RD	Received data	Blue	Orange
RTS	Request to send	Green	Green/White
CTS	Clear to send	Green/White	Green
DSR	Data set ready	Brown	Brown/White
SG	Signal ground	Orange/White, Blue/White	Orange/White, Blue/White
DCD	Data carrier detect	Brown	Brown/White
DTR	Data terminal ready	Brown/White	Brown

We chose the wire assignments to help minimize signal interference in the cable. The left and right wire color columns in the table reflect the crossed-over connections shown in Figures 4.4 and 4.5.

Now that everything is planned out for how to build the cable, you should cut one end of the cable to a clean, square edge; strip back about an inch of the outer insulation; hold the cable in the vise; and begin preparing the wires. For each wire, strip an eighth of an inch of insulation, twist the exposed strands together, and then heat the wire until solder will melt and tin the strands into a solid wire. Do this for all eight wires.

Next, load one of the connectors into the vise, slide the backshell onto the cable, and begin making connections. The tinned wires go into the cup at the end of the corresponding connector pin. You then heat the pin until it (not the soldering iron) melts solder; then melt in just enough solder to fill the cup and wick slightly up the wire. Apply heat a little longer, and then remove the iron. Do not move the connector or wire after you remove the heat or the solder will form a "cold" solder joint, which is unreliable. Figure 4.6 shows a wire being soldered into a partly assembled connector.

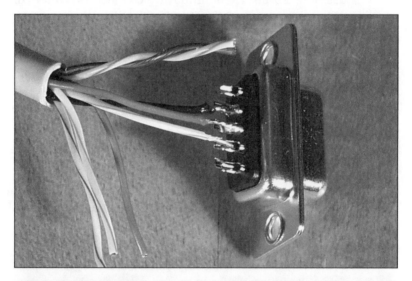

Figure 4.6: *Soldering wires into the D-subminiature connector.*

Repeat this for each wire, and then attach the backshell so it covers the connector and provides strain relief for the cable as it exits the backshell. Duplicate the process for the other end of the cable.

EXAMPLE

Example 4.3   Making a Serial Direct Cable Connection Cable

To make a direct cable connection cable, follow these steps:

1. Check the serial ports on the back of your computers to see if they use 9- or 25-pin D-subminiature connectors. Older computers used the 25-pin connectors; all computers built in the past four to five years are likely to use the 9-pin type.

2. Buy two female D-subminiature connectors and backshells with the right number of pins, along with a sufficient length of twisted-pair Ethernet cable. (You can use other cable as long as the wires aren't too big to fit the connector pins and there are enough wires.) We suggest stranded wire.

3. If you don't have a low-wattage soldering iron and the rest of the tools in Table 4.4, get them while you're buying cable parts.

4. Strip the outer insulation at one end of the cable about one inch back, and then strip each wire about 1/8 inch and tin with the soldering iron.

5. Put the backshell on the cable and solder the wires to the connector according to the wiring in Figure 4.3 through 4.5 plus Table 4.6.

6. Attach the backshell to the connector.

7. Repeat steps 1 through 6 for the other connector.

8. Use a multimeter set as a continuity checker to verify correct wiring, including that there are no shorts between adjacent pins.

Making one of these cables is a lot of work. Between putting the wrong wire on a pin or making a bad solder joint, there are lots of ways to make mistakes. If you're not very careful to get everything exactly right, the cable won't work or will be unreliable.

We recommend buying cables for serial direct cable connections.

Ethernet

It's reasonable to make your own Ethernet cables, unlike serial direct cable connections, because connectors and tools are available that permit reliable cable construction without soldering. Even so, we suggest you only bother to make cables when the wire needs to make a long run through a wall or when you can't purchase a cable in the length you need. Otherwise, you might as well buy them.

The construction techniques for 10Base-2 and 10Base-T cables are completely different, so we'll cover them separately. You'll also learn about extenders for 10Base-T LANs using fiber-optic cables in the section on 10/100Base-T wiring.

Pay attention to the type of outer insulation on the wire you get. There are two types of outer cable jackets: those made from PVC, which is less expensive, and those rated for use in the air plenum above ceiling tiles. Plenum-rated cable has a smoke-resistant jacket and might be required for ceiling installation by your local fire code (a *plenum* is an air space—in this case, it's the air space above the tiles and below the hard ceiling).

10Base-2

Coaxial cable is a pair of wires in a cable such that one wire is a foil or braid shield surrounding the wire at the center. The drawing at the left in Figure 4.7 shows a cross section of a coaxial cable including the signal wire, inner insulation, shield, and outer insulation. The photograph in the figure shows a length of coaxial cable with the outer layers stripped back to show each of those components.

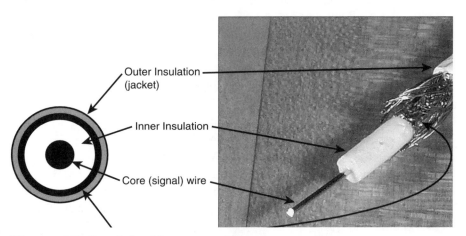

Outer Insulation (jacket)

Inner Insulation

Core (signal) wire

Figure 4.7: Coaxial cable cross section.

Ethernet (10Base-2) cables are mechanically very similar to television coaxial cables, with two important differences:

- **Different connectors.** Television coaxial cable uses a type-F connector that screws onto the connecting device (for example, television or VCR). Ethernet coaxial cable uses a BNC connector as shown in Figure 2.18.

- **Different cable impedance.** Television coaxial cable has an impedance of 75 ohms; Ethernet coaxial cable has an impedance of 50 ohms. If you connect television coaxial cable in an Ethernet, the impedance mismatch creates noise in the cable because signals bounce at the ends and at the connections to the network adapters.

You buy bulk type–RG-58 coaxial cable to make 10Base-2 cables. There are two different types of BNC connectors you can attach to the cable: crimp-on and screw-on. The good kind of crimp-on connectors require a crimping tool to secure to the cable (there are cheap ones with a ring you crimp with a pliers; they don't work well). The good crimp-on connectors might be more reliable. Strip and prepare the layers of cable according to the connector manufacturer's directions. You might be required to fold the shield back around the outer insulation. Crimp or screw on the connector according to the directions, being extremely careful that small shield braid wires don't end up shorted against the inner signal wire.

10/100Base-T

Twisted-pair wire and type–RJ-45 modular telephone–style connectors are the basis for all 10/100Base-T wiring (see Figure 4.8). There are four pairs (eight wires) in the cable, even though only two pairs are actually used. The RJ-45 connector, which is larger than the RJ-11 modular connector you'll find on your telephone, terminates all eight wires. The pieces you see in Figure 4.8 are from the Belkin Model F4F310 10Base-T/100Base-T Ethernet Installation Kit. In addition to the connector installation tool, RJ-45 connectors, and Category 5 bulk cable you see in the figure, the kit includes parts and equipment for running Ethernet cables in walls, too, which you'll learn about in Chapter 5.

There are several standards for the twisted-pair wire you'll use in your 10Base-T or 100Base-T Ethernet, the most common of which are called Category 3 and Category 5 cable. Those two categories characterize the signal-carrying performance of the cable, and are independent of whether the wire is solid or stranded or whether the outer jacket is PVC or plenum rated. There are two common signal-carrying characteristics of Ethernet cable:

- **High-Frequency Attenuation.** The faster the data rate on the Ethernet cable, the higher the maximum frequency carried by the cable. If important high-frequency components of the signal are attenuated too far by the time the signal arrives at the other end of the cable, the receiver can't recover the signal and data errors occur.
- **Near-End Crosstalk.** Figure 4.9 is a partial wiring diagram of one end of a twisted-pair Ethernet cable. There are two pairs of wires, one for transmit and one for receive. The signals in the wires are strongest

when they enter the wires, at the start of the transmit pair, and weakest when they leave the wires, at the end of the receive pair. Magnetic fields at the transmitter end of the transmit pair cross the receive pair, introducing noise into the receive signal. If the noise is strong enough, data-receive errors occur.

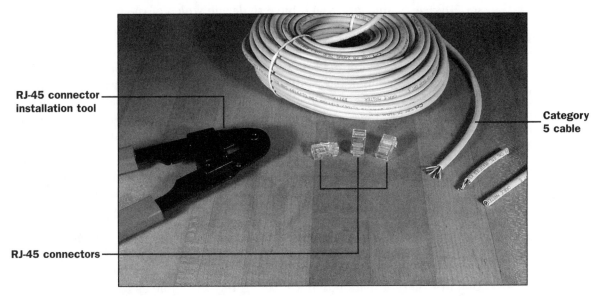

RJ-45 connector installation tool

Category 5 cable

RJ-45 connectors

Figure 4.8: *Twisted-pair wire and type–RJ-45 modular telephone style connectors.*

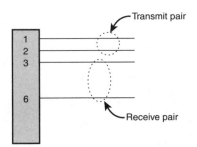

Transmit pair

1
2
3

6

Receive pair

Figure 4.9: *Minimal twisted-pair wire assignments to pins on an RJ-45 connector.*

Category 5 cable is better than Category 3 cable in both respects, attenuating high-frequency signals less and (because the wires are twisted more tightly and the insulation is better) allowing less crosstalk. Category 3 unshielded twisted-pair (UTP) cable is adequate for 10Mbps operation, but won't carry 100Mbps signals reliably. Category 5 cable is explicitly designed for 100Mbps operation, and even the Gigabit Ethernet technology is designed to work with good quality Category 5 cable.

All that boils down to our recommendation that you use Category 5 UTP for all your twisted-pair Ethernet cabling. You'll need to make the same decision about PVC versus plenum-rated outer jacket as you read about earlier for 10Base-2 cable, and you'll have to decide which of the following a given run should use:

- **Solid Copper Wire.** Doesn't bend as readily as stranded copper wire, and can weaken and break if bent too sharply or too many times. The punch-down blocks used for wiring termination on network jack wall plates are designed for solid wire; stranded wire doesn't attach well to punch down blocks at all. So long as you run the wire in walls around corners using a sufficiently large bend radius, solid wire is the choice for in-wall Ethernet cabling.

- **Stranded Copper Wire.** Bends readily and often, making it preferable for patch cords and other unprotected applications. The crimp-on RJ-45 connectors are designed for use with stranded wire.

Making twisted-pair Ethernet cables is relatively easy if you have the right parts and tools. Figures 4.10, 4.11, and 4.12 show what you'll need. Figure 4.10 is a close-up photograph of the crimp, cut, and strip tool from the Belkin Ethernet installation kit, separately available as the Model F4F198 Modular Crimp Tool.

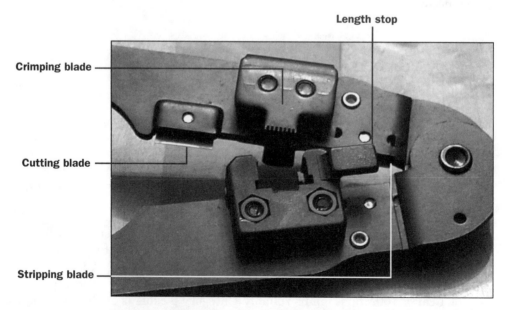

Figure 4.10: Belkin Model F4F198 Modular Crimp Tool.

You do the entire job of preparing cable and applying the RJ-45 connector with the tool in Figure 4.10.

Figure 4.11 shows the RJ-45 modular telephone connectors you'll use. Of particular importance in the figure are the wire channels and contacts you see in the middle—those eight channels are what route the individual wires in the Category 5 cable to the contacts in preparation for crimping. So long as you cut the cable end square, strip the outer cable jacket to the right length, and get the right color wire in the right channel, you'll have a working, reliable connection.

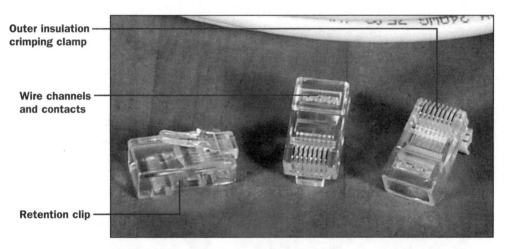

Outer insulation crimping clamp

Wire channels and contacts

Retention clip

Figure 4.11: RJ-45 modular telephone connectors.

Figure 4.12: Preparing Category 5 cable.

Example 4.4   Preparing Category 5 Twisted-Pair Ethernet Cable

Finally, Figure 4.12 and Example 4.4 illustrate the steps in preparing Category 5 cable before you attach the RJ-45 connector. Follow these steps:

1. Use the cutting blade on the crimp tool to cut the end of the cable squarely. If the cut angles across the axis of the cable, the wires won't all end at the same point, so some of the wires might not extend into the connector contacts properly. The lower wire in Figure 4.12 shows a properly trimmed cable end.

2. Figure 4.13 shows how you use the crimping tool to strip the trimmed end of the cable. Insert the trimmed cable from the side opposite the length stop (refer back to Figure 4.10) and push it through until it touches the stop. Your goal is to remove all of the outer jacket and *none* of the insulation on the individual wires, so close the jaws of the tool gently and remove the outer jacket. If you close the jaws all the way, you'll cut wire insulation. You'll probably want to rotate the cable a quarter turn so you can cut all faces of the outer jacket. When you're finished with this step, the cable should look like the middle cable in Figure 4.12.

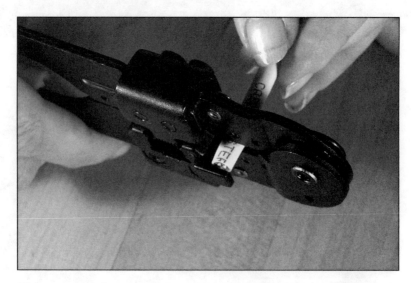

Figure 4.13: Stripping Category 5 cable.

3. You're going to untwist the wires (see the upper cable in Figure 4.12 where we've partially done that) and put them in a flat row in the right order for inserting into the RJ-45 connector. Table 4.7 shows how

to order the wires into the connector. Notice that the green and green/white wire pair is split across pins 3 and 6, matching the wiring you saw in Figure 4.9. You have to put signal pairs onto color pairs when you wire the connector so that the crosstalk minimization effects of the twisted wire work.

Table 4.7: Ethernet RJ-45 Wiring Table

Connector Pin	Wire Color	Function
1	Orange/White	Transmit +
2	Orange	Transmit -
3	Green/White	Receive +
4	Blue	
5	Blue/White	
6	Green	Receive -
7	Brown/White	
8	Brown	

If you're holding a connector with the contacts to the left and the retention clip facing away from you, pin 1 is at the bottom. The split in the pair between pins 3 and 6 makes it crucial that you identify pin 1 correctly. (We've seen references that put pin 1 at the other side; so long as you connect and number consistently, it won't matter.)

4. Figure 4.14 shows the wires properly ordered for insertion into the connector. You need to ensure the wires are in a flat plane, as shown in the figure, because that's the way they go into the connector. Pinch the end of the outer jacket to flatten the wires. When the wires are ordered and held properly, you'll see that solid and white wires alternate all the way across.

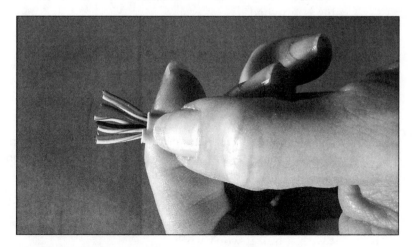

Figure 4.14: *Ordering Category 5 cable wires.*

5. Gently push the wires into the body of the connector. You might need to wiggle the outer jacket from side to side a little to make them all go in the contact holes. When you've inserted the wires properly, the connector will look like the photograph in Figure 4.15. If you look into the connector from the bottom, you'll see that each wire extends fully under its contact.

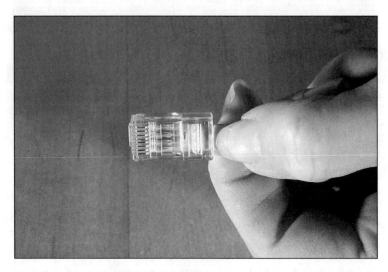

Figure 4.15: *Inserting Category 5 cable wires into the connector.*

6. Finally, check the wire ordering one last time, and then, keeping your hold on the cable, insert the connector into the middle part of the crimp tool, pushing the body of the connector until it stops, as shown in Figure 4.16. Crimp the assembly together firmly and one end of the cable is finished.

7. Cut the cable to the length you want, and then repeat steps 1 through 6 for the other end of the cable.

There are a lot of steps to making an Ethernet cable, and you have to get them all right. Practice a few times to get the feel of the steps before you make a cable you're going to use, and be sure to get good quality tools.

You learned in Chapter 2 that a crossover cable lets you connect two 10Base-T or 100Base-T computers together using twisted-pair wiring instead of a hub. You can use the same techniques you just learned to make an Ethernet crossover cable; simply wire the two ends differently, using Table 4.8 instead of Table 4.7. Be sure to label both ends of the cable to indicate it's a crossover and not a straight-through cable, because if you try to use it with a hub it won't work.

Figure 4.16: Crimping the RJ-45 connector.

Table 4.8: Ethernet RJ-45 Crossover Wiring Table

Left Connector Pin	Wire Color	Function	Right Connector Pin
1	Orange/White	Transmit +	3
2	Orange	Transmit -	6
3	Green/White	Receive +	1
4	Blue		4
5	Blue/White		5
6	Green	Receive -	2
7	Brown/White		7
8	Brown		8

The use of the wires on pins 4, 5, 7, and 8 isn't specified in the Ethernet standards, so almost no sources define what to do with those pins in a crossover cable. Table 4.8 specifies wiring the unused pins in a straight-through configuration, which follows an AT&T recommendation. Most of the sources we checked simply don't connect those four wires in a crossover cable, but because that makes it very difficult to route the wires into the connector, we suggest you follow Table 4.8.

Fiber-Optic LAN Extensions

You can use fiber-optic modules to extend segments of your twisted-pair Ethernet as far as two kilometers (over 1.2 miles). You'll learn what's in fiber-optic cables and how to choose the ones you need in this section. It's too hard to attach fiber-optic connectors to the cable; plan on buying any cables you need.

Fiber-optic cable has the internal construction shown in Figure 4.17. Fibers are specified in terms of the diameters of the core and cladding, in microns (one-millionth of a meter), so a 62.5/125 fiber has a core that's 62.5 microns in diameter and cladding that's 125 microns in diameter.

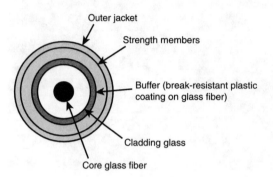

Outer jacket

Strength members

Buffer (break-resistant plastic coating on glass fiber)

Cladding glass

Core glass fiber

Figure 4.17: *Fiber-optic cable construction.*

More than one fiber is typically bundled in a cable, because one fiber only carries information in one direction. The bundling is done outside the buffer layer.

The size of the core glass fiber and the cladding glass surrounding the core determine the frequencies of light that will propagate down the fiber, along with the way in which the light propagates. There are two classes of fiber based on the way light propagates, called *multimode* and *singlemode* fiber. Figure 4.18 shows the difference. Multimode fiber (which has a larger core) permits the light to reflect off the sides of the core. Many different reflection angles are possible, each called a *mode*, leading the term multimode fiber. The core is typically very thin in singlemode fiber, so light can only pass straight through the fiber. Singlemode fiber avoids the small signal loss that occurs each time the light reflects, and so is capable of much longer range.

Table 4.9 shows you the performance you can expect from multimode and singlemode fiber cable. The wavelength in the table specifies the frequency of light being send through the fiber.

Light Transmission in Multimode Fiber

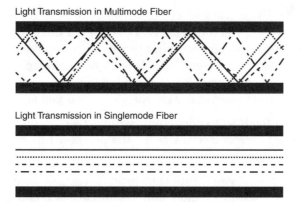

Light Transmission in Singlemode Fiber

Figure 4.18: *Light transmission in fiber-optic cable.*

Table 4.9: Typical Fiber Specifications

Fiber Type	Wavelength (nm)	Typical Specification	Typical Maximum Distance (km)
Multimode	850	62.5/125	2
	1300	62.5/125	5
Singlemode	1300	9/125	20

There are two main types of fiber-optic connector, too, called types SC and ST. SC is most often used with multimode fiber, whereas ST is most often used with singlemode fiber. (Both connectors can be used with either cable type.) Figure 4.19 shows what SC and ST connectors look like.

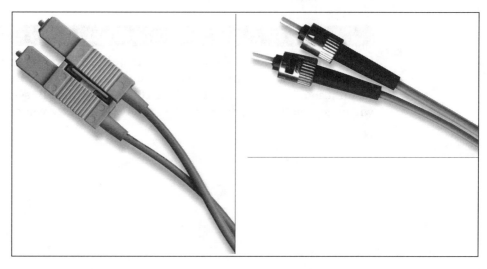

Figure 4.19: *Fiber-optic connector types (photos courtesy Belkin Components).*

Telephone Wiring

The telephone wiring you'll use for HPNA (Home Phoneline Network Alliance) compatible networks is simply whatever you have wired; there are no specific, unique requirements for HPNA system. Telephone wiring in North America typically uses RJ-11 modular telephone jacks and connectors, a four-wire version of the eight-wire RJ-45 version you saw in Figure 4.15.

Standard wiring for RJ-11 connectors permits two telephone lines to be wired, using the inner two contacts for the primary line and the outer two for the secondary one.

Look long enough and you'll find that most any small wire made has been used for telephone wire in homes and businesses. You can make a perfectly good telephone patch cord by connecting only the two middle contacts. At one time it was important to keep the two signals straight through and not crossed over, but telephone wiring has become so random in the last decades that equipment is now built to not care which of the two wires goes to which of the two middle contacts.

Summary

You've learned in this chapter that cabling is the foundation for your LAN, and that cables can be far more complicated than their simple appearance suggests. You learned how to make cables for serial direct cable connect networks, 10Base-2 networks, and 10/100Base-T networks. You learned the characteristics of fiber-optic cables and how they're specified, and learned the key elements of telephone wiring.

What's Next

In the next chapter, you'll see how to install LAN wiring in walls, including the hardware you'll want to use at the wall plates to create a neat, reliable installation. We'll look at installing 10Base-2, 10/100Base-T, and telephone wiring so you'll be ready, no matter what technology you select.

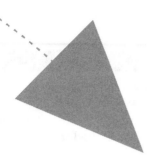

## 5

Installing Your LAN Wiring

In this chapter you will learn

- How to plan your network installation
- What techniques and parts you need to install LAN wiring

You'll learn in this chapter how to plan and install your network wiring. If you're simply wiring two computers together across a few feet, skip this chapter; otherwise, there's far more to do than simply throwing some wire in the walls.

The information you'll find in this chapter is targeted at people installing small LANs in homes and light commercial spaces. The guidelines you'd want to follow for large LANs, or for LANs in larger buildings, don't conflict with what you'll learn in this chapter, but they're more comprehensive and detailed.

Be sure to check the requirements of your local building codes before you do anything involving permanent cable installation in a building. Depending on where you live, there might be requirements for inter-floor fire stops and other safety-related precautions that you'll want to take into account.

Planning Your Network Installation

It's a nuisance to put holes in walls, discover you goofed, and then have to patch the holes. The best way to avoid unnecessary work and have a network you'll be happy living with is to plan everything you'll do before you start construction. The topics you'll want to think about include the following:

- **Understanding the Requirements.** Start by figuring out what computers you have to connect, where they are, and what equipment will be part of the network itself.

- **Mapping Your Network.** You'll want to (literally) draw a map of what buildings and rooms you'll be wiring, down to the level of where pieces of equipment are in the rooms. You'll compute the distances from computers to hubs and other network gear.

- **Routing Cables.** You can install your LAN wiring inside the walls or along baseboards. Either way, you can get parts and products to help keep the installation and to meet requirements for clearance away from noise sources.

- **Implementing Wall-to-Room Transitions.** It's entirely possible you'd like to avoid your home or office looking like a mad scientist's lair, with cables poking out of every available square inch of wall space. You'll want to design your installation to take advantage of outlet points for telephone and video signals.

- **Labeling Network Cables.** Networks don't stay constant; the connected equipment and the interconnections themselves change as your needs and constraints change. We'll show you ways to label your network cables so that when—not if—your maps of the network get out of date, you can still trace and understand the wiring.

The planning we recommend in this chapter need not take days or weeks of work; you can probably plan everything involved for a small LAN in a few hours.

Understanding the Requirements

Figure 5.1 shows an overview of what you need to think about to understand the requirements for your LAN. The figure shows a floor plan of the basement of a house, annotated to show where one computer, the LAN wiring wall faceplates, and the hub might reside. In-wall wiring connects from faceplates near the hub and the computer; patch cords connect the computer and the hub to the faceplates.

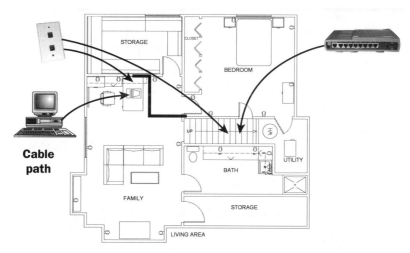

Cable path

Figure 5.1: *Requirements include what to connect, from where, and how.*

Ultimately, your network wiring plan will include a drawing like Figure 5.1, even if it's just a rough pencil sketch. We use Broderbund's 3D Home Architect for sketches such as these because it's easier to make changes neatly.

Your goal in defining the requirements for your LAN is to inventory all the computers you'll connect (present and future), where each one is or will be, where the wiring will run, and where the network equipment (such as hubs) will be. Example 5.1 shows you how to construct your inventory.

EXAMPLE 5.1   INVENTORY YOUR LAN REQUIREMENTS

Be as careful as you can constructing your inventory so you have an accurate picture of your requirements. The information will not only help you decide what to build, it will also help you maintain, expand, and troubleshoot the LAN later:

1. Make a list of all your computers, including ones you might add within the next year or two. For each computer, make a note of how much disk space it has (both total and available space).

    For Windows 95 and 98, you can get the disk space information by double-clicking the My Computer icon and looking in the resulting window. For Linux systems, you can get similar information from the df program at a command line. Figure 5.2 shows a typical Windows disk space display; the following is a typical Linux report from df:

```
/home/p/press >> df
Filesystem      1K-blocks     Used   Avail Capacity  Mounted on
/dev/da0s1a        198399    32177  150351     18%   /
/dev/da0s1e        727967       66  669664      0%   /tmp
```

```
/dev/da2s1e    3969982    434083  3218301    12%    /usr
/dev/da1s1e     893047    111716   709888    14%    /var
/dev/da3s1e   62593232  33111092 29482140    53%    /home
```

This df report shows that the /home part of the file system holds about 60GB total, with about 28GB free.

In Figure 5.2, Windows Explorer shows three local disks—C:, D:, and E:—with total sizes of about 2.2GB, 1GB, and 1.7GB, respectively. Those disks have free space of about 2.0GB, 334MB, and 496MB, respectively. You can also see a networked drive in the figure (Q:), which has a total capacity of 46.5GB and free space of 30.5GB.

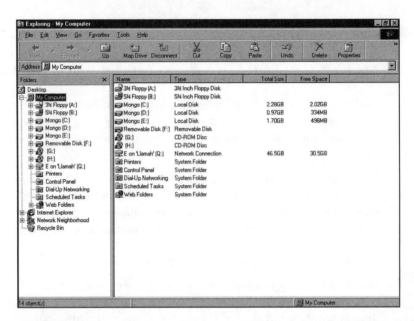

Figure 5.2: *The Windows Explorer shows total and free disk space.*

2. For each computer, record how much memory it has installed. You'll see this value reported onscreen as the computer starts; shut down Windows or Linux to a power-off state, and then turn the power on and watch the startup sequence.

   If the computer has a LAN adapter installed already, record the manufacturer and model number. You can get that information from the Windows Device Manager. Sequence through the commands Start, Settings, Control Panel, System, Device Manager, and then expand the Network Adapters entry. Figure 5.3 shows the result of that sequence on a machine with a 3Com Etherlink III Bus-Master PCI Ethernet Adapter installed.

Figure 5.3: The Windows Explorer shows total and free disk space.

You'll see the identification of the network card as Linux starts; other ways of finding that information (besides looking at the card itself) depend on the operating system; you'll learn how to do that in Chapter 6, "Picking and Installing Your LAN Adapters."

3. Record the operating system running on each computer, such as Windows 95 or 98, or Linux.

Mapping Your Network

The inventory is a list of all the devices you'll connect to your LAN—the requirements for what has to be tied to your network wiring. A map of the network—a drawing of the physical space the network spans and where each device is in that space—lets you understand where network access points need to be and where cables need to run. Example 5.2 describes how to start creating your network map.

EXAMPLE 5.2   MAPPING THE SPACE YOUR LAN WILL COVER

EXAMPLE

The physical network map is every bit as important as the inventory you did in Example 5.2, because it's the basis for deciding where to put cable outlets and where to run the in-wall cables. It's worth the effort to make the drawing reasonably accurate and to scale. Follow these steps:

1. Draw a map of where the computers are. The map doesn't have to be precise, but it's important to be able to use the drawing to know roughly where each computer is in the room, where walls are that might block or enclose LAN wiring, and approximate distances cables

will have to run. Be sure to note walls of unusual construction (such as cinder block) that might make cable routing difficult.

If you have more than one floor with computers, make a drawing of each floor.

2. Make an initial guess where the communications equipment (such as a 10/100Base-T hub) will be located, and add that to the map. If your network will be connected to the Internet, identify where the modem will be. Modems are often in computers, but they could equally be in a separate box containing a modem and a router.

There are several ways to identify computer locations on the map. For example, you can name each computer, adding the name to both the inventory listing and the map; or you can write all the information from the inventory directly on the map. You'll need a name for each computer anyhow, so we recommend the first approach. We also recommend choosing computer names that are acceptable on the Internet, which requires that the names satisfy each of these rules:

- Computer names must be no more than 15 characters long and must be unique on your LAN.

- You can construct names from the characters A–Z, a–z, 0–9, and the dash.

- The first and last character in a computer name must be alphanumeric (that is, not a dash). We recommend not using a number as the first character because some software we've seen has problems with names beginning with numbers.

Within those constraints, you can be as creative or ordinary as you like naming your computers. We've seen networks where the computers were named A, B, C, and so on, and a network where the computers were named beaver, ward, falcon, and viper. Our own network includes computers named netbert, mongo, and sarge. (It's common to use all lowercase names, but not required.)

After you locate each computer and your network equipment on the map, identify where the network cabling access point for each device will be. You'll likely be running the network cables through the walls or along baseboards; in either case, there's likely to be a point where the cable leaves the vicinity of the wall and runs to the computer itself. Add the telephone line you'll use for your Internet modem, too.

Routing Cables

If you have a 10/100Base-T network, you'll run cables from each computer to a hub. If you have more than one hub (or switch; see Chapter 16, "Enhancing Your Network," for more information on network switches and increasing network performance), you'll need to run cables between hubs. If you have a 10Base-2 network, you'll run a single cable path touching every computer in your network. Either way, use your map (and walk the building if necessary) to identify the routes each cable will take. It's often convenient to group cables together for runs through walls, especially as they approach the hub because it's as easy to pull several cables through the wall as one.

If you're interested in standards applicable to LAN wiring, and especially if your network is on the larger side, you'll probably want to take a look at these two standards from the Electronics Industry Association/ Telecommunications Industry Association (EIA/TIA):

- **EIA/TIA Standard 568A - Commercial Building Wiring Standard.** Specifies minimum requirements for telecommunications wiring within a building, including the telecommunications outlets, and between buildings. It recommends a wiring system topology and lengths, plus cable types, connectors, and pin assignments.

- **EIA/TIA 570 - Residential and Light Commercial Telecommunications Wiring Standard.** Addresses cabling in residential (single- or multi-family) and light commercial premises.

You can run cables in ceilings as well as in walls and along baseboards, but keep in mind that there might be more stringent fire safety requirements if you do.

As you plan your cable routes, watch for electrical devices that can inject noise into the wires. Table 5.1 shows some of the most common noise sources and the minimum recommended separation distance between the sources and your LAN cables. Table 5.1 only applies for circuits operating at 480V or less, which is typical of residential and light commercial spaces and segments the separation based on the maximum load in watts carried by the circuit.

Table 5.1   *LAN Noise Sources and Separation Distances*

Noise Source (480V or less)	Recommended Separation in Inches		
	<1500W	1500–3500W	>3500W
Unshielded power lines or electrical equipment in proximity to open or non-metal pathways	5	12	24
Unshielded power lines or electrical equipment in proximity to grounded metal conduit pathways	2.5	6	12
Power lines enclosed in a grounded metal conduit (or equivalent shielding) in proximity to grounded metal conduit pathway	0	6	12
Transformers and electric motors	40	40	40
Fluorescent lighting	12	12	12

You can translate the wattages in Table 5.1 to circuit breaker ratings by dividing the wattage by the voltage on the circuit (typically 120 or 240V; 480V circuits are rare in residential or light commercial spaces). Figure 5.4 shows a typical circuit breaker panel. Where you see two breaker handles mechanically ganged together, such as with the cap over two handles at the top of the figure, the breaker ratings (the numbers on the handle) should be identical and you're looking at a 240V circuit for most residential panels. Where the handles aren't ganged, even if the two breakers are paired in a single breaker module, you're looking at a 120V circuit.

30 amp breaker ganged to the one above it (240V circuit)

20 amp breaker in the same module as another, but not ganged (120V circuit)

Figure 5.4: *Circuit breaker panel and rating markings.*

Example 5.3 shows how you translate between the wattages in Table 5.1 and the voltages and ratings you find in the circuit breaker panel. (Note: there are lethal voltages behind the covers of circuit breaker panels. If you're uncertain working with the panel, consult an electrician.)

EXAMPLE

EXAMPLE 5.3   CONVERTING AMONG VOLTS, AMPS, AND WATTS

The math required to convert from among volts, amps, and watts is straightforward. Knowing how to do the conversions lets you make sure you have the right information to work with:

1. You calculate watts as volts times amps. The lower breakers in Figure 5.4 are rated for 20 amps (written on the handles), and are single-breaker circuits. In a residence or light commercial space, the breaker would be on a 120 volt circuit, so multiplying 20 amps times 120 volts equals 2400 watts maximum on the circuit. (In practice, you never want to run a circuit at maximum capacity.) You'd use the middle column in Table 5.1 for required spacing of LAN cables away from the power lines controlled by those breakers.

2. The ganged 30 amp breakers on the upper left of Figure 5.1, typical of a circuit for an electric oven or clothes dryer, together control a 240 volt circuit. Multiplying 30 amps times 240 volts gives 7200 watts, which requires you to reference the right-hand column in Table 5.1.

The interference between power lines and LAN cables travels through magnetic fields radiated by the power lines. Those fields don't travel well through metal shielding, which is why the different rows in Table 5.1 specify separation distances for different installations. The worst case is unshielded power lines—such as the insulation-covered power wires used in nearly every house built in the United States and Canada since 1975. The wire is formally called Type NM cable, but is generally known by its trade name, Romex. Older homes with power wires enclosed in metallic conduit have reduced separation requirements.

Unshielded twisted pair (UTP) cable for 10/100Base-T networks counts as LAN cable in "open or non-metal pathways" in Table 5.1. You might get away with reducing the separation distance if you're using 10Base-2 coaxial cable because the outer braid is a shield, but it's safest to use the full separation distance in the table.

Plan your cable routes on your map, taking into account the maximum distance limits for your network and the required separation distance. Draw the path each cable takes from computer to hub (for 10/100Base-T) or from one computer to the next (10Base-2). Try to group cables together when possible so you can install more than one cable at a time. When you're done, you'll have something like Figure 5.5. We drew one computer and the hub in the figure so it would be readable in print; your map should include all your computers and hubs. Don't forget the inter-hub connecting cables if you have multiple hubs. You'll draw the wiring between the network wall outlets if you're using plates like we've shown in the figure; if you're running cables directly to the computers without outlets, draw the wiring plan all the way to the computers and hub.

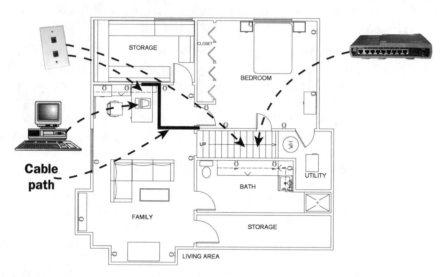

Figure 5.5: *Cable routing added to a network map.*

We routed the cable in Figure 5.5 starting at the left outlet, along the wall to avoid a power line, and then across the ceiling and over to the outlet for the hub. Routing through the ceiling let us avoid the door openings between the computer and hub, which simplified the installation. Routing in the ceiling was an easy decision to make in this case because when we mapped this network the walls and ceiling weren't built. The only compromise we had to make was that we needed to use plenum-rated cable instead of the more common type.

Implementing Wall to Room Transitions

In-wall cabling makes for a much neater and more durable installation than ones with wires strung helter-skelter across doorways and along the floor. Network cable connectors are easy to damage by kicking, tripping, or pulling on the cables, so cables protected inside walls are going to be far more reliable over time than ones that are exposed. If you can't run the cables in the walls, be sure to read the section later in this chapter on running cables in existing construction, where you'll learn about products to help you run your network cables safely along the baseboards.

Unless you know what products to use, one of the hardest problems you'll face when you install your network cables in the walls is finding a neat and reliable way to terminate the cables where they exit the wall. Outlets are common in hardware stores for telephone jacks and television coaxial cable type "F" connectors, but unless you live somewhere such as Silicon Valley, you might not find outlets for 10/100Base-T or 10Base-2 cable. Don't try to substitute telephone jacks and television coaxial cable connectors just because they're available—their electrical properties aren't what you need, and you're likely to make your network unreliable.

Instead, if you can't get outlets locally, order them from catalogs or on the Internet. We're using the Belkin (http://www.belkin.com) products as examples in this book; other companies making similar products include Panduit and International Connectors and Cable Corporation.

Figures 5.6 and 5.7 show the front and back of an outlet plate including two 10/100Base-T connectors suitable for use with Category 5 unshielded twisted pair cable. Plan on using solid Category 5 wire with the punchdown blocks you see in Figure 5.7. The bottom position in Figure 5.7 shows the Category 5 cable wired to the punchdown terminals on the connector.

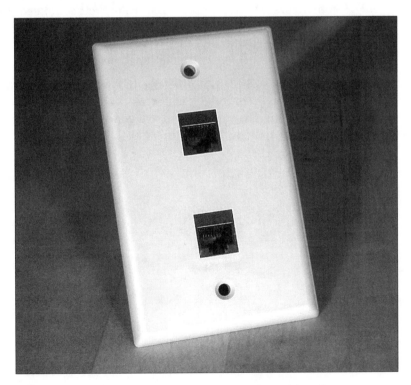

Figure 5.6: *Front view of dual 10/100Base-T outlet.*

Figure 5.7: *Rear view of dual 10/100Base-T outlet.*

Figure 5.8 shows a closeup of the punchdown terminals on the back of the RJ-45 connectors. If the photo were in color, you could see that the markings on the top of the punchdown terminals are color coded and marked to show how to connect the Category 5 wire; we've annotated the photograph to show you how the colors are positioned on the connector.

The overall strategy is to put one wire in each punchdown terminal, using a special punchdown tool to seat the wire in the terminal; there's no wire stripping required. Example 5.4 shows you how to wire solid Category 5 cable onto the punchdown terminals of the RJ-45 connector.

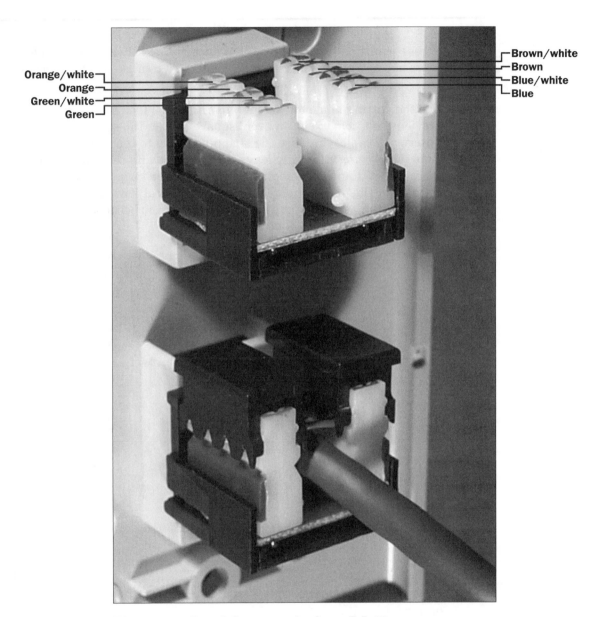

Figure 5.8: Punchdown terminals on RJ-45 connectors.

EXAMPLE 5.4 WIRING AN RJ-45 CONNECTOR USING PUNCHDOWN TERMINALS

The process seems awkward at first, but once you've attached a few RJ-45 connectors successfully, you'll have the confidence to make LAN connections whenever you need them. Follow these steps:

1. Use the cutting blade on your RJ-45 crimp tool (see Figure 4.10 in the previous chapter) to cut an even, square end on the solid wire Category 5 cable; then use the stripping blade to remove the outer insulation, being careful to leave the insulation on the individual wires intact. Figure 5.9 shows the result; we've stripped back about 1 1/4 inch in the photograph. It's not at all critical how far back you strip (as long as you expose enough of the wires) because you'll cut off the excess when you're done.

Figure 5.9: *Preparing solid Category 5 wiring for punchdown terminals.*

2. Figure 5.10 shows the steps to attach the wire. Starting with the part of Figure 5.10 in the upper left, spread the wires so they're untwisted and positioned to match the color and striping pattern of the connector.

3. The part of Figure 5.10 in the upper right shows the punchdown tool, which you'll use to push each wire onto the blade in its punchdown terminal. The part of Figure 5.10 in the lower left shows the tool in action, pushing the last of the eight wires into the connector.

4. Finally, put the covers over the terminals if your connector provides them, and then cut off the excess wire using a side-cutting wire cutter

as in the part of Figure 5.10 on the lower right. Snap the connector into the wall outlet and you're done.

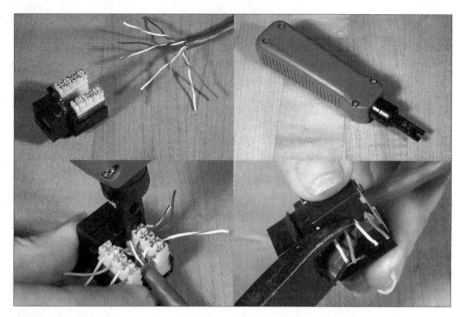

Figure 5.10: *Inserting solid Category 5 wire into the punchdown terminals.*

Most wall outlet products offer a variety of connectors to fit the wall outlet plates, including ones for telephone RJ-11 and video type F connectors. We'd suggest you use products with those options because it's very convenient to combine network, telephone, and video outlets together on a single wall plate.

Labeling Network Cables

You'll need to know how the cables connect to troubleshoot problems and maintain your network. You'll probably be able to remember what wall outlets connect to what other ones while you're installing the cables, particularly if you're installing into new construction and the wall board isn't up yet. Remembering what goes where a few months later, though, isn't terribly likely. You could make a drawing, but it's prone to getting lost.

A better approach is to label the cables and wall plates themselves. Labelers used to all be like the old Dymo Labelmakers, embossing letters into a relatively thick plastic tape. That was useful for flat surfaces such as a wall outlet, but wouldn't wrap around a wire well. Silly name notwithstanding, we use a Brother P-touch Home & Hobby II (Model PT-110) to make labels for both cables and wall plates (see Figure 5.11). The Model PT-110 prints on a thin Mylar tape that's flexible enough for cables.

Figure 5.11: *Brother Model PT-110 labeler.*

We label both cables and wall plates. You need to label the wall plates because you can't see the cable labels without removing the plate from the wall, but because you might move plates around, you'll want to label the cables to have a permanent naming record.

Think some about the naming scheme you print on the labels. Computers move around, so it's not a good idea to label the cable with the name of the computer it's connected to. It's probably not a good idea to use room names either because if you have more than one network outlet in a room the name could be ambiguous. One good scheme is to use room names combined with sequence numbers (OfficeA-1, OfficeA-2, OfficeB-1, and so on) because that way the name includes a geographic hint of where the cable runs in the unique name. Be sure to put the same name at both ends of the cable—you're naming the cable, not the end.

Although it might seem this approach fails for 10Base-2 coaxial cable because the cable forms one unbroken length when everything's wired up, you'll want to use the same approach. The cable you're naming is the segment in the wall, before you attach patch cables to the computer, and that segment (like the 10/100Base-T cable) has exactly two ends. You can't assume one end is always next to a hub, though, so you might want to modify your naming scheme some. One workable approach is to name outlets (using the OfficeA-1 scheme we suggested), and then combine outlet names to form the cable name. Using that scheme, OfficeA-1/OfficeB-2 would name a cable segment that went from outlet 1 in Office A to outlet 2 in Office B. Figure 5.12 shows a label wrapped along a Category 5 cable on the left, and a pair of labels on the front of a wall plate on the right. If you place the label along the axis of the cable, as on the left, you might have to secure the label with clear tape. Alternatively, you can wrap the label around the axis of the cable to form a tab with the name on it.

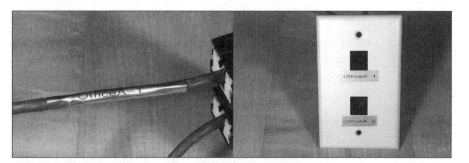

Figure 5.12: *Labels on wall outlets and cables.*

Installing the Cables

Whether you're wiring in new construction or adding a LAN to an existing building, what you don't do when installing cables is as important as what you do. You need to be careful how sharply you bend the cable and how hard you pull on the cable. Follow these guidelines:

- EIA Standard SP-2840A (a draft version of EIA-568-x) recommends a minimum bend radius for UTP of four times the cable outside diameter, or about one inch. For multipair cables the minimum bending radius is 10 times the outside diameter.

- If you're installing fiber optic cables, the minimum bend radius is 10 times the cable diameter if the cables are not under tension. Cables under tension may not be bent at less than 20 times the diameter. EIA Standard SP-2840A recommends that no fiber optic cable be bent on a radius less than 3.0 cm (1.18 inch).

- Cable pulling tension must always be less than 25 pounds because higher tension can stretch the cable and affect the twists in the pairs. The twists in the cable help improve high frequency response, so if you damage the twisting pattern, the high frequency response can be reduced. Kinking the cable by letting it get twisted or pulled around sharp corners can also damage its electrical properties.

It takes specialized equipment to measure the frequency response and near end crosstalk of an installed cable. For most people, your only indication of installation cable damage will be a connection that seems to have network problems more than others. The best repair approach is to not create the problem in the first place, being careful about bend radius and pulling tension when you install the cable. Following that suggestion might require making more openings in walls for existing buildings, but installation is a one-time problem, whereas an erratic network keeps on giving.

New Construction

Installing LAN wiring in new construction—before the wallboard goes up— is simpler than in existing buildings. You'll have to make a few decisions before you start:

- Will you use standard electrical boxes behind wall outlets? We've seen LAN outlets screwed directly into plasterboard, mirroring the typical telephone outlet installations we see.

- Will you use conduit, or run the cable exposed in the wall?

- How will you terminate cables at the hub, and how will you mount the hub?

Figure 5.13 shows your alternatives for attaching wall plates to the wall (check your building codes to see what's permitted in your area). The drawing on the left shows a side view cross section of an installation directly into the plasterboard, routing the cable through a hole into the wall. The hole should be large enough to clear the bodies of all connectors on the wall plate. You can secure the wall plate to the plasterboard with countersunk screws.

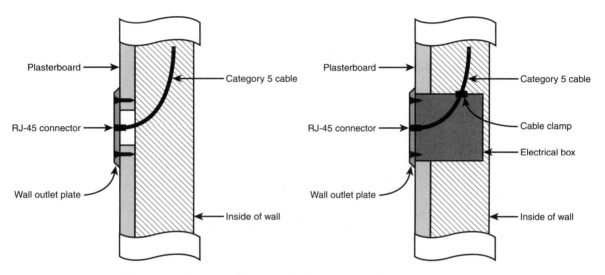

Figure 5.13: *Attaching wall plates to walls.*

Two problems with the approach on the left are that 1) you can only remove and replace the wall plate so many times before the screws fail to bite into the plasterboard, and 2) there's no strain relief on the cable to protect the RJ-45 connector. Anyone pulling on the cable in the ceiling or elsewhere could pull a wire loose.

The second way to mount a wall plate, shown in the side view cross section on the right in Figure 5.13, is to attach it to a standard electrical box you in turn attach to a wooden stud in the wall. If you run the cables exposed in the wall, much like Romex power cable, you should be able to use the same cable clamps as for Romex to anchor the LAN cable to the box. If you run the cable in plastic or metal conduit, you don't need separate cable clamps because the conduit provides all the protection required.

You can drill smaller holes through the studs if you're running exposed cable, which might make installation easier. If you're running conduit, you'll either want to use plastic conduit and large-radius corners, which can be a nuisance to install, or flexible metal conduit. No matter what, don't ever use an electrical box as a corner junction and then cover the box up with plasterboard—if you do, you'll never be able to remove and replace the cable because the cable is likely to get stuck in the box.

You have two options for how to install a hub and route cables to it. You can terminate all the incoming cables at RJ-45 jacks and then run patch cords from the jacks to the router, or you can mount the hub in a relatively large enclosure that mounts in the wall and receives the incoming cables. Figure 5.14 illustrates the first idea—you install a RJ-45 jack in the wall near the hub for each cable, and mount the hub either on a shelf on the wall or in a rack near the jacks. A patch cord connects each jack to the corresponding jack on the hub.

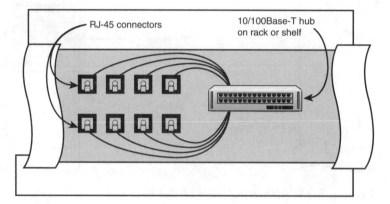

Figure 5.14: *Rack or shelf mounting and wiring a LAN hub.*

Figure 5.15 illustrates mounting a large electrical box, possibly one large enough to hold a medium-sized circuit breaker panel, in the wall and using it to enclose the hub and the incoming cables. This approach has the advantage that you don't need to wire a lot of RJ-45 jacks in the wall and then use patch cords—you can run the incoming cables directly to the back of the hub. Be sure to make provisions for an electrical power circuit in the box to power the hub.

Existing Construction

You'll use the same ideas installing LAN cabling in an existing building as in new construction, but you'll be further constrained by the possibilities for where you can manage to run wires. The problem is that you're likely to have to make holes in the walls to run cables inside walls, and although patching painted plaster or plasterboard isn't all that hard, patching wallpaper and wood or vinyl paneling is probably out of the question.

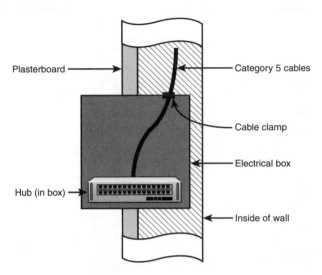

Plasterboard

Category 5 cables

Cable clamp

Electrical box

Hub (in box)

Inside of wall

Figure 5.15: *In-wall electrical box mounting and wiring a LAN hub.*

If you're going to make holes in plaster or plasterboard, there are two basic approaches to making a repairable hole. Oddly enough, one is to make a very small hole, and the other is to make a very large one.

The idea behind making a very small hole (up to 1/2 inch, perhaps) is that, if a hole is small enough, you can patch it with plaster patch simply by filling, smoothing, sanding, and painting the hole. You're limited how you can use a small hole because it's typically very hard to find a wire in the wall with only a small hole to look or reach through. You can reach a "fish line" (a stiff coiled wire) through the hole, and if that lets you reach to a larger opening where you'll be installing a wall plate, it might be enough to pull the cable through.

If a small hole won't do, make a big one. Specifically, make one that spans two wooden studs in the wall. Figure 5.16 shows what you want to do, which is to make a cut that spans the two studs so you'll have a way to support the cut out panel when you go to repair the hole.

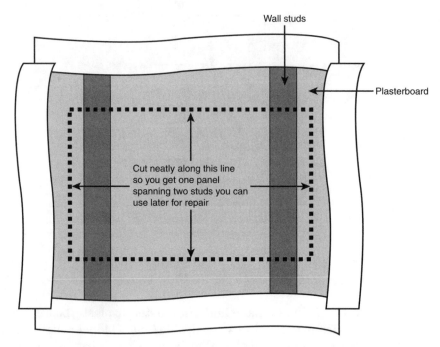

Figure 5.16: *Making a large, patchable hole in a wall.*

Example 5.5 describes how to work in walls using large holes.

EXAMPLE

EXAMPLE 5.5   WORKING WITH A LARGE HOLE IN A WALL OR CEILING

Decide where you need to put repairable holes. You probably don't need an additional hole where the wall plates mount, but you'll need holes anywhere you have to run the cable through a stud or around a corner. Then follow these steps:

1. Neatly cut out a section of wall or ceiling panel with a dry wall saw or another saw, making the cut all the way around narrow enough that you can fill it with plaster patch. Try not to dent or otherwise damage the panel any more than necessary.

2. Complete whatever work you have to do inside the wall. If possible, you'll want to finish wiring, connecting, and testing the LAN before closing up the hole so it's easy to make cabling repairs.

3. When you're done working inside the wall, mount the panel back onto the studs with nails or screws. Orient the panel the same way it was when you removed it, and center it in the opening, to minimize the gaps between the panel and wall.

4. Patch and paint all the way around the panel, including the heads of the nails or screws. Remember that it's a lot easier to clean up excess patch material with a damp paper towel, rag, or sponge than to sand it off later.

The other way to install LAN cabling in an existing building is to use "raceway" products—plastic or metal strips shaped to look like wall molding. Because the raceway runs along the floor against the wall, it's neat and out of the way. Raceway manufacturers include Belkin (`http://www.belkin.com/products/product_index/lan/products/Raceway.html`), Panduit (`http://www.panduit.com/products/solutions/raceways.htm`), and International Connectors and Cable Corporation (`http://www.icc.com/rss.htm`).

The Belkin Signal Point raceway system provides hollow molding that carries wiring and provides space for connections (see Figure 5.17). In this figure, for example, you can see the RJ-45 LAN connectors on the left of the open area at the top of the molding.

Figure 5.17: *Belkin Signal Point molding with connectors.*

Figure 5.18 is a close-up view of an opening drilled in the molding; the inside is hollow, providing room for signal cables. The Belkin system supports audio, telephone, infrared signaling, video, and cable television signal distribution in addition to 10/100Base-T networks.

Figure 5.18: *Belkin Signal Point molding internal view.*

All signal distribution with this system is based on a central wiring cabinet. Figure 5.19 shows the cabinet itself, which is built much like the standard cabinet used to hold circuit breakers.

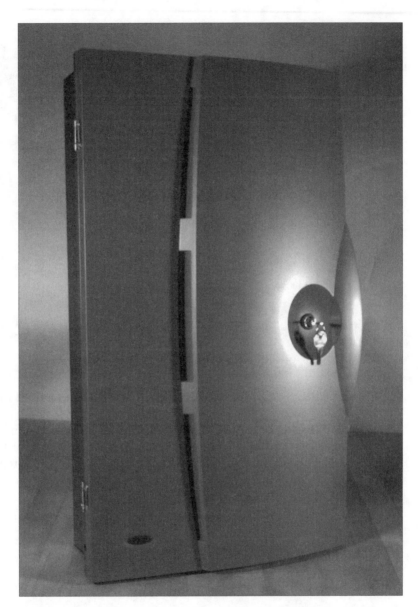

Figure 5.19: *Belkin Signal Point wiring cabinet.*

The insides of the Signal Point cabinet are far different than a circuit breaker panel, holding modules used to connect the wiring for all the signal types you install. Figure 5.20 shows (top to bottom) audio, 10/100Base-T, telephone, and infrared distribution modules installed in the cabinet.

Figure 5.20: *Belkin Signal Point wiring modules installed in cabinet.*

The 10/100Base-T module (closeup in Figure 5.21) is designed as a patch panel used with a hub. You connect incoming in-wall cables to the punch-down blocks at the top of the module, and then you use patch cables to connect the corresponding RJ-45 jacks in the signal module to the hub, which itself resides in the cabinet.

Figure 5.21: Belkin Signal Point 10/100Base-T module.

Summary

Planning, good techniques, and the right parts are the keys to a reliable, professional LAN installation. Your plan should include an inventory of the machines that will be on the LAN, a drawing of the building spaces, and a schematic of where the cables will run. Good techniques include labeling LAN connections so you'll know what's where and planning cable runs to minimize interference from power wiring. Choosing the right parts includes deciding how to terminate each LAN connection—whether at the back of machines or at wall plates—using the right cable and connectors for your LAN technology, and installing the cables carefully to make sure you're careful about bend radius and pulling tension limits.

What's Next

What you've learned in this chapter gives you the ability to construct the wiring that will connect your computers together. In Chapter 6, "Picking and Installing Your LAN Adapters," you'll learn how to choose and install the hardware your computers need to communicate across the network.

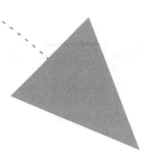

## 6

Picking and Installing Your LAN Adapters

In this chapter you will learn

- The basics of how your computers work and what's inside the case

- How to choose a network adapter that meets your requirements

- What tools and techniques you should use to install a LAN adapter

For some people, the scariest part of building a network is having to work with new hardware. If your experience goes no farther than turning on the power switch, new hardware can be intimidating. If that's a good description of you, this chapter is what you need because you'll learn what goes on inside your computer, what the funny-looking things inside it are, and how to choose and add in the network hardware you need.

If you're already up to speed with computer hardware, you can skip the introduction to PC hardware and the guide to installation, focusing on the section on choosing a LAN adapter.

PC Hardware

You should know both how your computer does what it does and what the physical pieces are that make up your computer. The next two sections explain those topics; you can read them separately or in order.

How Your Computer Works

Think of your computer as an extremely capable but very simple and literal assistant. It will do almost anything you want, but you have to be very precise about what you want, you have to explain everything in the computer's language, and you have to explain in excruciating detail.

Example 6.1 should give you an idea of how extreme a statement this last paragraph really was. The topic of Example 6.1 is to paint an image on the screen of your computer. There are programs to help you do that, of course, but let's do this as a thought experiment where you'll paint the picture the way the program would, not the way you would using the program. The image on your color monitor is itself made up of many, many color dots. Just like a color TV, each dot is the combination of three smaller dots in a triangle: one red, one green, and one blue. You can make your computer display any color by setting the brightness of those three colors appropriately. You get white by setting red, green, and blue to full brightness; black by setting all three to zero brightness. Red and blue in differing brightness combinations give shades of purple. You get the entire color palette by choosing the right combination of those three primary colors. (Don't be fooled by our statement that red, green, and blue are primary colors; that's true in an *additive* color model. The usual *subtractive* model, such as applies to filters or paints, uses red, yellow, and blue, although the red is more properly magenta.)

EXAMPLE

EXAMPLE 6.1   PAINTING A PICTURE BY COMPUTER

There are thousands of dots on your computer's screen; if you look closely enough at the face of the monitor, you can see the individual dots. Many people run the displays on their computers at 800 dots horizontally by 600 dots vertically, so they have 480,000 dots total onscreen. We have to set the precise color in your picture for each one of them to draw that picture over the entire screen:

1. Setting one dot on screen involves storing three numbers (red, green, and blue intensity) into your computer's *memory*, a place where the computer can remember things while it's running. Do that for the first dot, the second one, the third one, and (from left to right) on up to the 800th one. When you're done, you've painted one row onscreen.

2. Repeat step 1 for each of the 600 rows.

Not only did you have to set the color for 480,000 dots in Example 6.1, you had to do three operations for each dot. The total work you had to do, then, was 480,000 dots times three operations per dot, or 1,440,000 operations. If you did that by hand, with a pencil and paper, the entire example would likely take you hours. Your computer can do many millions of simple operations, such as storing a color value, every second. What would take you hours takes the computer fractions of a second.

Let's take the idea of carrying out Example 6.1 with pencil and paper a step further and match all the items involved with elements of your computer, giving us Example 6.2.

EXAMPLE

EXAMPLE 6.2   MATCHING PENCIL AND PAPER TO COMPUTER COMPONENTS

We've written artificial intelligence software, and we understand how far computers are from the level of what people commonly do, so we're not about to claim that computers think or are equivalent to people. Nevertheless, many features in a computer are similar to human characteristics:

- The paper you wrote on corresponds to the *memory* in your computer. Memory stores values and the results of computations.

- Your brain corresponds to the *processor* in your computer. The processor carries out instructions.

- Your eyes are the equivalent of the *input devices* for your computer. Input devices such as keyboards, mice, or scanners translate actions or objects in the real world into electrical signals.

- Your hands are the *output devices* in the example. Output devices such as printers convert electrical signals in the computer into physical representations.

Figure 6.1 is another view of the inside of your computer, showing a more complete version of a computer's functions using the model that a computer is made up of blocks for processing, storage, memory, input, and output. The figure includes annotations of examples of devices you'll find in each category. You'll find modems and networks in both the input and output categories, reflecting the fact that they both send and receive information.

You're probably familiar with what the common terms such as disk, CD-ROM, keyboard, mouse, and others represent. The processor and memory terms might not be so familiar:

- **Processor.** There are two processor manufacturers—Intel and AMD—who, between them, sell nearly all processors in PCs running Windows or Linux. (Macintosh computers use a completely different processor that is incompatible with the Intel and AMD chips.)

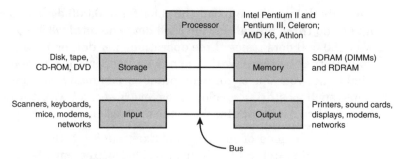

Figure 6.1: *Functions making up a computer.*

The commonly advertised processor characteristic is its clock speed, which is a measure of how fast things happen inside the device. Different processors accomplish more or less work per clock, which is why you can expect a Pentium III to be faster than a Pentium II or Celeron, and an Athlon to be faster than a K6. The comparison between the two companies' top-line processors, the Intel "Coppermine" Pentium III and the AMD Athlon, is more complex. Which is faster for a given clock rate probably depends on whom you ask.

• **Memory.** Computer memories are devices that hold millions of distinct numbers, letting the processor read and write numbers hundreds of millions of times per second. The very high speeds at which memories talk to the processor have required the invention of new, higher-performance memory.

The memories in systems built since the introduction of the Intel Pentium processor all come on small circuit boards about an inch high and six inches or more long. Different memory technologies spawned different types of memories. Essentially all processors based on Pentium and K6 systems required single inline memory modules (SIMMs). Most Pentium II, Pentium III, Celeron, and Athlon systems use dual inline memory modules (DIMMs). The very newest, high-performance Pentium III systems use Rambus inline memory modules (RIMMS; Rambus is simply a name for a new, fast memory technology).

DIMMs proved to be an excellent package for memory, with a relatively long lifetime—long enough that several generations of DIMM speed grades and compatibility specifications have come and gone. The initial DIMMs followed no particular specification and were quickly replaced by PC66 memory (which ran with a memory clock speed of 66 million cycles per second, or megahertz; abbreviated MHz). PC66 memory gave way to PC100, clocking at 100 MHz, which in turn is being replaced by PC133, clocking at 133 MHz.

In most ways storage and memory are the same because they serve to remember things. The difference is that memory (sometimes called RAM or random access memory) forgets everything stored in it when the power goes off, whereas information stored on disk, tape, CD-ROM, or DVD is preserved.

There's one other key component of your computer, the software. The word *software* was made up in contrast to hardware and describes the series of instructions the processor carries out—the programs—to do the work you want. You'll learn a lot about the software it takes to make your network operate in Part III, "Setting Up Your Network Software."

That's the essence. The processor carries out instructions (software), telling all the other components what to do. Memory provides a fast workplace; storage is a vast container that can hold information without power. Input and output devices let the computer communicate with you and with other computers.

The Nuts and Bolts Inside

Theory aside, it's worth having a working knowledge of what's inside your computer. The difference is much like that of knowing how an internal combustion engine works versus recognizing all the bits and pieces when you open the hood on a car. Knowing the theory lets you think about what goes on; knowing the practice lets you work with the equipment.

Figures 6.2 through 6.7 show you the key elements outside and inside a typical computer case. What you find inside your computer will likely differ in layout and in fine detail, but the elements we've highlighted with annotations in the figures will be present in similar form.

Before you open your computer, be sure to shut it down and unplug it from the wall. Try not to disconnect or dislodge any wires inside the computer. You'll want to get an antistatic wrist strap at Radio Shack or a computer store; the wrist strap (when clipped to the chassis of the computer) helps make sure no static electricity can build up that would damage the electronics inside the computer.

Figure 6.2 shows the back of the computer, with annotations describing the functions of the switches and connectors. Starting in the upper right and following around clockwise, the major quadrants in the figure are the power supply, vents for airflow, the panel for access to adapter cards, and the input/output connector panel. You'll connect the power cord to the power connector on the back of the power supply. The keyboard, mouse, external modem, Universal Serial Bus (USB) devices, and printer connect to the input/output connector panel; with the computer in Figure 6.2, the display monitor and speakers also connect to the input/output connector panel. We've installed an internal network adapter card in this computer; you can see its RJ-45 connector in the middle of the adapter-card access panel.

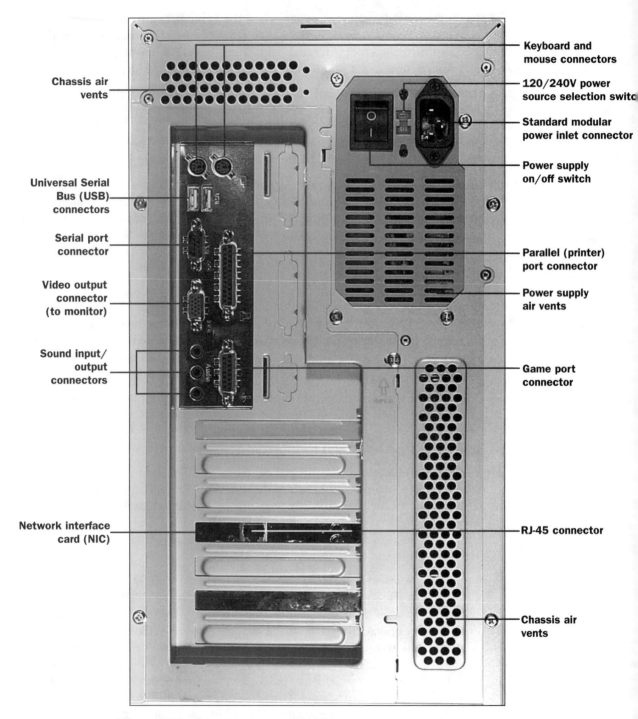

Figure 6.2: *Computer rear panel layout.*

The input/output connector panel is directly attached to a large electronics board inside the computer called the motherboard. The adapter cards plug into connectors on the motherboard, too. Figure 6.3 shows a side view of the inside of the computer in Figure 6.2. The complex-looking area in the lower left is the bottom half of the motherboard. Annotations in the figure show you where and what the visible components in the view are, including the processor, memory, Peripheral Component Interconnect (PCI) bus slots on the motherboard, CD-ROM or DVD, hard drive, and floppy disk.

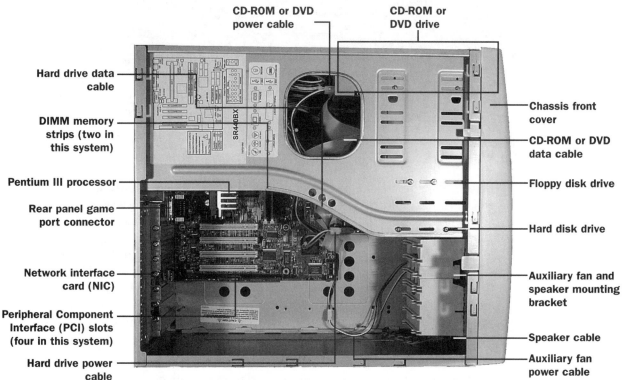

Figure 6.3: *System internal side view.*

Figure 6.4 is a close-up of the visible part of the motherboard to make its key components clearer. You can see the bottom of the Pentium III processor in the top middle, the four PCI slots and one ISA slot immediately below the processor, and the two memory slots to the right of the processor. (The ISA slot is holding the network adapter, so the connector is only barely visible.) The connectors at the upper-left edge are part of the input/output connector panel. (The other black rectangles—chips—on the motherboard don't directly affect operations you can see, so we've ignored them.)

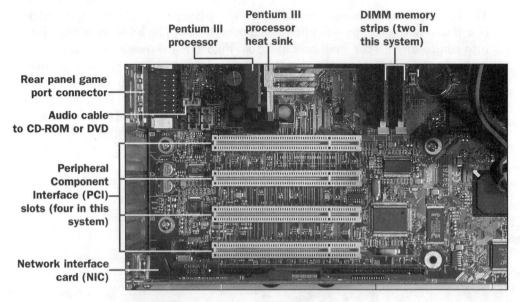

Figure 6.4: *Close-up of motherboard.*

Figure 6.5 is another close-up of part of the motherboard, only with the chassis panel that had blocked view of the rest of the processor moved out of the way. You can see the entire Intel Pentium III processor running from top to bottom of the middle of the photograph. The processor module is the black vertical rectangle at the left of that assembly, which also includes the silver-finned heat sink attached on the right side of the module. The fan in the middle of the heat sink helps draw heat away from the processor by ensuring a continuous supply of cooler air. More of the two memory strips is visible to the right of the photograph, while more of the connectors forming the input/output connector panel are visible on the left edge.

Figure 6.6 is a side view of the motherboard near the processor, showing the two memory strips, the main power supply connector, and more of the wiring inside the chassis.

Figure 6.7 shows a close-up of the back of the hard disk drive. The drive itself is just visible extending toward the center from the middle-right edge of Figure 6.2. Figure 6.7 shows the typical data cable and power cable wiring for a disk drive, including the stripe on one edge of the cable used to ensure the cable is turned the right way in its mating connector on the drive. The pins in the connector are numbered; the stripe indicates the end of the connector with pin number 1. The orientation of the power connector is equally important; rounded corners on the connector ensure it can only go into the drive in one orientation.

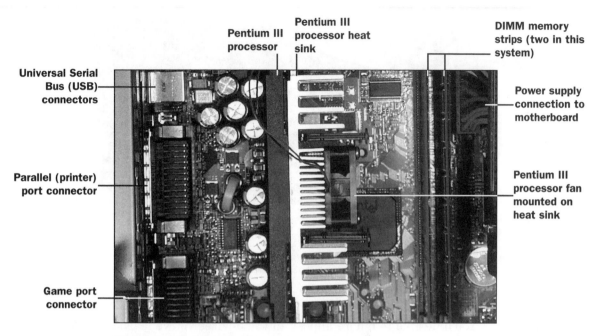

Universal Serial Bus (USB) connectors

Parallel (printer) port connector

Game port connector

Pentium III processor

Pentium III processor heat sink

DIMM memory strips (two in this system)

Power supply connection to motherboard

Pentium III processor fan mounted on heat sink

Figure 6.5: Close-up near processor.

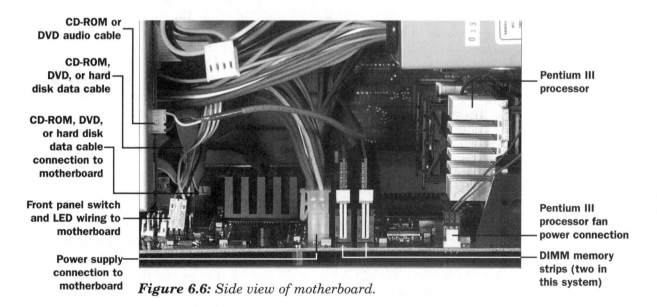

CD-ROM or DVD audio cable

CD-ROM, DVD, or hard disk data cable

CD-ROM, DVD, or hard disk data cable connection to motherboard

Front panel switch and LED wiring to motherboard

Power supply connection to motherboard

Pentium III processor

Pentium III processor fan power connection

DIMM memory strips (two in this system)

Figure 6.6: Side view of motherboard.

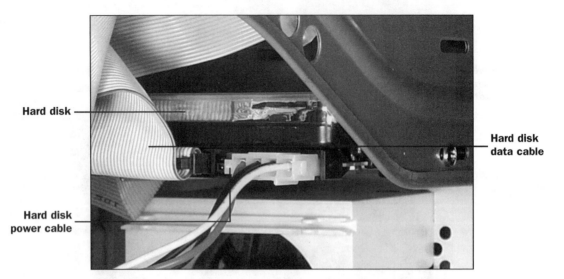

Hard disk

Hard disk
data cable

Hard disk
power cable

Figure 6.7: Close-up of hard disk and cabling.

You'll be able to ignore almost all the devices you've learned to identify in this section; you can do everything in this book and at most have to open your computer only to add an internal network adapter (bottom edge in Figure 6.4). Knowing what the other items inside the case are helps you know where to look for the slot the adapter will occupy and helps you understand the computer as more than an impenetrable box.

Choosing a LAN Adapter

Although most computers sold to corporations include a LAN adapter, and although you can order a new computer with a LAN adapter from Micron, Dell, Compaq, and others, most computers in homes and small offices lack that essential network component. You'll solve that problem in two steps:

1. Select and purchase the LAN adapter.

2. Install the new adapter.

Like everything else you're going to learn in this book, choosing a LAN adapter successfully is the result of deliberate planning and analysis. There are hundreds of LAN adapter manufacturers and thousands of models to choose from, and not all are products you'd want to live with. Eventually your selection will come down to one based on price, but before that happens you'll want to narrow the field based on five criteria:

- Device driver availability
- Internal or external device

- Electrical computer interface
- Network technology
- Manufacturer reputation

All five of these criteria are directed at a single goal: to select adapters that meet the requirements of your computers and network and that will be dependable over the long run. In our opinion, little else matters in the decision.

Device Driver Availability

You learned in Chapter 3, "Understanding and Evaluating Network Services," that developers build software in layers. Figure 6.8 reproduces Figure 3.1, showing the typical layers in a networked PC.

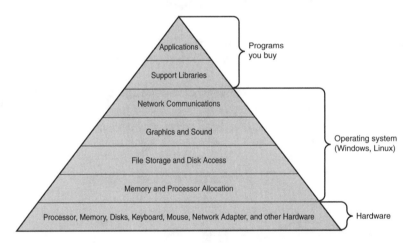

Figure 6.8: *Different programs layered one on another make your computer work.*

Windows and Linux themselves don't talk to the hardware devices at the bottom of the pyramid; they talk to specialized programs called device drivers, which in turn talk to the hardware. Windows device drivers are usually written by the hardware manufacturers, whereas Linux device drivers are typically written by a programmer who happened to have one of the devices and needed it to work.

You need to know about device drivers because, if no driver is available for the operating system you use, you won't be able to use the hardware. We've seen network adapter cards, for instance, that the manufacturer "targeted" at Windows 98, steadfastly refusing to provide drivers for Windows NT or Windows 2000. If you had one of those cards and wanted to upgrade your operating system, you'd be sunk.

For that reason, you'll want to check on driver availability for the operating systems you care about before you buy a network adapter. Keep in mind that Windows 95 drivers might not work with Windows 98 or Windows 98 Second Edition, that Windows NT drivers are different from those for Windows 95 or 98, and that Windows 2000 drivers are different from all of those. There is no commonality between Linux drivers and Windows drivers, either.

You can usually get the driver information you need from the manufacturer's Web site.

EXAMPLE 6.3 CHECKING DEVICE DRIVER AVAILABILITY

Example 6.3 shows how to get driver availability information on the 3Com 3C905C-TX-M PCI adapter from the 3Com Web site. Microsoft also maintains a Windows hardware compatibility list at `http://www.microsoft.com/ hcl/default.asp`:

1. Connect a computer to the Internet and go to the manufacturer's Web site. The one for 3Com is `http://www.3com.com` (see Figure 6.9).

Search controls ———

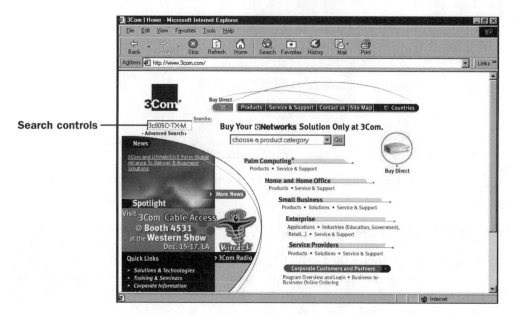

Figure 6.9: *Starting a 3Com Web site search.*

2. Having the model number for the LAN adapter (in this case the 3Com 3C905C-TX-M) is half the battle. As you see in the upper-left corner of Figure 6.9, you can start a search directly from the 3Com home page. We searched for 3C905C-TX-M—3C905C would work as well—and

found downloadable device drivers for the card in the list of search results. The description specifically states that the drivers support Windows 95, Windows 98, and Windows NT. (Windows 2000 also has drivers, but the page hadn't been updated when we wrote this chapter.)

The lesser market share and freeware basis of Linux mean you can't do a straightforward search for drivers you'll need with Linux. We use the Linux-Mandrake distribution of Linux; on its Web site (`http://www.linux-mandrake.com`) under the Supported Hardware link is (a ways down the page) a list of supported network adapters. The list includes the 3C900 series, and although it's likely from that information the 3C905C is supported, you might want to alter your choice to a card for which you have precise model number confirmation.

Internal or External Device

Your second decision factor is whether to use an internal or external LAN adapter. You're generally constrained to use an external adapter with a laptop computer unless one's already built in, but you can go either way with a desktop computer. External adapters are easier to install because you don't have to open the computer, but unless they use the PCMCIA/Card Bus/PC Card interface (see the next section), they'll be limited to at most 10Mbps. Few desktop computers have a PCMCIA/Card Bus/PC Card interface, so if you're using 100Base-T network technology, you'll want to pick internal adapters.

External adapters, because they amount to extra electronic bits and pieces on your desk, are also more vulnerable to being knocked around and broken. Internal adapters are safely enclosed by the computer case, with the cabling at the back of the case.

Computer Interface

Every network adapter has two interfaces: one to the computer and one to the network. The electrical interface to the computer is to a *bus*, which is a standardized port for high-rate data communication. The PC industry has had a long history of buses, of which you're likely to use one of these four:

- **Industry Standard Architecture (ISA).** The ISA bus, used to add cards within the computer, dates back to the original IBM Personal Computer of the early 1980s. It's prone to all the failings you might imagine from an interface designed before anyone had an inkling of what people would extend the PC to do. Shortcomings of the ISA bus are that it's too slow, it's less reliable than the PCI bus, it doesn't support automatic device configuration in its original form, and the automatic configuration mechanism added to the bus late in its life is unreliable.

You won't find 100Base-T network interface cards for the ISA bus because ISA is incapable of transferring data that fast.

- **Peripheral Component Interconnect (PCI).** The PCI bus is the standard internal adapter slot interface in computers today. You can see PCI slot connectors in Figure 6.4. The PCI bus supports automatic detection and configuration of new hardware by the operating system, simplifying both hardware and software installations. Following the recommendation of Intel and Microsoft, manufacturers started shipping computers in 1999 with no slots except PCI, eliminating the ISA entirely.

- **Universal Serial Bus (USB).** USB is an external interface standard designed in response to the problems people encounter trying to add devices using the printer and modem (serial) ports on computers since the original IBM PC. USB can transfer data at over 10Mbps, supports many simultaneously connected devices, and permits devices to be plugged in or disconnected without shutting down the computer. Following a relatively slow start in the late 1990s, USB exploded in popularity in 1999 with devices including network adapters, mice, keyboards, printers, digital cameras, scanners, game controllers, speakers, microphones, telephones, modems, serial and parallel ports, external CD-ROM and DVD drives, video capture ports, uninterruptible power supplies, fingerprint recognition sensors, security ID keys, and radios.

  Although a faster USB specification is under development, USB network adapters are presently limited to 10Mbps operation. They're without question the easiest adapters to install, though, making them attractive for smaller systems.

- **Personal Computer Memory Card International Association (PCMCIA).** Laptop computers present unique problems adding in new hardware because their compact packaging usually precludes using the larger industry standards for desktop computers such as ISA or PCI. USB is an option for newer laptops; prior to that, the laptop industry invented a credit card–sized hardware format called PCMCIA (since renamed to PC Card). PCMCIA-card network adapters plug into small bays inside laptop computers, but often have cables vulnerable to damage at the point the cable connects to the PCMCIA card.

In practice, your decision-making should be pretty straightforward, as you'll learn in Example 6.4.

EXAMPLE 6.4   PICKING A NETWORK ADAPTER COMPUTER INTERFACE

If you're adding a network adapter to a file or other server, use an internal PCI adapter. You wouldn't want to sacrifice server performance on a 100Mbps network that a USB or ISA adapter would require, and the internal adapter leaves fewer parts hanging out to be knocked around and damaged:

1. Add a network adapter to a desktop computer with an internal PCI or external USB adapter. Both are capable of operation on 100Mbps networks if required; the USB adapter is easier to install.

2. Choose a USB or PCMCIA adapter to connect your laptop computer to a LAN.

No matter what type of computer you're working with, we recommend you avoid an internal adapter using the ISA bus at all costs unless there are no other slots inside the computer and no USB port is available. ISA is simply too prone to setup and configuration problems to be worth dealing with any longer.

Network Interface

Your fourth network adapter selection criterion will be the interface you require to the LAN. Like the computer interface, the network interface is usually a black-or-white choice; you'll have one or two specific interfaces you can use, and no others. LANs using 100Mbps technology can often accommodate 10Mbps products (and vice versa), but you'll have to check the specific products you use to verify their compatibility with the alternative speed. You can get network adapters—called *combo* adapters—that support 10Base-2 and 10Base-T, but it's unusual to find combo cards supporting 100Base-T too.

Similarly, it's uncommon to find a telephone-line LAN adapter that can also connect directly to a 10Base-T network. If you're using telephone-line networking for your LAN cabling, you're limited to products with that interface.

To be safe, you're even more restricted with wireless LAN adapters; until the market for IEEE 802.11–compliant technology matures, you'll probably want to make sure all your equipment is from the same manufacturer.

Manufacturer Reputation

Too many people seem to believe that all computer equipment is essentially the same and that you can buy strictly on price. In our experience that's a risky approach; the computer industry is riddled with manufacturers who ship buggy products, ship products they quickly abandon, fail to provide competent customer support, or deliver proprietary products locking customers into expensive upgrades.

For that reason, we suggest you follow a policy of keeping track of the manufacturers whose products serve you well and whose products serve you poorly. Knowing that lets you return to the former and shun the latter.

PC networking products are prone to all the same problems. You might save a few bucks buying strictly on price; we've found 10/100Base-T network interface cards for as little as $13, which is admittedly a lot less than the $40 we've paid for the 3Com 3C905C-TX-M NICs we use. We typically buy NICs from 3Com, Intel, and Actiontec, and although we don't regard that as a fixed, inviolate list, it's served us well. We've *never* had a NIC from one of those manufacturers fail, even though we've had our share of problems with other products.

Example LAN Adapter Products

In the spirit that pictures make ideas more definite than words, this section shows you what typical LAN adapters, ones we recommend at that, look like. Figure 6.10 shows a 3Com 3C905C-TX-M internal 10/100Base-T PCI network adapter. The adapter is only for 10/100Base-T networks, with no connectors usable with 10Base-2 wiring, but adds capabilities not found in other adapters, including the ability to pull your computer out of low-power standby state when there are network messages to process using the new *Wake on LAN* standard. Looking at the construction of the card in Figure 6.10 should convince you of the competition to reduce price and improve reliability in the NIC market. Aside from an optional chip shown on the right of the card that lets your computer start from the network instead of a local hard disk, there's only one (large) chip on the 3C905C-TX-M. All the functionality of the NIC hardware is in that chip; the rest of the tiny components spread around the card serve to match electrical characteristics of the chip with the network and otherwise condition electrical signals on the board. Available drivers for the 3C905C-TX-M support Novell NetWare, Microsoft Windows For Workgroups (a predecessor to Windows 95), Windows 95 and 98, and Windows NT and 2000.

Figure 6.11 shows a representative external USB network adapter, the 3Com 3C460 Home Network USB Ethernet adapter. Installing the 3C460 (which you'll read about in a later section of this chapter) is about as simple as it can be: You merely plug one end of the USB cable into the back of your computer, plug the network RJ-45 cable into the body of the adapter, install software drivers, and you're finished. Drivers for the 3C460 only support Windows 95 and Windows 98, largely due to the absence of good USB support in other operating systems. Whether 3Com provides driver support for Windows 2000 will probably depend on whether they conclude that versions of Windows 2000 are likely to be used in the home market.

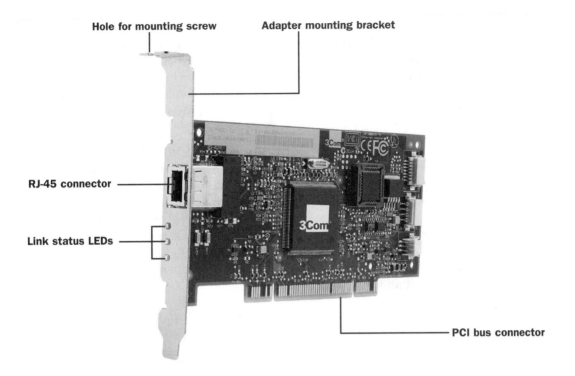

Hole for mounting screw

Adapter mounting bracket

RJ-45 connector

Link status LEDs

PCI bus connector

Figure 6.10: 3Com 3C905C-TX-M 10/100Base-T PCI Ethernet adapter. (Photo courtesy 3Com Corporation.)

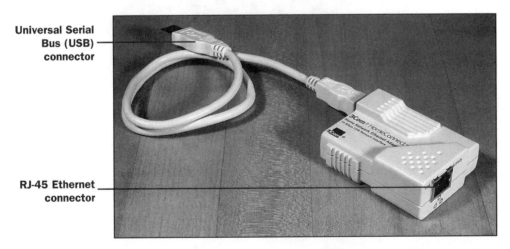

Universal Serial Bus (USB) connector

RJ-45 Ethernet connector

Figure 6.11: 3Com 3C460 Home Network USB Ethernet adapter.

You can use a crossover cable (see Chapter 5, "Installing Your LAN Wiring") to let the 3C460 USB Ethernet adapter do the same job as a serial Direct Cable Connect (DCC) cable or a pair of similarly cross-connected internal network adapter cards. The USB Ethernet adapter is over a hundred times faster than the DCC cable approach and doesn't require opening up the computer case (which you'll have to do to install internal cards).

Figure 6.12 shows a PCMCIA (also known as PC Card) external network adapter option for laptop computers, the 3Com 3CCFEM556B PCMCIA Ethernet adapter and 56Kbps modem. In addition to supporting both 10 and 100Mbps Ethernets, the card can upgrade a laptop to 56Kbps operation from the 33Kbps standard common in many machines. The card comes with a pair of cables that convert from the dense, flat connectors on the edge of the card to standard modular RJ-45 network and RJ-11 telephone connectors. Like most desktop computer LAN adapters, the NIC in the 3CCFEM556B automatically detects the network operating speed—10 or 100Mbps—and adjusts itself accordingly.

Ethernet and modem phone-line connectors (both require external adapter cables)

PCMCIA bus connector

Figure 6.12: *3Com 3CCFEM556B PCMCIA Ethernet adapter and 56Kbps modem.*

We've shown both external and internal telephone-line network adapters in Figure 6.13: the Intel AnyPoint Home Phone Line Network external adapter and the Actiontec ActionLink Home Network internal PCI card adapter. The two are compatible with each other, using the Home Phoneline Networking Alliance (HPNA) standard. The Intel product is available with a printer (parallel) port or USB computer interface. Both let you use the telephone line normally while the network is in operation, and both provide software to support letting any computer on your network access the Internet through a shared modem (more about that in Chapter 12, "Sharing an Internet Connection").

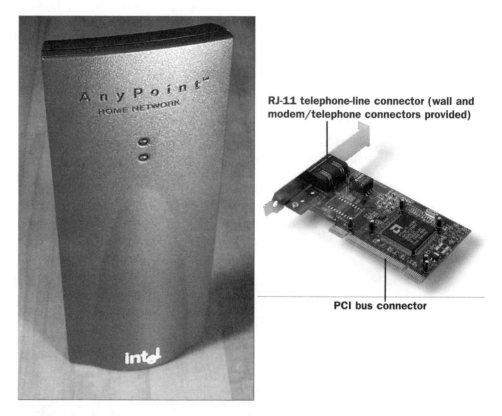

RJ-11 telephone-line connector (wall and modem/telephone connectors provided)

PCI bus connector

Figure 6.13: *Intel AnyPoint Home Phone Line Network adapter and Actiontec ActionLink Home Network adapter (internal adapter photo courtesy of Actiontec).*

Installing LAN Adapters

The key to success for any work you do changing your computer is a planned, careful, methodical approach; know what you're going to do, do the work precisely, and explain (plus, if necessary, correct) any unexpected behavior before you go on. Those work habits are doubly important when you're working with network hardware because you're affecting more than one computer through the network.

Internal Adapters

Installing an internal adapter isn't difficult, but you should have the right tools. The following are the ones you'll need for the installation:

- Antistatic wrist strap to prevent static electricity damage to computer components

- Appropriately sized hex driver or Phillips or slot screwdriver to remove and replace adapter mounting screws

You might need a needle-nose pliers to retrieve dropped screws, too.

Don't take our recommendation to use an antistatic wrist strap lightly. You can't even feel static electricity strong enough to kill computer chips, and the only dependable way to guard against static electricity buildup is to use a wrist strap. Figure 6.14 shows the parts of a typical one; use the elastic wrist strap to make sure the metallic wrist contact is snug against your skin, and then attach the alligator clip at the other end of the ground cord securely to the computer chassis or a metal cold water pipe.

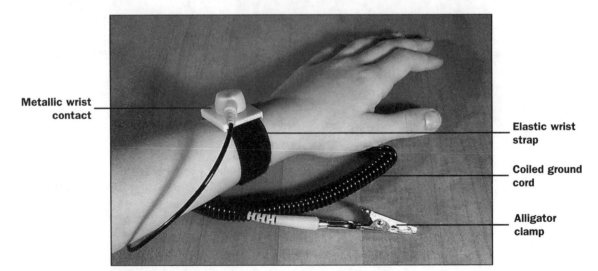

Figure 6.14: Antistatic wrist strap.

There's a right way and many wrong ways to insert or remove adapter cards from your computer. Figure 6.15 shows the right way: Hold the card at both ends between thumb and forefinger, holding the card itself and not components on the card. Using a gentle rocking motion (from left to right and back in the photograph) ease the card into or out of the slot connector, making sure the bracket (on the left in the photo) fits properly into the allowed space in the chassis. Figure 6.15 shows an adapter card in an ISA slot to illustrate the difference between ISA and PCI; note the connector (which will be black) is smaller than the PCI connector above it.

Hold adapter card by printed circuit board ──

Figure 6.15: Inserting or removing an adapter card the correct way.

Whichever slot type your card requires, PCI or ISA, you'll install the card following the steps in Example 6.5.

EXAMPLE 6.5   INSTALLING AN INTERNAL NETWORK ADAPTER IN ITS SLOT

EXAMPLE

After doing one or two adapter installations, you'll realize they're all the same, and none of them are very difficult. You have to pay attention to the details, though, including the safety and computer protection guidelines in steps 1 and 2. Follow these steps:

1. Shut down your computer and disconnect the power cord.

2. Put on your antistatic wrist strap, clip it to the computer (possibly in an air vent hole), and open the computer case.

3. Choose the empty slot you'll use to hold the adapter, and remove the cover plate for that slot from the back of the computer. It's not likely

to matter which of several identical slots you choose; we tend to keep cards spaced away from one another if possible to improve airflow within the case. Save the screw you remove for use in step 5.

4. Gently insert the card into the slot following the technique of Figure 6.15. You'll never want to force the card, but do make sure the card seats completely in the slot. You can tell it's seated when essentially all the gold strips on the bottom of the card disappear into the slot connector on the motherboard.

5. Secure the adapter to the chassis back panel with the screw you removed in step 3. Figure 6.16 shows the retaining screw being replaced using a hex driver. We prefer hex drivers and hex head screws for computer work because they make it less likely that the tools will slip off the screw head and damage some of the components inside the computer.

Adapter mounting screw under hex driver

Figure 6.16: *Securing an adapter card with a retaining screw.*

6. We typically don't close up the computer case until after we've finished software installation. (You'll learn how to do that in Chapter 8, "Configuring Your System Software.")

Be careful where you put your hands and what you move inside the case; accidentally stretching or disconnecting a data or power cable, or bending a card to the point that it cracks internally, can cause problems that are very hard to troubleshoot. If you must disconnect a cable to make room to work, be sure to draw or write down precisely how it was connected so you can replace it later. Be very gentle removing and replacing cables, too, so you don't break wires or bend pins.

External Adapters

Plugging in an external adapter, be it USB or PCMCIA, is simply a matter of finding the port on the computer, orienting the cable or adapter card the right way, and plugging the device in. Figure 6.17 is a close-up of part of the input/output connector panel of the computer in Figure 6.2. (We've rotated the photograph a quarter-turn counterclockwise to make it bigger on the page, too.) There are 2 USB ports in the middle of the photograph, bracketed by the keyboard and mouse ports on the left and the serial and parallel ports on the right. The flat USB connector from the network adapter (such as the 3Com 3C460 in Figure 6.11) plugs into either of the two. There's a top and bottom to the connector, so it will only go in one way. Don't force the connector if it doesn't want to fit; try turning it over instead.

Figure 6.17: *USB port on back of computer.*

Summary

In this chapter, you've gained some understanding of how your computer works and what's inside your computer. You've read about five key factors you should consider when selecting network adapters to buy and examined five products representative of top-quality adapters. You've learned what precautions to take while installing an internal network adapter, and covered the steps in the installation.

What's Next

You'll learn the details of network software operation in the next chapter, including the differences between Novell, Microsoft, and TCP/IP (Internet) networks. That foundation will provide the background knowledge you need to understand what's going on in Chapter 8, where you'll learn how to configure the operating system software for the LAN adapters you installed in this chapter.

Part III

Setting Up Your Network Software

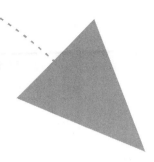

## 7

Network Software—Protocol Stacks and Applications

In this chapter you will learn

- How computers use highly structured conversations to communicate with each other

- That computer protocols operate in layers, with lower layers providing services for the upper ones

- About addresses—the techniques computers use to identify each other—and to route messages across the planet

You learned in Chapters 2, "Kinds of Networks," and 4, "Picking Your LAN Cable Technology and Speed," how the physical hardware works, including the different network technologies and cabling. In this chapter, you'll learn about the "languages" computers speak to each other when they talk across networks—that is, the messages and protocols that implement your network.

The ideas and examples in this chapter get a little bit technical. If you're willing to accept cookbook recipes for how to make your network operate, you can skip directly to Chapter 8, "Configuring Your System Software." We'd suggest eventually reading the material here, though, because it can help you understand what's happening inside your network and diagnose problems when the network doesn't respond the way you expect.

Network Protocols

The thoughts inside your head are different from conversations between people; when you're just thinking to yourself, the information and context is all present and you can jump directly to what you want to think about. When you talk to someone else, you have to make sure you both share the information and context needed for the ideas you say to make sense. Because of that, people carry on conversations with an underlying structure to communicate information. One common pattern is that people introduce themselves or acknowledge the presence of someone they already know, state what they want to talk about and then get down to the meat of the discussion in which information and questions will flow both ways. Following that pattern helps ensure that when something is said both people already have the necessary background information to interpret the statement in the same way.

Computers have to solve the same problems to communicate with each other. Although a computer might have all the information it needs to do work locally, it will still have to identify itself and carry on a "conversation" with another computer to cause that remote computer to do some work. Because computers lack the flexibility of people, those conversations consist of precisely formatted messages sent between the computers following a strict, rigid pattern called a protocol.

What Do Network Protocols Do?

The precise details of what protocols do depend on the protocols and tasks you're asking the computers to do, but the overall functions that protocols accomplish on your network are common:

- Send and receive messages of any type across the network hardware
- Identify the sender and destination of the message, and determine whether the receiving computer is the end destination
- For computers with multiple network connections, forward received messages along the way to their ultimate destination if possible
- Verify that the received message arrived intact, or request retransmission of corrupted messages
- Discover the computers operating on the local area network
- Convert names of computers to addresses used by the network software and hardware, and vice versa
- Advertise services offered by this computer and inquire about the services offered by other computers

- Receive user identification and authentication information and control access to services

- Encrypt and decrypt transmitted information to maintain security across an insufficiently secure network

- Transfer information back and forth according to the requirements of specific application software and services

It's not always apparent, but protocols are organized in layers: There's not just one massive specification covering all the functions we listed; there are typically many. Software implementing protocols works the same way; programs that worry about computer naming, for instance, are separate from those that worry about reliable delivery, and both are separate from those that worry about encryption.

Because network developers worldwide have to talk to each other to make their systems work together, there's a common way to describe network layers called the Open Systems Interconnect (OSI) Reference Model. Figure 7.1 shows the layers in the OSI model, from the hardware-level functions at the bottom of the stack (layer 1) to the application-specific functions at the top (layer 7).

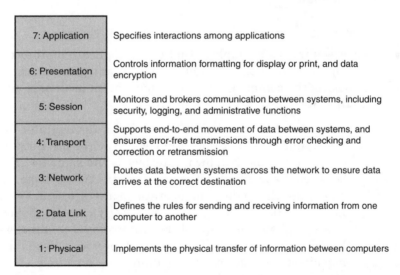

Figure 7.1: *The Open Systems Interconnect (OSI) Reference Model.*

You've already encountered parts of your system operating at the lower levels in the OSI reference model—the network interface adapter (or network interface card, NIC) and its device driver implement the layer 1 physical and layer 2 data link functions. The IP protocol in TCP/IP is an implementation of the layer 3 network functions, whereas the TCP protocol in TCP/IP implements the layer 4 transport.

It's possible to have more than one implementation of any layer in a single computer. Installing two dissimilar network interfaces, such as a NIC and a modem, results in two physical and data link layer implementations. Installing support for both Microsoft and Internet networking results in two parallel implementation stacks for the network and transport protocol layers.

Software at layers 5 (session) and up is often independent of the lower-level implementation, requiring merely that a protocol exist with a minimum set of capabilities. The intercomputer file transfer functions built into Microsoft Windows Explorer, for example—a layer 7 application function—can operate over any standard protocol (Microsoft, Novell, and Internet). The relative independence of application functions and underlying network implementation results in there being a few standard network protocol suites and many specialized application protocols. The common network protocols are Microsoft, Novell, and Internet; you can discover application protocols following Example 7.1 by looking at the networked functions on your computer.

EXAMPLE

EXAMPLE 7.1   DISCOVERING APPLICATION NETWORK PROTOCOLS

The lesson in this example is that every application protocol requires some application program to implement it and give you control over it. Cataloging the common networked application programs gives you insight into their application-level protocols:

- **File transfer.** We already noted that intercomputer file transfer functions built into Microsoft Windows Explorer use network protocols; even though the graphical interface is the same for moving files between disks on a local machine and between disks on two different machines, the underlying operations are different. On the local machine, the Windows Explorer directly invokes the local file system to accomplish your request. For intercomputer transfers, the Windows Explorer invokes one of the network protocols available on both machines to cause the information to be sent from one computer to the other, using the local file system to store information received from the network or get information to be sent over the network.

- **Computer discovery.** If you open the Windows Explorer by double-clicking the Network Neighborhood icon, you'll see a list of all the computers visible on your LAN from your computer. If instead you click the Network Neighborhood icon with the right mouse button and choose Explore, you'll see the more interesting display in Figure 7.2, in which the left pane in the Explorer shows disk drives, special Windows folders, and Network Neighborhood; whereas the right pane shows the visible computers.

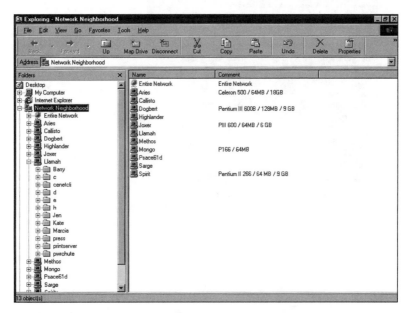

Figure 7.2: *Computer browsing with Windows Explorer.*

If you expand Network Neighborhood in the left pane (click the plus sign next to the Network Neighborhood icon), you'll see the computers listed. Expand one of the computers (as we've done with the computer named Llamah in Figure 7.2) and you'll see the shared resources on the computer. The one we've expanded in the figure (the computer is named Llamah) has a variety of shared resources, including drives C, D, E, and H.

It took no fewer than three protocols to generate the display in Figure 7.2: one to discover the computers visible on the network, one to associate names with the numbers the first protocol returned, and one to discover the services and resources being made available by a computer on the LAN.

- **Advertise and inquire about services, identify and authenticate users, encrypt and decrypt data, and transfer information.** Figure 7.3 shows an image from a video conference using Microsoft NetMeeting. Beyond the underlying layer 3 and 4 protocols, establishing the conference call required application-specific protocols to discover the computers could initiate and accept NetMeeting calls, to scramble the data for network transmission, and to transfer the video and audio data of the conversation.

Figure 7.3: *Video conference using Microsoft NetMeeting.*

The following three sections describe the capabilities and limitations of each of the three common layer 3 and 4 protocol suites. We'll assume the existence of layer 1 and 2 functions such as sending and receiving messages or identifying sender and receiver because they're common functions usually handled by the network hardware and device drivers rather than these protocols. Similarly, we'll ignore the functions and services at layers 5 through 7 until later in this chapter because they can often operate on any of the three protocols we'll cover. Of the general protocol capabilities listed earlier, then, the following are the ones you'll learn about for the three major protocols:

- Forward received messages (layer 3)

- Verify that the received message arrived intact, or request retransmission of corrupted messages (layer 4)

- Discover the computers operating on the local area network (layer 3)

- Convert names of computers to addresses used by the network software and hardware, and vice versa (layer 4)

NetBEUI

NetBEUI is Microsoft's protocol for simple Windows networks. Its advantage is that it's simple to set up and use, requiring almost no work on your part. Its disadvantage is that it's strictly limited to the LAN, with no support for crossing between two connected networks. People often confuse NetBEUI and its related component NetBIOS with the application protocols Windows uses to permit file and printer sharing. Those protocols, known as SMB (Server Message Block) and supported by the Samba software under Linux as well as the native Windows software, can run over NetBEUI, Novell, and Internet protocols.

NetBEUI is a specific implementation of the essential layer 3 and 4 capabilities, with benefits and restrictions appropriate to small LANs:

- **Forward received messages.** NetBEUI doesn't forward messages. It relies on the LAN hardware to transport messages from the sender all the way to the destination. That restriction means that LAN devices such as hubs and switches operating at layer 2 (you'll learn about network switches in Chapter 16, "Enhancing Your Network") work fine with NetBEUI, but routers and switches operating at layer 3 do not.

- **Reliable delivery.** NetBEUI includes the ability to verify that received messages arrive intact and will request retransmission of corrupted messages. Corrupted messages occur for innocent reasons, such as collisions on the network, even if all the hardware and software is working perfectly, so all three of the protocols you're learning about have the ability to ensure reliable delivery.

  All three protocols also support transmission using unreliable delivery. Odd as it sounds, unreliable delivery is ideal for information transfers where the data are sent repetitively or are regularly updated, such as for video conferencing. Rather than ask for retransmission of a corrupted message carrying sound or images during a video conference, the software relies on the fact that there's always more audio and video coming. You might hear slight glitches or briefly see some blocky artifacts on the screen, but the transient goes away quickly to be replaced by newer, good data.

- **Computer discovery.** NetBEUI supports *broadcast* messages, which are messages sent without a specific destination address. Every computer receiving a broadcast address processes the message; if the receiving computer has information or services relevant to the sender, it responds with a message including the receiver's network address. Broadcasts are the basis for being able to discover what computers exist on a LAN; the inquiring computer sends a broadcast requesting all computers to respond with their name and address and then waits for responses. The responses come back as direct, point-to-point messages using reliable delivery.

- **Name and address resolution.** NetBEUI doesn't provide a centralized service for computer name and address resolution, as does TCP/IP, but the discovery process we mentioned before gives each computer a list of names and addresses it can use. Computers can also send out specific broadcasts asking for the computer having a specific name to respond and can send messages to a specific address asking for the name of that computer.

NetBEUI is a small, fast protocol that's easy to use. Its lack of routing abilities make it appropriate only for small LANs; bigger LANs will use IP or IPX/SPX, whereas LANs connected to the Internet must use IP.

The lack of routing in NetBEUI isn't necessarily a detriment because it makes the protocol secure against outside attack (there's no way to get a NetBEUI message across a wide area network to attack a computer using only that protocol). Example 7.2 shows how you might take advantage of that characteristic.

EXAMPLE

EXAMPLE 7.2   USING NETBEUI TO HELP SECURE A LAN

Suppose you have a LAN with multiple computers, but can restrict Internet access to just one of the computers on the LAN. You can exploit the lack of routing in NetBEUI to help secure your LAN from attack through the Internet with NetBEUI by following these steps:

1. Figure 7.4 shows all the computers on the LAN (represented by Computer A) implementing only the NetBEUI protocol and not TCP/IP. The computer used for Internet access (Computer B) implements both NetBEUI and TCP/IP.

2. The presence of TCP/IP on computer B means it's visible on the Internet and therefore vulnerable to attack. All the rest of the computers are invisible, though, because they have no way to transmit or receive Internet messages.

3. Although the network in Figure 7.4 is generally more secure than one using TCP/IP everywhere, you won't want to assume it's bulletproof. Successful attacks on Computer B are possible that make NetBEUI resources seen by Computer B accessible from the Internet. You should make sure you have kept Computer B up to date with the latest security patches for its operating system.

4. Although a healthy concern for network security is good, paranoia isn't. You'll learn more about how to secure your network in Chapter 14, "Advanced Internet Access."

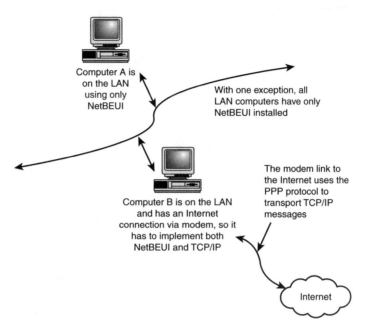

Figure 7.4: Using NetBEUI to isolate computers for security.

You should also keep in mind that threats to your computers and network can originate from inside as well as out. Companies that ignore the problems that malicious or ignorant users can create are likely to receive personalized instruction in ways that they would never suspect could cause problems. Even home networks are worth some thought about security. Giving a four-year-old unrestricted access to files all over your networked computers is dangerous not because the child might try to damage or delete files, but because in exploring what the computer is and does it's possible to do damage unintentionally. Limit file access to safe areas and you're less likely to have a repair problem.

IPX/SPX

In the same way that NetBEUI is a protocol Microsoft invented to meet the needs it perceived for Windows, IPX (Internetwork Packet Exchange) and SPX (Sequenced Packet Exchange) are protocols Novell derived from work at Xerox to meet the needs of the Novell NetWare products. The fact that there are two different protocols named doesn't imply more functionality than NetBEUI—it's just naming. IPX is the underlying, unreliable layer 3 protocol, while SPX is the reliable protocol running on top of IPX.

IPX and SPX have many of the benefits of NetBEUI, but add capabilities appropriate to larger LANs:

- **Forward received messages.** IPX provides message routing services based on a combination of assigned network numbers and hardware addresses. Every distinct network segment, equivalent to the span reachable by a NetBEUI network, requires its own NetWare network number (or IPX segment number). That number must be unique across all the interconnected networks.

- **Reliable delivery.** SPX uses the facilities of IPX to provide reliable packet delivery. Packets are guaranteed to be received by the destination in the order they were sent. The protocol limits the rate packets are sent to ensure communications links aren't overloaded.

- **Computer discovery, and name and address resolution.** NetWare includes an explicit protocol running above the level of IPX or SPX to support computer and services discovery. That protocol is known as SAP (Service Advertising Protocol) and is the mechanism by which file servers, print servers, and application servers make known their services and addresses. Servers broadcast a SAP packet every 60 seconds onto their local network segment. Each router tracks the information in the broadcasts, so clients can always access a nearby router to discover computers and services.

IPX/SPX requires relatively little setup and administration; the defaults take care of unrouted networks, and unless you have a lot of separate network segments, tracking network numbers yourself for assignment isn't very hard. There's no mechanism or organization that makes global network number assignments corresponding to the work done for IP by the Internet Assigned Numbers Authority (IANA). A network administrator can provide that function for individual organizations and corporations, so IPX/SPX is capable of supporting worldwide network operations.

Your IPX/SPX-based network isn't likely to be attacked from outside because of the lack of global network number assignment. Attacks from within are still possible, so you'll still want to be conscious of network security.

TCP/IP

TCP/IP isn't the invention of any company; it evolved over time, with origins in an American defense project to connect multiple networks together into a larger, survivable whole. The initial network of networks was the ARPAnet, using a computer-to-computer protocol called the Network Control Protocol (NCP). NCP was replaced by the Transmission Control

Protocol (TCP) and the Internet Protocol (IP) by 1974, both of which have been revised and extended since then. The original ARPAnet used 50Kbps telephone lines for the network backbone, evolving to the multigigabit-per-second fiber-optic backbone of the Internet today.

Much of the strength of TCP/IP comes from the fact that the protocols defining the suite—far more than just TCP and IP (see Figure 7.5)—are publicly proposed and evaluated. Changes and extensions to TCP/IP are managed by a volunteer organization called the Internet Engineering Task Force (IETF). Anyone can propose a change or extension to TCP/IP, but unless the proposal successfully progresses through the IETF standardization process, it's likely to be ignored.

The TCP/IP protocol suite doesn't correspond exactly to the seven-layer model in Figure 7.1, combining several of the layers together in a single protocol when it's convenient. Figure 7.5 matches the key Internet protocols against the seven-layer model. Of the protocols shown in the figure, Telnet, File Transfer Protocol (FTP), Simple Mail Transfer Protocol (SMTP), and Domain Name Service (DNS) are the upper-layer protocols you'll learn about later in this chapter.

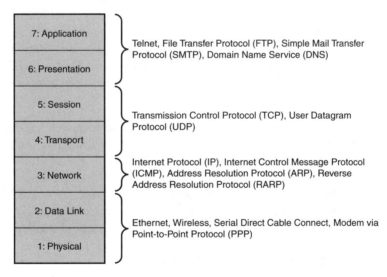

Figure 7.5: *TCP/IP is an extensive suite of protocols working together.*

TCP/IP implements all the general capabilities you learned about earlier in this chapter, and does so in a more robust, scalable manner than NetBEUI or IPX/SPX:

- **Forward received messages.** IP itself is the basis for message routing and delivery in TCP/IP, with much the same function as IPX in the

Novell protocols. The protocols use both hardware and network addresses; messages sent across a TCP/IP network are sent to specific hardware addresses, but at the receiving computer a comparison is made between the receiver's IP network address and the destination IP network address. If the receiving computer isn't the ultimate destination but has routing capabilities, it passes the message along on the network segment leading to the destination. The forwarding process continues for as many hops as are required to reach the destination.

- **Reliable delivery.** Although IP provides basic unreliable delivery services, programs generally work with two other protocols. TCP is the protocol for reliable, in-order packet delivery (corresponding to SPX in the Novell protocols), whereas the User Datagram Protocol (UDP) is the method for low-overhead unreliable delivery.

- **Computer discovery, and name and address resolution.** TCP/IP provides both broadcast messages and explicit protocols for computer discovery. Broadcast messages are typically limited to the network segment of the sender, but can be forwarded by routers by special arrangement. The Address Resolution Protocol (ARP) converts network addresses to physical hardware addresses using broadcast messages; the inquiring computer sends out a broadcast message containing the IP address it wants translated, and receives back from that computer a message including the corresponding hardware address. The Reverse Address Resolution Protocol (RARP) does the inverse job, converting a machine's hardware address to an IP address.

IP addresses were managed globally by the Internet Assigned Numbers Authority (IANA) prior to the creation of the Internet Corporation for Assigned Names and Numbers (ICANN). The global standardization provided by the IETF, combined with the global management functions provided by IANA and ICANN, have been the basis by which TCP/IP has had the strength to scale to support the worldwide Internet, a network of millions of interconnected computers and hundreds of millions of users.

Picking Your Network Protocol

Your decision of what protocols to run on your LAN is driven by what you expect your network to do. You can use the simple, straightforward NetBEUI protocols if you're simply setting up a new, small LAN for file and printer sharing, but you'll want heavier-duty protocols for more powerful applications. Example 7.3 shows you how to decide what protocols you need to implement.

EXAMPLE

EXAMPLE 7.3   CATEGORIZING YOUR LAN AND CHOOSING YOUR NETWORK PROTOCOL

Choose the best network protocol for you based on the following types of systems:

- **Small standalone LAN with Windows-based computers.** A small LAN with only Windows computers and with no Internet connection needs only the NetBEUI protocols. The small size of the LAN implies only hubs and switches are needed, not routers, while independence from the Internet implies TCP/IP is not a requirement.

- **Small standalone LAN with a mix of Windows and Linux computers or with print servers.** It's easiest to run TCP/IP on Linux machines. Not only does it take extra work to run NetBEUI, it's almost impossible not to run TCP/IP on Linux. Many standalone print servers, such as the Intel InBusiness Print Station you'll learn about in Chapter 11, "Sharing Printers and Fax," support only TCP/IP and IPX/SPX. Consequently, if you run a LAN with non-Windows devices you'll likely want to use TCP/IP on the network. You'll learn in the next chapter how to set up TCP/IP addressing on both standalone and Internet-connected LANs; after you get past assigning addresses and names for each computer, TCP/IP on a standalone LAN is little more complicated than NetBEUI.

- **LAN connected to the Internet.** Aside from Linux-based computers and standalone print servers, there are two reasons you might want to run TCP/IP on your LAN: multiplayer games, and the Internet. Older multiplayer games used to use the IPX/SPX protocols, but because multiplayer gaming over the Internet became popular, nearly all the games now published use TCP/IP.

  As soon as you connect your LAN to the Internet, you run the risk of people attacking your systems. For Windows computers, one of the easiest ways to help secure shared files is, as you saw in Figure 7.4, to only run NetBEUI. In Chapter 14, you'll learn how to run both NetBEUI and TCP/IP but make file sharing available only to NetBEUI-connected computers.

- **LAN connected to the Internet through a firewall.** The destination address in network messages received by your computer specifies the requested function—for example, file sharing messages have a part of the destination address that's different from print-sharing messages. As Figure 7.6 shows, you can improve your network security by adding a device known as a *firewall* between your LAN and the Internet to filter out messages from the Internet asking for services you only want to be accessible to local computers. You'll learn about firewalls in Chapter 14, too.

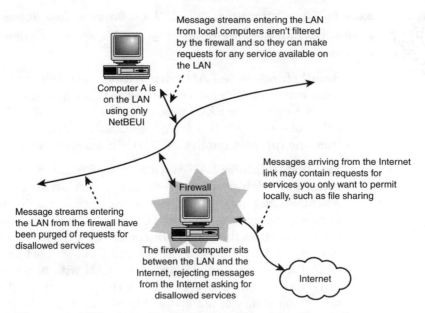

Message streams entering the LAN from local computers aren't filtered by the firewall and so they can make requests for any service available on the LAN

Computer A is on the LAN using only NetBEUI

Messages arriving from the Internet link may contain requests for services you only want to permit locally, such as file sharing

Firewall

Message streams entering the LAN from the firewall have been purged of requests for disallowed services

The firewall computer sits between the LAN and the Internet, rejecting messages from the Internet asking for disallowed services

Internet

Figure 7.6: *Blocking disallowed traffic with a firewall.*

We've recommended NetBEUI, TCP/IP, or both in all cases; there's simply no reason to bother with the Novell protocols unless your LAN already has NetWare file servers that haven't been upgraded to TCP/IP, or unless you install standalone print servers that only support older Novell protocols.

Network Plumbing

Much as there's a lot of plumbing in the walls and under the streets that makes your sinks, tubs, and whatnot work, there's a lot of plumbing underneath network transport services that makes all the applications you use work. You'll learn about those network-transport services in this section, using TCP/IP as the specific protocol in the discussion because it separates the various functions out most clearly.

Physical and Logical Addresses

If you go to visit your next-door neighbor, you simply go out your door and walk down the street. You don't need to know your neighbor's street address because you know physically where the house is.

If you plan on driving to visit your uncle who's just moved into a new house across the country, though, you're going to need to know the state, city, street, and house number. You'll use the city and state information to decide what highways to travel, and use the city and street address to home in on the right house. After you've seen the house you'll be able to drive around in the local neighborhood without referring back to the house address.

Networks operate in exactly the same way. The *physical address* of a computer on a LAN, fixed in the network interface card by the manufacturer, works like physical knowledge of where a house is. Messages sent on the same LAN segment, corresponding to a house's neighborhood, can get to a specific physical LAN address. If you want to send a message across the country or around the world, though, you need the equivalent of a country, state, city, and street address. In network terms, the address you need is called a *logical address*. The key difference between physical addresses and logical addresses is that, although physical addresses are scattered randomly around the world, logical addresses follow a pattern determined by network administrators and stored in *routing tables*. Routing tables (used by routers) are the equivalent of street maps, guiding messages to their destination.

Current versions of TCP/IP represent logical network addresses as a sequence of four decimal numbers, each ranging from 0 to 255. The four numbers are typically written with dots separating them; a typical TCP/IP address is 192.246.40.185. Figure 7.7 shows how messages get from your computer to anywhere in the world using routers and the notion of a *default route*. Whenever your computer needs to send a TCP/IP message to a computer not part of your LAN, it instead sends it to the computer defined as the default TCP/IP route. That computer (or router) has the responsibility to forward the message on a communications link leading to the destination, using routing tables to identify the correct link. In practice, the message goes out by default from your LAN through a computer or router with a link to your Internet service provider (ISP). A router at the ISP looks in the Internet core routing tables, selects the ISP's Internet link most directly connected to the end destination of the message, and sends the message down that link. The forwarding process continues until the message finally arrives on the LAN hosting the destination computer.

Example 7.4 explores how the Internet sends messages through intermediate hops to get from one place to another halfway around the world.

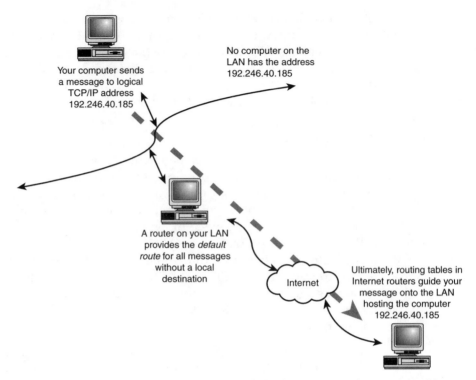

Figure 7.7: *Worldwide routing using default routes and routing tables.*

EXAMPLE

EXAMPLE 7.4   WATCHING NETWORK MESSAGE ROUTING

A standard TCP/IP utility called traceroute (tracert under Windows) lets
you discover the hops a message takes passing from the originating computer to the destination. Follow these steps:

1. Assuming you have a computer hooked to the Internet, open a Web
   browser and go to the address http://wwwcs.cern.ch/public/status/
   tools/traceroute.html, which is a public service maintained by the
   Communications Systems Group of the European Laboratory for
   Particle Physics (called CERN) in Geneva, Switzerland.

2. Enter the destination TCP/IP address (192.246.40.185 in the earlier
   example).

3. Click the Send button and wait for the results. The following listing
   shows the results we received:

```
Traceroute from wwwcs.cern.ch to 192.246.40.185

1 r513-c-rci47-15-gp2 (137.138.28.129)  1 ms  1 ms  0 ms
2 cgate1 (128.141.200.10)  3 ms  2 ms  2 ms
```

```
 3 cgate2-dmz (192.65.184.94)  3 ms  3 ms  2 ms
 4 cernh9 (192.65.185.9)  3 ms  3 ms  3 ms
 5 ar1-chicago-gva (192.65.184.149)  310 ms  305 ms  307 ms
 6 bordercore4-hssi5-0-0-1.WillowSprings.cw.net (166.48.34.5) 305 ms 302 ms 305 ms
 7 corerouter2.WillowSprings.cw.net (204.70.9.146)  309 ms  308 ms  302 ms
 8 corerouter1.Dallas.cw.net (204.70.9.149)  323 ms  325 ms  324 ms
 9 core2.Dallas.cw.net (204.70.4.69)  319 ms  329 ms  333 ms
10 borderx1-fddi-1.Dallas.cw.net (204.70.114.52)  348 ms  147 ms  147 ms
11 diamond-net.Dallas.cw.net (204.70.114.106)  149 ms  148 ms  147 ms
12 idsoft-1.CR-1.usdlls.savvis.net (209.176.32.178)  163 ms  148 ms  149 ms
13 charon.idsoftware.com (192.246.40.185)  149 ms  149 ms  150 ms
```

4. Following down from the top of the listing, you see that the first four lines were within CERN itself. The times listed are how many milliseconds were required for a roundtrip from the originating computer to the listed point and back; in lines 1–4, that was 0–3 milliseconds.

5. At line 5, the messages have hopped across the Atlantic Ocean from Switzerland, being routed to Chicago, Illinois in the USA. The roundtrip times have jumped to 310 milliseconds, suggesting that a satellite link is being used.

6. The messages then transit through Willow Springs (near Chicago) to Dallas, where they eventually reach the destination computer at id Software. That computer's name is charon.idsoftware.com; you'll see later in this chapter how TCP/IP translates computer addresses to names and back.

After a message gets to the destination computer, the operating system has to deliver it to the proper software running on that computer, the software implementing the service requested by the sender. Network protocols implement the idea of *ports*, which are identifiers for different message receivers running on a machine. Just as a surface mailing address includes the person to whom the mail is sent along with the street address, a complete network address includes the port number along with the TCP/IP address. The World Wide Web operates using port 80, for example, so connecting to the id Software Web server on the computer charon.idsoftware.com requires the complete address 192.246.40.185:80. The software you use almost always takes care of providing the port numbers, but it's important to understand that network addresses are a three-step process: logical addresses let the message travel to the destination LAN; physical addresses (derived from the logical address) get the message onto the destination computer; and port addresses get the message to the right software.

Domain Name Service and Address Resolution Protocol

Making network addresses useful requires several key software elements. You've learned that computers on networks can be referenced by name, by logical address, and by physical address. Names are required by people using computers; it's hopeless to try and remember that 192.246.40.185 is charon.idsoftware.com, and what's worse is that changes in the id Software LAN structure could alter the numeric address of the computer, invalidating what everyone using the numeric address knew.

Wide area networks (WANs) require logical addresses, so there have to be methods to convert between the names people use for computers and those addresses. Similarly, LANs require physical addresses, so there also have to be methods to convert between logical and physical addresses.

Every protocol suite uses different methods for those conversions. NetBEUI and IPX/SPX don't explicitly separate out the protocols doing those conversions, but in TCP/IP there are two key protocols for that work:

- **Domain Name Service (DNS).** TCP/IP uses DNS to convert between computer names and logical addresses. Your computer can send a message to a Domain Name Server computer, also called a DNS, and receive back the requested translation. A DNS can translate from names to numbers or numbers to names.

- **Address Resolution Protocol (ARP).** Messages to be delivered locally on a LAN require the correct physical address. TCP/IP uses ARP to perform a logical-to-physical address translation. The ARP mechanism sends a broadcast message including the logical address to all receiving computers on the LAN segment. If one of those computers recognizes the transmitted logical address as its own, it replies with a confirmation message to the sender including the necessary physical address.

The global scope of the Internet required that DNS be organized hierarchically, which determines the structure of computer names on the Internet. The top of the hierarchy is unnamed; immediately underneath are what are called the top-level domains. There are two forms of top-level domain: generic domains, such as .com, .org, or .net; and country code domains, such as .us (USA), .jp (Japan), and .au (Australia). The authorized set of country codes is defined by the International Standards Organization (ISO) and available at http://www.din.de/gremien/nas/nabd/iso3166ma/codlstp1.html.

Specific organizations are designated to register names (such as idsoftware.com or yahoo.com) under each top-level domain. The owners of specific names have the ability to use the names directly (you can send mail to addresses at yahoo.com, for example), or to further subdivide the domain with a finer-grained structure (`charon.idsoftware.com` is an example of that).

Domain Name Server computers exist and are organized to match the Internet name structuring. There are master Domain Name Servers, with subservient DNS computers handling each top-level domain. Owners of names within domains provide Domain Name Servers underneath the top-level domain servers. The entire structure resembles a branching tree in which requests are passed as far along the tree towards the unnamed root as needed to resolve a request. The set of computers forming the DNS system act in concert, sharing information about computer names and their corresponding logical network addresses.

TCP/IP resolves logical-to-physical addresses using an entirely different, far more local scheme, with the ARP protocol described earlier in the chapter performing the actual translation. Figure 7.8 shows the outer structure of a message on an Ethernet, called a *frame*. The physical and data link layers of Ethernet require the frame header and trailer to surround the actual message data. The preamble lets the hardware detect and synchronize with the arrival of the message across the LAN cable. The destination and source physical addresses identify the Ethernet network interface cards sending and receiving the message. The packet type informs the protocol stack how to process the message. The packet data is the actual message content (an IP or NetBEUI message, for instance). The error check data lets the physical and data link layers detect if there were errors in the transmission or reception of the message.

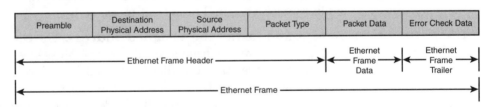

Figure 7.8: *The outer wrapper of a network message defines destinations.*

Detection of message transmission or reception errors by the physical or data link layers has to be independent of the protocol riding on those layers because multiple protocols can operate at the same time.

Dynamic Host Configuration Protocol (DHCP)

We mentioned earlier that, except for having to assign network addresses to computers, TCP/IP can be as simple to use on a standalone network as NetBEUI. With the right software using the Dynamic Host Configuration Protocol (DHCP), the address assignment process for a standalone network can be completely automatic. (You'll learn in Chapter 12, "Sharing an Internet Connection," how you can use the same automatic services for networks connected to the Internet.)

Having learned that TCP/IP most often uses client and server computers to do work, you'd probably design a protocol to automatically assign TCP/IP addresses using that idea. Example 7.5 shows the steps you might design into the interchange between the client (wanting an address to be assigned) and the server (the machine responsible for handing out network addresses).

EXAMPLE

EXAMPLE 7.5   AUTOMATIC TCP/IP ADDRESS ASSIGNMENT

Protocols invariably build up information in the requesting computer, starting with basic elements and progressing to the ultimate goal by building on the basics. Steps following that principle for TCP/IP address assignment use this pattern:

1. **Discover a server and ask for an address.** The first problem is finding a server, a problem easily solved with a broadcast message. The message is a little awkward because the sending computer can't fill in an existing TCP/IP address, so instead the software could use all zeroes.

2. **Receive an address from the server.** Assuming the broadcast message finds a working server, a message should be sent back from the server directly to the client containing the allocated TCP/IP address. The message can be sent directly back to the client using the physical address in the original broadcast message.

3. **Accept and install the assigned address.** The client might receive address assignments from several servers. Messages need to be sent to the chosen server that the client accepted the address and to the rejected servers that they can make the address available for reassignment. The client then installs the TCP/IP address into the protocol stack as the local computer address.

The three steps in Example 7.5 are what DHCP does, but the real protocol has been enhanced to provide some additional information:

- **Netmask.** Even though a segment on a LAN is defined as the collection of computers reachable on a cable without intervention by a router, it's convenient for routed protocols to acknowledge the partitioning into segments in the logical network addresses. The Novell protocols use a network number in conjunction with the physical hardware address, whereas TCP/IP separates the numeric address into a network address and a node or computer address. The partitioning of the overall address into network and node sub-addresses is dynamic, controlled by a number called the *netmask*. Figure 7.9 shows the relationship between a TCP/IP address and a netmask. The netmask acts as a filter; portions of the TCP/IP address at the rightmost end not overlapped by the netmask are stripped off, leaving just the *subnet* address portion of the overall address. In the example in Figure 7.9, the netmask (which in the example would be written 255.255.255.0) removes the 185 part of the overall address, leaving a subnet address of 192.246.40.0. The node address is the part of the overall address not selected by the netmask, so it's 185.

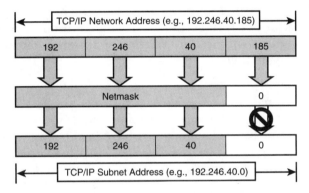

Figure 7.9: *Network and node addresses in TCP/IP.*

The subnet address is valuable because it identifies TCP/IP addresses guaranteed to be on the same LAN segment. Such addresses are then made unique on the segment by the node address.

- **Default gateway.** Typically, computers on a LAN won't know the details of how to route messages for other subnets; they're usually set up to assume a computer or router called the *default gateway* will do the routing. The default gateway has to have an address directly reachable from the sending computer. DHCP provides that address along with the address assigned to the requesting computer.

- **Name server address.** A computer requesting automatic TCP/IP address assignment typically doesn't know the address of a local Domain Name Server, so DHCP responses include the DNS address too. After the DNS address is known, the computer can use the server to look up TCP/IP addresses for any required computer name.

- **Address lease expiration.** Computers are commonly moved around or connected to and disconnected from networks. Computers crash, too; all these actions present the opportunity to cause TCP/IP addresses to fall out of use. Any given DHCP server will have a limited range of TCP/IP addresses it's permitted to hand out, so the protocol includes a timer that, when it expires, causes the assigned address to become invalid and revert to being the property of the DHCP server. In DHCP terms, assigning an address to a client is called leasing the address to the client; when the timer runs out, the lease is said to have expired. At that time the client is required to request a new TCP/IP address from the server. There's a provision in the protocol to request the same TCP/IP address as the client had before, so it's possible for renewed leases to be invisible to computers communicating with the DHCP client over a lease renewal.

If your LAN is connected to the Internet through a router, you'll be assigned a block of TCP/IP addresses by your Internet service provider (ISP) that you can configure into the DHCP server. If you're using a stand-alone network, you have two choices:

- **Use arbitrary addresses.** If you know you'll never connect your LAN to the Internet, you have the option to use any TCP/IP address what-soever. Should you change your mind and go to connect to the Internet at some later time, though, you'll have to change the TCP/IP address of every computer on your LAN. That's not too hard if you've used DHCP; it can be a nightmare if you configured all the addresses man-ually.

- **Use defined private addresses.** The Internet Assigned Numbers Authority (IANA) reserves three blocks of the TCP/IP address space for private networks. You can use addresses from any of the three blocks, which themselves differ in how many hosts they permit within a subnet.

The IANA-reserved blocks are shown in Table 7.1.

Table 7.1: Private TCP/IP Network Addresses

Subnet Address	First Node Address	Last Node Address	Number of Usable Addresses
10.0.0.0	10.0.0.1	10.255.255.254	16,777,214
172.16.0.0	172.16.0.1	172.31.255.254	1,048,574
192.168.0.0	192.168.0.1	192.168.255.254	65,534

The first node address is reserved as part of the formal subnet address, while the last node address is reserved as the broadcast address for the subnet. Because those two addresses are reserved in every address block, a block of 16 node addresses (for example) has only 14 usable addresses. The number of usable addresses column at the right of Table 7.1 shows the maximum number of addresses less two, so it's the maximum number of computers and other devices you could connect to one subnet in the block.

There are three subnets available to provide options for different numbers of attached nodes. Legitimate TCP/IP addresses formed from the subnet address in the second row would be 172.16.0.1, 172.16.0.2, and so on up to 172.31.255.254.

The addresses in these three subnets cannot route directly onto the Internet because in practice they're in use in many different places. You'll learn in Chapter 12 that a technology called Network Address Translation (NAT) lets you use addresses from these subnets on your LAN yet connect to the Internet through a router performing NAT. Using NAT means you can later connect all your computers to the Internet and not have to change a single IP address.

PPP

The other key protocol forming part of your network plumbing you should know about is the Point-to-Point Protocol (PPP). You're likely to use PPP only over the modem connection you use to your Internet service provider; PPP is a layer 2 (data link) protocol similar in function to the Ethernet protocols you learned about earlier in this chapter. You might encounter a similar protocol, the Serial Line Interface Protocol (SLIP); PPP is more capable and should be used in preference to SLIP. Key functions of PPP include the following:

- Encapsulation of TCP/IP packets for transmission over the modem link. The exact format of PPP frames is different from the Ethernet frame you saw in Figure 7.8, but it serves the same purpose.

- Data link configuration, including specifics of how specific characters must be transmitted.

- Transport of multiple higher-level protocols. For example, it's possible to transport the Novell protocols with PPP as well as TCP/IP.

- Header compression, which can reduce the size of the combined IP and TCP headers from 40 bytes to about 4.

There are other key benefits of PPP, not the least of which is the ability of a newer version, Multi-Link PPP (MLPPP) to let you connect multiple modems in parallel for higher connection speeds.

Network Applications

Layers 5 through 7 (session, presentation, and application) in the seven-layer model implement the services computer users normally interact with directly. Only some of these services have been implemented on top of the Microsoft or Novell protocols.

You'll see the commonly supported protocols in the section titles for each application. Other user-level applications (such as fax sharing) are common, but might use vendor-specific implementation protocols.

File Transfer and Sharing (Microsoft, Novell, TCP/IP)

File transfer and sharing is supported on all three of the common transport protocols. File sharing protocols, which give you shared remote disk access, permit file transfer too because they permit file copy between remote and local disks. File transfer protocols, such as the TCP/IP File Transfer Protocol, do not support file sharing because they only serve to copy files from one computer to another. The three standard transport protocols have these characteristics for file transfer and sharing:

- **Server Message Block (SMB, Microsoft).** The Microsoft native implementation of file and disk sharing uses the Server Message Block (SMB) protocol, implementations for which are built into Windows and are available for Linux.

- **NetWare (Novell).** The Novell protocols use their own file transfer and sharing protocols, implementations for which are available for Windows and Novell NetWare.

- **Network File System (NFS, Linux standard) and File Transfer Protocol (FTP).** Linux and other versions of UNIX natively provide NFS. Implementations of NFS are available for Windows as well as the UNIX variants. Windows, Linux, and probably all other TCP/IP-enabled operating systems provide FTP.

The distinction between file transfer and file sharing is only readily apparent on systems using the TCP/IP protocols and FTP plus either SMB or NFS. Example 7.6 shows you the difference between the two.

EXAMPLE

EXAMPLE 7.6   COMPARING FILE TRANSFER AND FILE SHARING

You'll need a working Windows-based LAN to follow this example on your own computers; if your LAN isn't ready yet, follow along with the figures we've included, come back and rework the example after your own network is up and running.

You'll need an FTP server and client too. If you have a machine running Windows NT or Windows 2000 Server, you'll likely have an FTP server to use; if not, you can install the WFTPD FTP server using the instructions in Chapter 9, "Sharing Fixed Drives and Setting Access Controls." You can use the DOS-like FTP client tools in Windows; in Chapter 9 we'll show you how to install and run a graphical FTP client (WS_FTP), which is what you'll use in this example.

After you're all set up, follow these steps to compare file transfer and sharing:

1. On the machine you'll connect to (the server) make sure a disk is set up for sharing, and set up the FTP server access permissions. If you haven't set up sharing and FTP yet, refer to the instructions in Chapter 9.

2. Open Network Neighborhood. You'll get the same two-pane window format as in Figure 7.10 if you click with your right mouse button on Network Neighborhood and then select Explore rather than Open.

3. If you've configured the LAN protocols and file sharing correctly, you'll see a list of visible computers underneath Network Neighborhood in the left-hand pane of Windows Explorer. Expand the list underneath the computer you want to look at for shared files. In Figure 7.10 we've expanded the view for the server named Llamah; underneath the computer name, you can see the various shared resources; C, D, E, and H are drives local to the Llamah server, whereas the other resources are specific shared directories on those drives. This particular server offers no shared printers, but if it did they'd show up in the resource list too.

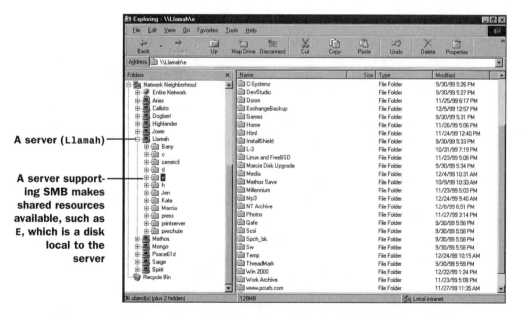

A server (Llamah)

A server supporting SMB makes shared resources available, such as E, which is a disk local to the server

Figure 7.10: *The list in the right pane of Windows Explorer shows directories and files on the server disk just as if they were local to the client computer, with all the same operations supported.*

4. If you click one of the shared drives (drive E is clicked in Figure 7.10), the right-hand pane changes to show the directories and files on that drive. Just as you would with a local drive, you can further expand underneath the drive in the left pane (or double-click directories in the right pane). Everything you can do with local files is possible with remote files on the shared file server.

5. You can further show yourself the equivalence of local files and shared files on a file server by right-clicking the drive letter in the left pane and choosing the Map Network Drive option (see Figure 7.11). The dialog box you see in the middle of the figure lets you pick the drive letter that will, on your client machine, represent the shared drive on the remote server. The drive letter on the server and the drive letter on the client need not be the same and will often not be.

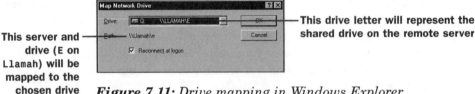

This server and drive (E on Llamah) will be mapped to the chosen drive letter

This drive letter will represent the shared drive on the remote server

Figure 7.11: Drive mapping in Windows Explorer.

6. Figure 7.12 shows the WS_FTP client in operation. FTP operates using a current directory on both the client and the server and permits file transfers between the two. The left pane in the window shows files in the current directory on the local machine (the client), whereas the right pane shows files in the current directory on the remote machine (the server). You can do many of the operations possible with file sharing, such as copy, delete, and rename, but can't execute a program through the FTP client and can't map a drive letter.

Printer Sharing (Microsoft, Novell, TCP/IP)

Printer sharing is, like file sharing, supported by all three common network transport protocols:

- **Server Message Block (SMB, Microsoft).** As with file and disk sharing, the Microsoft native implementation of print sharing uses the Server Message Block (SMB) protocol. Implementations of SMB print sharing are built into Windows and available for Linux.

- **NetWare (Novell).** The Novell protocols use their own print sharing protocols, implementations for which are available for Windows and Novell NetWare.

- **Line Printer Daemon (LPD, Linux standard).** Linux and other versions of UNIX natively provide the Line Printer Daemon (LPD) protocol. Implementations of LPD are available for Windows as well as the UNIX variants.

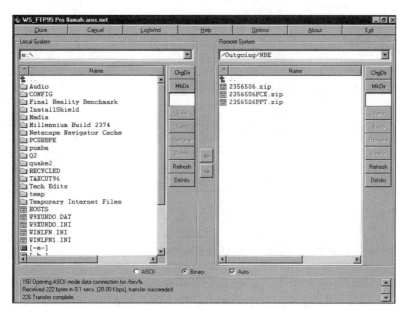

Figure 7.12: *Graphical FTP client.*

You learned in Chapter 3, "Understanding and Evaluating Network Services," that normal application programs use printer device drivers to send data to locally attached printers and that when the printer is remote and shared over the LAN, the device driver accesses the network to transport the print data to the remote print server computer. Now that you've learned about protocol layering, you'll understand that the network interface can occur in several different ways.

Figure 7.13 shows additional detail of the application print process to make the options evident. The vertical flow in Figure 7.13 is the process of generating print; applications create content and then use built-in page formatting routines to create printed pages. Those formatting routines make requests to graphics and text output routines in Windows or X Window (the graphical user interface for Linux and other UNIX variants). If you're printing to a network printer, the first option for the protocol is to divert the printing pipeline at that high level and do the work on the server.

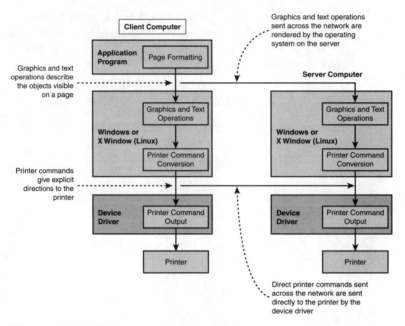

Figure 7.13: *Printer networking options.*

The output of the printing pipeline is a sequence of commands in the unique language required by the specific printer. Those commands can be generated in either the client or server computer; if the commands are output on the client computer to an attached printer, you have local print; if they're output on a server computer to a printer attached there, you have network print.

Whether network printers generate the command sequences on the client or server computer often depends on the server. If the server is a fully capable computer, you can save time and processing power on the client by processing on the server. If the server is a limited-function device that really exists to connect printers to the network (such as the Intel InBusiness Print Station you'll learn about in Chapter 11) the command sequence will be generated in the client. There's more complexity in a protocol that lets the graphics operations be done in the server.

Electronic Mail (Microsoft, Novell, TCP/IP)

Before the explosion of applications onto the Internet, individuals typically sent email using proprietary services such as America Online (AOL), whereas businesses sent email using proprietary systems they installed on their own computers. That's all changed due to the Internet, but some of the proprietary legacy lives on. The email application protocols associated with the standard transport protocols offer different features and capabilities:

- **Exchange Server (Microsoft).** Companies often want email-related services beyond what's possible with the standard Internet email protocol. Many companies offer enhanced email services; one of the most popular has been Lotus Notes (since acquired by IBM). Microsoft's proprietary enhanced email system comparable to Notes or Novell's GroupWise is Exchange, which includes its own protocols for clients to communicate with the Exchange Server. Interoperability with the Internet email protocols is an option with Exchange Server. Individuals and small companies might find these products too complex to be worth the time to set up and keep them running.

- **NetWare (Novell).** Novell offered a complete, proprietary email suite from the advent of NetWare. The Novell offering, GroupWise, now supports group collaboration as well as email and can run over TCP/IP, making it one of the competitors in the product space that includes Exchange Server and Lotus Notes.

- **Simple Mail Transfer Protocol (SMTP, Internet standard).** The Internet standard for email is the Simple Mail Transfer Protocol (SMTP). SMTP is itself limited to text message transfer, but widely supported enhancements permit programs, Web pages, images, video clips, and any other data to be sent through the protocol. Appropriately enhanced SMTP email readers are available for all TCP/IP-capable operating systems.

  One of the changes to SMTP has been the introduction of protocols specifically designed to let clients get messages from email servers, leaving SMTP to the job of transferring mail between servers. The most common client-to-server email protocol is Post Office Protocol version 3 (POP3), although some Internet service providers support the newer Internet Message Access Protocol (IMAP).

Like other protocols, Internet email transactions progress according to a defined sequence: The sender connects to the receiver and then the sending computer transmits *header* information, which identifies the message sender, destination, subject, relaying path, and other facts and then transmits the message itself.

The extensions built on top of SMTP to transmit arbitrary data all affect the structure of the message data. The most common are the multipurpose Internet mail extensions (MIME), which can encode several arbitrary data items into one message.

World Wide Web (TCP/IP)

Even though email remains the most common Internet application, the one people identify most with the Internet is the World Wide Web. Whether used over the global Internet, corporate intranet, or standalone LAN, Web technology has let more people make more information readily available than ever before. The Web is only available through TCP/IP; no other protocols support Web access.

Whether you're connecting to a local or a distant server, Web access involves three things: a client computer running a Web browser (such as Netscape Navigator or Microsoft Internet Explorer), messages sent using the Hypertext Transfer Protocol (HTTP), and a Web server (such as Apache for Linux or Internet Information Server for Windows). The interaction between client and server is similar to that for SMTP in the previous section, in that the transaction involves both headers and content data. The headers characterize the conversation between client and server; the content data (using the Hypertext Markup Language, HTML) becomes what you see onscreen.

HTTP supports several security and encryption methods, from basic security, such as asking for a username and password, to fully encrypted transactions across the network.

Some sites and pages on the Web are in very high demand by many people. The Web implements a mechanism called a *proxy server* to cache copies of high-demand pages at your ISP. Figure 7.14 compares normal Web operation to that with a proxy server. The ability of the proxy server to keep local copies reduces the traffic at the busiest Web servers and reduces your response times.

You have to configure client computers to request access through the proxy. The operation is usually no more than identifying the proxy name and port number to the client (the port number is usually 8080 in contrast to the usual port 80 for a direct Web server).

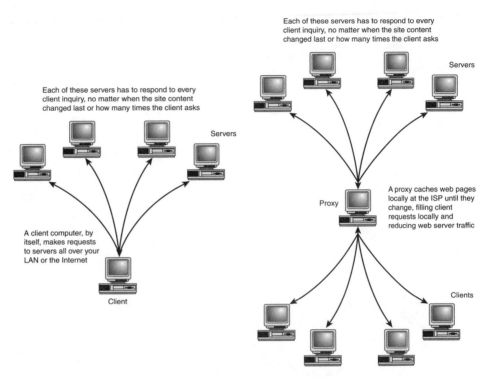

Each of these servers has to respond to every client inquiry, no matter when the site content changed last or how many times the client asks

Servers

Each of these servers has to respond to every client inquiry, no matter when the site content changed last or how many times the client asks

Servers

A proxy caches web pages locally at the ISP until they change, filling client requests locally and reducing web server traffic

Proxy

A client computer, by itself, makes requests to servers all over your LAN or the Internet

Client

Clients

Figure 7.14: Direct Web client access compared to Web access through proxy server.

Summary

Computer communication is similar in many ways to human communication; the computers must speak a common language (a protocol), and must have enough mutual context (shared information) for the conversation to make sense. The most common protocols for message transport are NetBEUI, Novell, and TCP/IP NetBEUI is a good choice for very small LANs; TCP/IP is the common language of the Internet.

Protocols above those three are application dependent. Common network applications with specific protocols include file transfer and sharing, printer sharing, email, and the Web.

What's Next

You'll learn how to set up the basic networking software on your computers in the next chapter. When you've finished the chapter, you'll be ready to go on to Chapter 9, in which you'll start to set up and use the applications your network will provide.

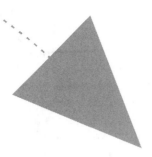

8

Configuring Your System Software

In this chapter you will learn

- How to install and configure device drivers for your network interface cards
- How to choose and configure your network protocol stacks
- How to install and configure file sharing software
- How to configure Linux networking and file sharing

Even if we can't convince you in this book, you'll discover from experience that building your network is like every other engineering project; you specify and design what you want from the top down and then build and test from the bottom up. In the case of networks, that means you specify and design starting with what you want the network to do for you, but you build and test starting with the network interface cards (NICs) and proceeding through device drivers and protocols to applications. That sequence is part of why this book is organized the way it is: You learned how to install wiring in Chapter 5, "Installing Your LAN Wiring," and to pick and install NICs in Chapter 6, "Picking and Installing Your LAN Adapters." This chapter covers how to install device drivers and protocols; Chapter 9, "Sharing Fixed Drives and Setting Access Controls," starts the application installation work by showing you how to set up file sharing.

The Windows examples in this chapter are based on Windows 98 Second Edition and both Windows NT 4 and Windows 2000. (We've ignored Windows 95 because in our opinion there are no good reasons to continue to use Windows 95 in homes or small businesses; we've included both Windows NT 4 and Windows 2000 because Windows 2000 is still too new; there will remain a significant Windows NT 4 installed base for years to come.)

You're likely to find some differences in Windows 95, either in the details of dialog boxes or in finding the place in the software where you make the necessary settings and changes. We recommend Windows 98 Second Edition or Windows 2000 for new network developments; we find Windows 98 Second Edition far more stable than Windows 95 or Windows 98, and we find Windows 2000 easier to use than Windows NT 4. We'll use Windows 2000 Professional in our Windows 2000 examples, but for what we'll cover you're likely to find Windows 2000 Server to be the same. The differences in Windows 2000 Server are more important for medium-to-large networks.

Linux setup is vastly different from setup for Windows, so we'll cover it separately. There are a surprising number of Linux distributions, such as the ones from Debian, Mandrake, Red Hat, Slackware, and SuSE. The distributions are more similar than they are different, but even subtle differences can be major problems if you don't have time to research problems. You can match our examples by installing Mandrake Linux version 6.1 (http://www.linux-mandrake.com) because we've used Mandrake for all the examples in this book. Mandrake Linux is based on Red Hat Linux (http://www.redhat.com), so many Linux users should be able to work with the examples directly.

Adding Device Drivers

One reason we recommended using PCI internal NICs or USB external ones whenever you can is that those buses support automatic device recognition and configuration, making device driver installation much simpler.

The steps you'll go through adding device drivers to either Windows 98 or Windows NT/2000 are similar, but the details, tools, and procedures are different. We'll start with Windows 98.

Windows 98

There are two main tools you'll use when working with your network hardware and low-level network software setup in Windows 98. Both are Windows Control Panel applets; one is System, the other Network.

Within the System applet (on the left in Figure 8.1), the tool you want is the Device Manager tab, shown on the right in Figure 8.1. The General tab that appears first when you start the Device Manager gives some basic system information, one of the key items of which is the version of Windows you're running. You can see in Figure 8.1 that the system was running Windows 98 Second Edition; Example 8.1 shows you how to recognize the different Windows versions you'll see. Example 8.2 shows you several ways to open the Device Manager.

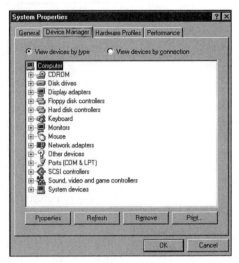

Figure 8.1: *The Windows 98 System Applet (left) and Device Manager (right).*

EXAMPLE 8.1   RECOGNIZING WINDOWS 9X VERSION NUMBERS

To learn what version of Windows you are running, look for the Windows version number on the General tab of the System control panel applet:

- Systems running Windows 95 are version 4.10.0950.

- Windows 95 Service Pack 1 (widely available) and Service Release 2 (only available with a purchased computer) correspond to versions 4.10.0950 A and 4.10.0950 B.

- Systems running the original release of Windows 98 display a version of 4.10.1998.

- Systems running Windows 98 Second Edition have a version number of 4.10.2222 A.

EXAMPLE 8.2   OPENING DEVICE MANAGER

You can reach the Device Manager in any of several ways. The most-often documented way is through the Control Panel. Follow these steps:

1. You'll open Windows Explorer through Start, Settings, Control Panel. After the Explorer opens on the Control Panel, you'll see a list of the available applets. Double-click System to open the applet, and then click the Device Manager tab at the top.

2. If you have a keyboard with a Windows key—that would be a key with the Windows logo flag on it—you can reach the Device Manager by holding down the Windows key and pressing the Pause or Break key

(usually in the upper-right part of the keyboard). Doing that should open the System applet, after which you can click the Device Manager tab at the top.

3. A third way to reach the Control Panel is by opening Windows Explorer in the Explorer view (by right-clicking My Computer and then choosing Explore, or by choosing Start, Programs, Windows Explorer), and then selecting the Control Panel in the left pane.

4. Finally, you can open Device Manager by right-clicking on the My Computer icon on your desktop. When you do, you'll see a small menu appear; click Properties to open the System applet and then click the Device Manager tab at the top.

The Device Manager itself, shown on the right in Figure 8.1, gives you a hierarchical list of all the devices in the computer that's your view into the hardware in your computer. As with other hierarchical lists in Windows (such as the left pane in Windows Explorer), you can expand any entry in the list by clicking on the plus sign next to the icon. Expanding the Network adapters entry in Figure 8.1 results in the display on the left of Figure 8.2; double-clicking the line for the specific adapter (a 3Com Etherlink III Bus-Master PCI Ethernet Adapter in the figure) results in the dialog box on the right side of the figure.

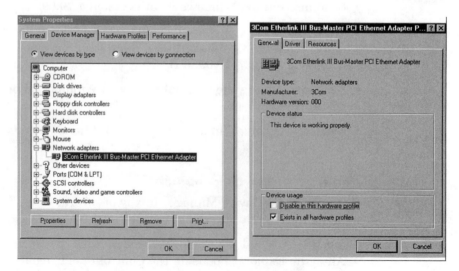

Figure 8.2: *Expanding a category in Device Manager (left) and viewing an adapter's properties (right).*

The General tab for the device indicates that the device is working properly so far as Windows knows; the Driver and Resources tabs provide more specifics on the installed device drivers and on the computer resources the device uses (see Figure 8.3). The Driver tab reports the author and date of the installed drivers; you can get more information on individual driver files by clicking the Driver File Details button near the bottom. You can sometimes use the Update Driver to install a new driver for the device, although your success with that approach will depend on whether the driver provider wrote it to support the Windows 98 installation conventions.

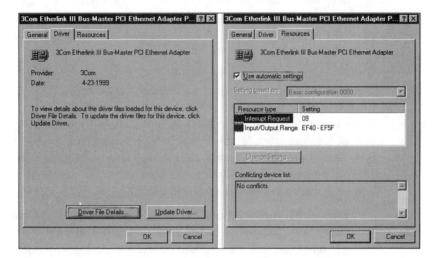

Figure 8.3: *Driver (left) and Resources (right) tabs for a specific device in Device Manager.*

You won't find a Resources tab for USB device you've plugged in, such as the 3Com 3C460 USB Ethernet adapter you learned about in Chapter 6, because the devices listed under Universal Serial Bus controllers in Device Manager provide all the resources required inside the computer for any attached USB devices. Specific devices that show up in Device Manager might have additional tabs. For example, you'll find a Settings tab for the disk drives in your computer.

If a yellow caution or red problem icon appears next to the device in the Device Manager, the problem might be due to a lack of *resources*—which is a catch-all name for mechanisms software uses to talk to hardware devices. Categorically, there are four kinds of resources you might encounter:

- **Interrupt Request (IRQ).** Interrupts are signals from an attached device to the computer's processor indicating the device needs help. Devices on the computer's PCI bus (see Chapter 6) can be capable of sharing the same IRQ. There are 16 different IRQs in a PC, many of which are dedicated to specific purposes. Every device that uses an IRQ to communicate with its device driver requires Windows assign an IRQ.

- **Input/Output (I/O) Port.** An I/O port is a shared place through which the processor can send a command or data word to the device, or through which the device can return status or data words. Nearly all devices use I/O ports or memory for command and status communication; many use one or the other for data exchange, too. There are 65,536 possible I/O ports, numbered from 0 to 65,535. The addresses are shown as base 16 numbers in the Resources page, so in addition to the usual digits 0–9, you'll see the letters A–F used as digits in base 16 numbers. Written in base 16, I/O port numbers (also called addresses) range from 0 to FFFF.

- **Memory Address.** You learned in Chapter 6 that memory is a collection of storage locations, each with an address. There are tens of millions of unique memory locations on the SDRAM strips in your computer. In addition to that memory, individual cards in your computer can provide small blocks of memory the device driver uses to pass commands, status, and data back and forth. Windows assigns addresses to the memory on those cards so the device driver can read and write the on-card locations.

- **Direct Memory Access (DMA) Channel.** A DMA channel is a high-speed way to access an I/O port or a block of memory. The DMA channel does the same thing the processor would, storing or reading multiple characters in succession when the device says it's ready, but does so much faster than the processor can, and without any intervention on the part of the processor while the transfer is in progress.

You can get a summary of all resource usage in your computer by selecting Computer in Device Manager and then clicking Properties. When you do, you'll get a display like that in Figure 8.4. You can get a display for each of the resource categories by clicking the category at the top of the Computer Properties dialog box; Figure 8.4 shows the IRQs used.

Your other key tool is the Network applet (see Figure 8.5). Start the applet with the sequence Start, Settings, Control Panel, Network, or by right-clicking the Network Neighborhood desktop icon and then selecting Properties. The list of components near the top of the dialog box shows you what network adapters, protocols, and (in some cases) applications are installed and running on the computer. In the case of Figure 8.5, you can see the 3Com Etherlink III Bus-Master PCI Ethernet Adapter (a network interface card), NetBEUI and TCP/IP (protocols), and both Client for Microsoft Networks and File and printer sharing for Microsoft Networks (applications).

You'll learn to use the Network Control Panel applet to add, remove, and configure protocols and applications later in this chapter; its ability to add and remove adapters gives it capabilities for networks similar to what you can do in the Device Manager.

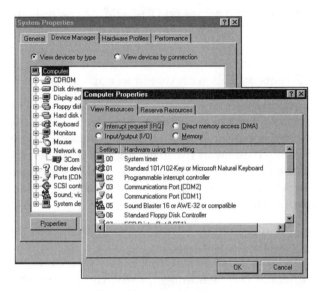

Figure 8.4: *List of all IRQs used in a computer.*

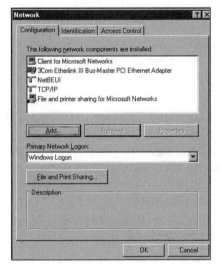

Figure 8.5: *Network Control Panel applet.*

Adding device drivers is similar for both PCI and USB network interface cards (NICs). Depending on how the manufacturer wrote the installation, some require device driver installation before you plug in the NIC, whereas others expect you to install the NIC before you install the drivers. Your best bet is to follow the manufacturer's installation instructions instead of forging on blindly.

Software now most often comes on CD-ROM. If you're instructed to run a software-setup routine before installing the device, you'll most likely insert the CD-ROM into your drive and, if the installation routine doesn't start automatically, run the SETUP.EXE program you'll find there. (If the manufacturer's instructions conflict with this procedure, follow those instructions.)

If the installation sequence requires you to install the device first, both PCI and USB devices should be detected as New Hardware Found as Windows starts. If that happens, the manufacturer's instructions are likely to want you to insert the CD-ROM in the drive and let Windows search the CD-ROM for the drivers it wants. After the drivers are installed this way, you might (depending on manufacturer) still have to run a setup program to finish installation.

After you complete the manufacturer's instructions, you can return to the Device Manager and Network applet to verify that Windows sees no problems with the install. If you do find problems with an internal card, look for resource conflicts in Device Manager, using the Resources tab; if you look again at the right-hand dialog box in Figure 8.3, you'll see a part of the dialog box at the bottom titled Conflicting Device List. You can select resources one at a time using the resource list in the middle of the dialog box and then check for problems below. If you do come up with a conflict using a PCI card with the automatic settings option checked, you'll probably have to get some help troubleshooting because fixing that problem is likely to require low-level machine changes.

If the conflicting device is a card you can remove without crippling the machine (a sound card, for example), one option you have is to remove the conflicting card and see whether that fixes the problem. You'll still have to get some help to sort out how to have all your devices installed at once, but at least you'll be able to verify that the network works.

Windows NT 4 and Windows 2000

One unfortunate characteristic of Windows NT 4 (and one of the compelling reasons to use Windows 2000 instead) is that Windows NT 4 has no support for the Universal Serial Bus. Your choices for a NIC you'll use with Windows NT 4 are therefore more limited; plan on installing a PCI NIC if there's no NIC already in your computer. The details of PCI hardware detection and driver installation under Windows NT 4 should be much the same as for Windows 98, but the tools that correspond to Device Manager and the Network applet are different. Example 8.3 shows you how to get to the Windows NT 4 Diagnostics, the equivalent of the Device Manager.

EXAMPLE

EXAMPLE 8.3   INVESTIGATING THE WINDOWS NT 4 DIAGNOSTICS

You can reach the Windows NT 4 Diagnostics dialog box through the Start button in the Windows taskbar. Follow these steps:

1. Choose Start, Programs, Administrative Tools (Common), Windows NT Diagnostics.

2. Figure 8.6 shows an initial display for the Windows NT 4 Diagnostics. The tabs at the top of the dialog box are different from the ones in the Windows 98 Device Manager, and in fact there's no one tab that's equivalent to Device Manager. Instead, you'll use several of the tabs to get the same functions.

Figure 8.6: Windows NT 4 Diagnostics.

3. You can reach the function in the Windows NT Diagnostics that's closest to Device Manager, listing many of the devices known to Windows, by clicking the Resources tab and then the Devices button. When you do, you'll see a display like the left side of Figure 8.7. The list of devices you see doesn't include disk drives or all the other detailed system devices in Windows 98, but it's otherwise similar.

4. Double-click a device in the device list of Figure 8.7 and you'll get a Properties dialog box, as on the right in Figure 8.7, which lists the properties for the 3Com 3C905 Fast Etherlink XL Adapter installed in the machine.

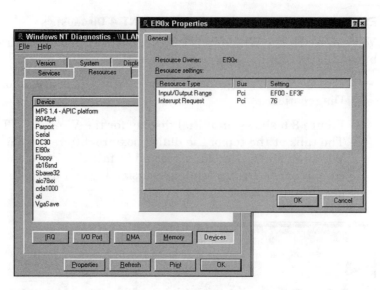

Figure 8.7: *Windows NT 4 Diagnostics Resources and Device Properties displays.*

5. Windows NT 4 doesn't offer the same list of conflicting devices and resources as does Windows 98, but you can use the other buttons at the bottom of the resources dialog box to discover what resources are assigned to what devices. The set of resources—IRQs, I/O Ports, Memory Addresses, and DMA channels—is identical to what you found in Windows 98 because the structure of the underlying computer is identical.

The Network Control Panel applet is in the same place for Windows NT 4 as for Windows 98 (Start, Settings, Control Panel, Network), but as with the Windows NT Diagnostics is structured differently than its Windows 98 equivalent. The key difference is that the elements you found all in one list in Windows 98 are spread across several tabs. Figure 8.8 shows the applet on the left with the Services tab selected, and on the right with the Adapters tab selected. The services listed are very different from those for Windows 98 (for which you'll typically see Client for Microsoft Networks and little else), reflecting the added capabilities of Windows NT. Typically, you'll accept the default set of services installed at setup time.

The Protocols tab in the Windows NT 4 Network applet looks much more familiar when compared to Windows 98, as you can see in Figure 8.9.

Windows 2000 device-driver installation is like Windows 98 too, but Windows 2000 reorganizes the Windows NT 4 tools to be much more like Windows 98. Figure 8.10 shows the initial view of the System Control Panel applet on the left. The tabs in the dialog box are different from those for Windows 98, but if you select the Hardware tab, you'll get the display on the right, which includes a button labeled Device Manager. (You can also get to Device Manager through the Start button menus using the sequence Start, Programs, Administrative Tools, Computer Management; then select Device Manager in the left pane of the resulting window.)

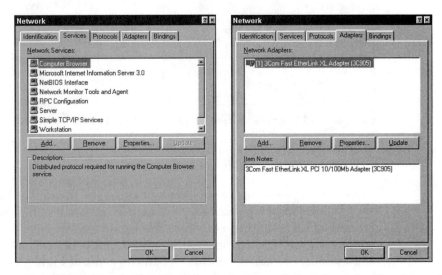

Figure 8.8: *Windows NT 4 Network Control Panel applet Services tab (left) and Adapters tab (right).*

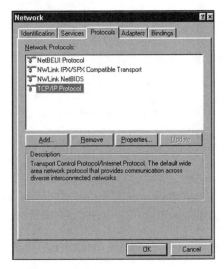

Figure 8.9: *Windows NT 4 Network Protocols tab.*

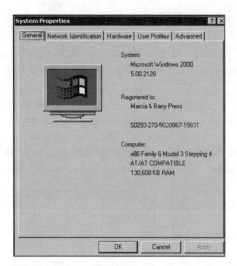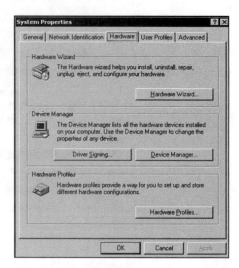

Figure 8.10: *Windows 2000 System Control Panel applet General tab (left) and Hardware tab (right).*

Click the Device Manager button and you'll get the dialog box on the left of Figure 8.11. Expand a category (as with Windows 98) and you'll see the individual devices in the category. We expanded the Network adapters category in the left side of Figure 8.11, and then double-clicked the 3Com network adapter to get the dialog box on the right of Figure 8.11. That dialog box is essentially identical to the ones you'd expect to see in Windows 98, including a list of resources, a check box to use automatic settings, and a list of conflicting devices.

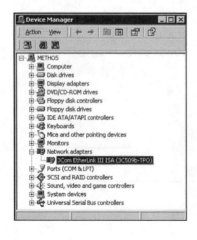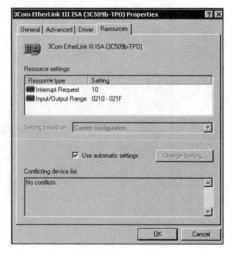

Figure 8.11: *Windows 2000 Device Manager (left) and individual device properties (right).*

Adding Protocols

Windows adds a default set of protocols to the system when you install a network interface card or adapter. That set of protocols might not be what you've planned, and the default setup for the protocols might not match what your LAN requires. The protocols and parameters you'll set are essentially the same for Windows 98, NT 4, and 2000, but (as with the hardware tools you learned about earlier) the mechanisms to configure the system are different. You'll want to assign a unique network name to each computer using the identification capabilities in your operating system, no matter what protocols you install:

- **NetBEUI.** There's nothing to configure for the NetBEUI protocol after it's installed on your system. Operation is completely automatic because addresses are simply the hardware adapter addresses.

- **Novell.** Assuming you're only using a single LAN number, rather than multiple routed IPX/SPX LANs, the Novell protocols are also automatic. Network addresses are a combination of the network number (typically 0) and the network adapter hardware address, so no manual assignments are required.

- **TCP/IP.** Implementing the TCP/IP protocol on your LAN requires assigning addresses to each network adapter. As you learned in Chapter 7, "Network Software—Protocol Stacks and Applications," you can do the assignment manually on each computer, or can use the DHCP protocol on your LAN to make the assignments automatic.

Example 8.4 shows you how to set the machine name for each of the operating systems, independent of the specific protocols you use.

EXAMPLE

EXAMPLE 8.4   SETTING THE MACHINE NAME

The machine name is only used for network applications, so you'd expect to find the tools to set or change it in the Network control panel applet. Follow these steps:

1. In Windows 98, open the Network Control Panel applet and choose the Identification tab. Type the computer name you want to assign in the first field. You can leave the Workgroup field set to the default (which is WORKGROUP), or you can fill it in with a workgroup name you'd like. A workgroup is simply a name for a collection of computers; unless you have a whole lot of computers, it's not likely to do you much good. For small LANs, making sure all your computers are set to the same workgroup makes finding them on the network easier.

2. In Windows NT 4, open the Network Control Panel applet and choose the Identification tab. If you want to alter the assigned computer

name or workgroup, click the Change button and make the necessary changes. (You'll also find the capabilities in the Change dialog box to set up the computer to work with a domain—a more sophisticated version of a workgroup—but unless you have a computer running Windows NT Server, you won't be able to work with domains.)

3. In Windows 2000, open the Control Panel System applet—choose Start, Settings, Control Panel, System; or right-click the My Computer icon, choose Properties, and then click the Network Identification tab. The resulting dialog box is much like the one described earlier for Windows NT 4, providing options to change the computer name and workgroup.

Make sure to set the machine name no matter what protocols you'll use, and make sure you know what machine has what name.

The next sections explain how to add and delete protocols, and how to configure TCP/IP.

Windows 98

You saw the Windows 98 Network Control Panel applet in Figure 8.5; we've shown it again here on the left side of Figure 8.12 after clicking the Add button. You pick whether you intend to add a client application, a network adapter, a protocol, a service, and then you click Add. (What Microsoft here calls *clients* and *services* both fit under the category we've called *network applications*.) If you were to select Protocol from the left side of Figure 8.12 and click Add, you'd get the dialog box on the right side of Figure 8.12.

In the resulting dialog box, you simply pick the protocol you want to add and click OK.

You can also remove protocols using the Network Control Panel applet; simply click the protocol you want to eliminate and click the Remove button. Changes you make adding and removing protocols don't take effect until you click OK to exit the dialog box. You'll always have to reboot the system after changing the installed protocols, but don't be surprised if it takes Windows a few seconds to figure that out.

You configure the TCP/IP protocol by selecting it in the list of components and then clicking Properties. When you do, you'll see the configuration dialog box shown in Figure 8.13. The IP Address tab gives you the choice of using DHCP (the Obtain an IP Address Automatically option) or filling in the configuration manually. If you use the manual option, you'll need to set the IP address and subnet mask (see Chapter 7) along with the gateway and DNS if your LAN is connected to the Internet. The map you made of your LAN (see Chapter 5, "Installing Your LAN Wiring") will be invaluable for manual TCP/IP configuration because it lets you track in one place all the TCP/IP addresses you've assigned.

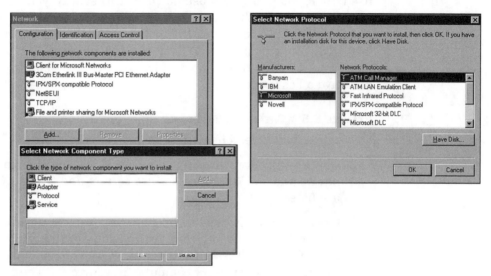

Figure 8.12: *Windows 98 Network Control Panel applet (left) and Add Protocol dialog box (right).*

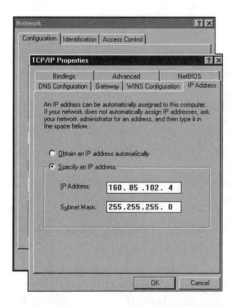

Figure 8.13: *Windows 98 TCP/IP configuration dialog box.*

After you finish making and checking all the settings, click OK until the last dialog box closes and then reboot when Windows finally asks.

If your LAN is connected to the Internet, you'll use the Domain Name Server (DNS) provided by your Internet service provider; if not, or if you use DHCP, you'll probably use no DNS. Either way, your LAN computers won't be known by the names you chose in a DNS unless you've made special arrangements with your ISP or (for standalone networks) to run your own DNS. You can still use TCP/IP services by computer name, though; you simply need to construct a hosts file. Example 8.5 shows you how to create and save a hosts file.

EXAMPLE

EXAMPLE 8.5   CREATING A hosts FILE

To create a hosts file, follow these steps:

1. Check your network map for accuracy, making sure the machine names and TCP/IP addresses are correct and that all your machines are listed.

2. Open Windows Notepad (choose Start, Run, Notepad), and type a file that looks like the following listing, substituting your computer names and TCP/IP addresses for the ones we've shown. Make sure there's a line in the file for every computer in your map. The localhost line is a TCP/IP convention that means the computer the referencing program is running on.

```
#
#     Press network
#
127.0.0.1        localhost
160.85.102.1     netbert
160.85.102.2     mongo
160.85.102.3     highlander
160.85.102.4     aries
160.85.102.5     callisto
160.85.102.6     spirit
160.85.102.7     xena
160.85.102.8     llamah
160.85.102.9     joxer
#

#
```

3. Store the file in the C:\Windows directory on every Windows 98 or Windows 95 system. (Most Windows computers store the Windows software in C:\Windows directory. If yours is set up to keep Windows somewhere else, substitute that place for C:\Windows.) Store the file from Notepad using Save As, navigating to the correct directory, changing the file type to All Files, setting the filename to hosts.

(don't omit the period), and clicking Save. If you don't follow those instructions, Notepad can append .txt to the filename.

4. Store the hosts file in C:\Winnt\system32\drivers\etc on Windows NT 4 and Windows 2000 systems.

The Windows Explorer will reference computers by name without a hosts file because it's using the SMB protocol, but standard TCP/IP applications won't have that information. After you get the hosts files set up on all your computers, you'll be able to reference each computer by name using standard TCP/IP applications.

Windows NT 4 and Windows 2000

If, running Windows NT 4, you select the TCP/IP protocol and click Properties, you'll get the dialog box shown in Figure 8.14 on the left; Windows 2000 gives you the dialog box on the right after you open Network and Dial-up Connections in Windows Explorer and then select Local Area Connection, right-click, and choose Properties. The way you use the available settings is the same as for Windows 98 even though they're organized differently among the tabs in the dialog box. Make sure the right network adapter is selected and then either choose Obtain an IP Address from a DHCP Server if your network uses DHCP or fill in the TCP/IP address, subnet mask, gateway, and DNS just as you learned for Windows 98. Windows NT 4 and Windows 2000 likely won't require you to reboot the computer when you change these settings.

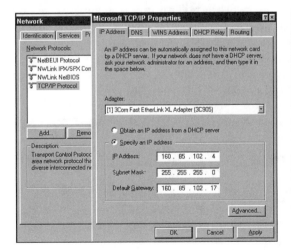
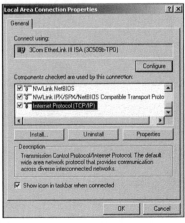

Figure 8.14: *Windows NT 4 (left) and Windows 2000 (right) TCP/IP configuration dialog boxes.*

It doesn't matter what order you add and remove protocols, but be sure to install your network adapters before trying to set up the protocols.

Adding Applications and Clients

With what you've learned so far in this chapter, you've been able to add the layer 2, 3, and 4 software that will power your network. The device drivers provide layer 2, controlling the link between your computer and the network. Elements of NetBEUI, the Internetwork Packet Exchange (IPX), and the Internet Protocol (IP) provide layer 3 support, moving packets across the network. Layer 4 processing depends on the Server Message Block (SMB), Sequenced Packet Exchange (SPX), and Transmission Control Protocol (TCP) to reliably move packets in order.

Getting useful work done requires that you install software operating at layers 5 through 7—applications providing services on the network. Microsoft calls some of the applications you'll learn about in this section *clients*, reflecting the fact that they are clients to servers on other computers. The clients, and the associated servers, fall in the category of what we're generically calling *applications*.

You'll want to add both clients and servers on computers on your LAN. You might choose to designate specific computers as *file servers*, as shown in Figure 8.15, or you might load the server software on all the computers on your network so they're all capable of sharing files. The advantage of having designated file servers is that you can focus your investment in large volumes of disk storage in a single place rather than on many computers spread across the network, and can install a tape drive on the file server for maximum backup performance. File servers simplify the job of people looking for files, too, because by design the files they want are ones someone else put on the file server to be shared. When you make all the computers on your LAN capable of file sharing, it's harder to know where to look for shared files.

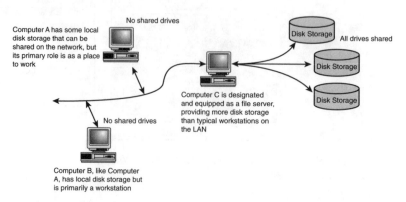

Figure 8.15: Using a file server to simplify finding shared files.

File servers should be computers you put in a corner and don't use directly because computers people use to run programs are more likely to crash. When a file server crashes, you can affect the work of everyone else on the LAN. Setting up a computer as a file server, therefore, requires the added expense of a dedicated computer. If you have a very small LAN, perhaps one with only two or three computers, letting any or all of the computers share files is reasonable and avoids the cost of an additional dedicated computer.

Windows 98

If you look again at the dialog box in Figure 8.5, you'll see two application-level networking components: the Client for Microsoft Networks and File and Printer Sharing for Microsoft Networks. Each has a well-defined purpose:

- **Client for Microsoft Networks.** The client software lets you *browse* your network for other computers, meaning it finds all the computers visible through protocols loaded on the local computer, and lets you access shared resources (files and printers) on remote computers. The presence of a client program on a Windows computer is what makes the Network Neighborhood icon appear on your computer's desktop and lets you see remote computers and their resources in the Windows Explorer.

- **File and Printer Sharing for Microsoft Networks.** The server software corresponding to the Client for Microsoft Networks is File and Printer Sharing for Microsoft Networks. The file and printer sharing software adds the support necessary to make files and printers on the local computer accessible to clients on remote machines.

The Client for Microsoft Networks and File and Printer Sharing for Microsoft Networks implement the Server Message Block (SMB) application protocols. For access to Novell file and print servers, you can also install the Microsoft Novell client software, Client for NetWare Networks. You can make a Windows computer function as a NetWare-compatible file and print server by installing File and Print Sharing for NetWare Networks.

In most cases, you won't want to install the NetWare client or server software unless you have an actual Novell NetWare server on your LAN; the Novell protocols introduce additional message traffic you can avoid with the Microsoft protocols. You'll especially want to avoid installing File and Print Sharing for NetWare Networks by accident on an existing LAN; if you introduce a new NetWare server, existing NetWare clients on other computers will think that the default server is *your* computer. That change might prevent the redirected clients from finding files they need to operate.

Whichever client you install, make sure that there's a common set of protocols on the client and server. If you install only the NetBEUI protocol on a client along with the NetWare client, the computer won't be able to see or talk to NetWare services with only IPX/SPX or TCP/IP loaded. To access that server, the client would itself have to have one or both of IPX/SPX or TCP/IP loaded.

Example 8.6 shows you how to install and configure client and server application software on a Windows 98 computer.

EXAMPLE 8.6 INSTALLING APPLICATION SOFTWARE

EXAMPLE

The default network configuration for Windows installs TCP support and the Client for Microsoft Networks and assumes automatic TCP/IP address assignment. If you want to deviate from that default, you'll want to follow this example:

1. Start the Network Control Panel applet with the sequence Start, Settings, Control Panel, Network, or by right-clicking the Network Neighborhood desktop icon and then selecting Properties.

2. Most likely Windows will install the Client for Microsoft Networks automatically when you add the network adapter. If not, as shown in Figure 8.16, click Add to get the dialog box shown in the middle of Figure 8.16 and then click Client and click Add in that dialog box. The result of that will be the Select Network Client dialog box you see at the front of Figure 8.16. Select Microsoft and then the Client for Microsoft Networks. Click OK and you'll return all the way back to the Network applet.

Figure 8.16: Adding the Client for Microsoft Networks.

3. Windows doesn't install the file and print sharing server software by default. If you want it loaded, click the File and Print Sharing button in the Network applet and then select the services you want in the dialog box you see in Figure 8.17. Click OK and then click OK on the Network applet. You'll need the Windows CD-ROM so Windows can load the additional software. Wait until Windows figures out you have to reboot and let the machine restart.

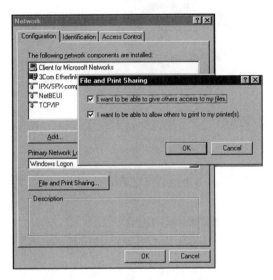

Figure 8.17: *Installing File and Print Sharing for Microsoft Networks.*

4. There's nothing useful to configure under Windows 98 for the file and printer sharing component after it's installed because the defaults are what you want, but you should check the settings for the client. Figure 8.18 shows the configuration dialog box. Assuming you identified the machine as using a workgroup earlier in the chapter, you'll leave the Log On to Windows NT Domain box unchecked. The choice you'll want to consider is whether to require the computer to validate any permanent connections you might make to disks on other computers (you'll learn how to do that in Chapter 9. If you choose Quick Logon, Windows will simply start and ignore the remote machine until you first try to access it. That choice lets Windows start up faster, but postpones any warnings that the server isn't reachable. If you choose Logon and Restore Network Connections, Windows checks all the permanent drive connections (although not ones to printers). If it finds a problem you receive a warning dialog box.

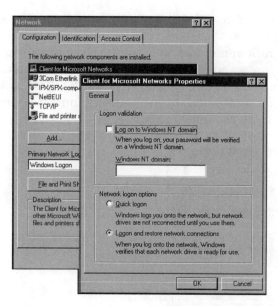

Figure 8.18: *Configuring the Client for Microsoft Networks.*

Windows NT 4 and Windows 2000

By default, Windows NT 4 adds the client and server software for Microsoft networking, including both file and printer sharing. There are no useful options to configure, although in the next chapter you'll learn how to set access permissions to make sure the people you want to get to your files (and only those people) can do so. Figure 8.19 shows a typical set of services for Windows NT 4 Workstation. There's no particular correspondence between this list and the one for Windows 98 or Windows 2000; fortunately, you can safely ignore it.

Windows 2000 is much closer to Windows 98 in most respects, including the Network Control Panel applet (see Figure 8.20). The order in which components show up in the list is different from that for Windows 98, but once again you can see Client for Microsoft Networks and File and Printer Sharing for Microsoft Networks. The dialog boxes you get if you select one of the two and click Properties are very different from Windows 98, though; you'll likely want to leave those settings at the defaults. Using the Install button, you can also install Gateway (and Client) Service for NetWare; you get the equivalent of the Windows 98 File and Print Services for NetWare by installing the SAP Agent (Service Advertising Protocol) service.

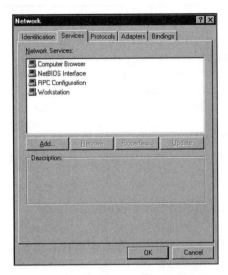

Figure 8.19: *Windows NT 4 Workstation services.*

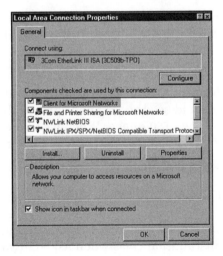

Figure 8.20: *Windows 2000 Professional Network Control Panel applet.*

Configuring Linux Networking

No matter what version of Linux you might have, setting up and configuring Linux is completely different from setting up and configuring Windows. In this section, you'll learn about the key settings you'll make on an initial installation of Mandrake Linux version 6.1 and then about how to modify those settings after your system is up and running. If you're looking for information on how to configure Samba, which is the Linux software for file and printer sharing with Windows, you'll want to look in Chapter 9.

Initial Networking Settings for New Installations

The Mandrake Linux installation sequence we'll talk about in this section is from a CD-ROM. If you have a computer connected to the Internet with a CD-Recordable (CD-R) drive and Adaptec's widely available EZ-CD Creator software (we've even seen it included with a box of blank CD-R media), you can download a ready-to-record image of the Mandrake Linux CD-ROM for free from one of the sites listed at http://www.linux-mandrake.com/en/ftp.php3. Example 8.7 shows how to download a CD-ROM image; after you've done that, double-click the resulting file (it will have an .ISO extension) to start the writing process.

EXAMPLE

EXAMPLE 8.7 **DOWNLOADING AND RECORDING MANDRAKE LINUX**

You'll need a computer with a CD-R or CD-RW drive and a connection to the Internet. The file you'll download is over 600MB, so you might not want to try this with a 28.8Kbps modem. We do it with a 128Kbps ISDN connection, and the download takes about 12 hours. If you do choose to download Mandrake Linux, follow these steps:

1. Open a Web browser and navigate to http://www.linux-mandrake.com/en/ftp.php3. Scroll down the list of sites until you find one near you. In this example, you'll click the link for ftp://ftp.tux.org/pub/distributions/mandrake.

2. After the Web page for ftp://ftp.tux.org/pub/distributions/mandrake opens, you should see the ISO folder. Click that link, and you should see a file that's the .ISO image. When we wrote this, the filename was named mandrake61-1.iso and was 611MB in size.

3. Use your Web browser to download the file to a directory on your disk.

However you get an installation CD-ROM, go ahead and start the install. You'll have to make some decisions about where on your disks to put Linux; this is easiest if you're dedicating a machine to Linux and using the entire disk. We chose a Custom installation class when asked; if you choose Workstation or Server you might get a different set of questions to answer.

At the screen allowing selection of the software components to install, we chose these network-related components, and did not choose to select individual packages within the components:

- Networked Workstation
- SMB (Samba) Connectivity
- Anonymous FTP Server

We also chose to install the X Window System and KDE so we could work with a graphical desktop.

Somewhat later in the installation you'll reach a screen asking whether you want to configure your LAN networking. Choose Yes. Example 8.8 walks you through the choices you'll make.

EXAMPLE

EXAMPLE 8.8   CONFIGURING LAN NETWORKING DURING INSTALLATION

The first LAN networking configuration screen you'll see lets you define the network interface card (NIC) in your computer. If your NIC isn't listed, you'll need expert help to find and install a driver. If you don't have a captive Linux expert, we suggest replacing the NIC with one that's supported. Follow these steps:

1. Find the list of NICs supported by Mandrake at `http://www.linux-mandrake.com/en/fhard.php3#network`.

2. You'll then be asked to either manually enter the configuration data for your NIC or to let Linux probe for the card. The information Linux wants is the same resource information you learned about in the Windows Device Manager earlier in this chapter: interrupt request, I/O port, memory addresses, and DMA channels. We suggest probing to let Linux try to find the right information automatically; if you have a PCI NIC installed, this should always work.

3. After Linux has the NIC set up, it will ask you how you want the TCP/IP network address to be assigned for this computer. Your choices are to assign a specific address, called a *static IP address* or to let the machine use the BOOTP or DHCP protocols to get an assignment from another machine. (BOOTP is another TCP/IP protocol used to allow diskless computers to start. One of its included functions is assignment of the TCP/IP address, netmask, and related parameters.)

   We chose to specify a static IP address for the example installation, which led the setup program to ask for the TCP/IP address, netmask, default gateway, and primary domain name server (DNS). (Both Linux and Windows systems let you define multiple addresses to use for DNS services. You need one DNS; the others are only used if the primary DNS doesn't work.)

4. Setup then will ask for the domain name, hostname, and numbers for secondary and tertiary DNSs. The names can be arbitrary if you're not connected to the Internet; if that's the case, after your system is running you'll want to reconfigure it to use a hosts file and not try to reference a DNS.

5. After specifying the time zone, you'll be asked to examine and possibly modify a list of services to start. Table 8.1 shows the network-related services and the start/do-not-start status we assigned, along with the reason for that choice.

Table 8.1: Linux Network-Related Services

Do Not Start	Start	Reason
	inet	Basic TCP/IP processing.
	netfs	Network file access support.
	network	Basic network support.
nfs		Network File System; only required if you'll be using the NFS protocol on your LAN.
routed		Routing between subnets. Only required if you're using this computer to connect different subnets.
sendmail		Email send/receive processing. Not required for email access through an ISP.
	smb	SMB protocol. Required for access to file and print services on Windows machines (unless you run NFS), and required for Windows machines to access files on the Linux machine.
		You should be able to leave the non-network services at their default settings and have the machine work fine.

After you complete the rest of setup and reboot, the machine should be able to access Web servers elsewhere on your LAN or out on the Internet if your LAN is connected through an ISP. If that doesn't work, you can check the settings you made using the tools in the next section, and can apply the techniques you'll learn in Chapter 17, "Troubleshooting Network Problems."

Modifying Existing Networking Settings

If you chose to not configure LAN networking when you installed Mandrake Linux, or if you want to check and modify any of the settings your Linux computer now has, you'll use the tools you'll learn about in this section. All the tools we'll describe run in the KDE graphical desktop environment, which in turn runs on top of the X Window System. You can think of KDE as the *shell* in Windows; the component that changed the desktop appearance so radically between Windows 3.1 and Windows 95. X Window and the rest of Linux correspond to the rest of Windows—the code that controls the hardware, loads and runs programs, and communicates on networks.

The tool you'll use to begin examining and reconfiguring network settings is the *network configurator*. The easiest way to start the network configurator running is to start linuxconf using the icon on the KDE desktop and then start the network configurator from there. Linux requires you be logged in as root to make network and system configuration changes (you created the root password when you installed the system); if you logged in with another account, linuxconf will prompt you for the root password when it starts.

Figure 8.21 shows `linuxconf`; click the Networking button to start the network configurator.

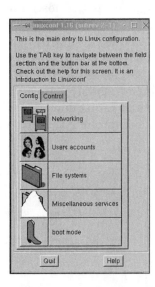

Figure 8.21: *Mandrake Linux* `linuxconf`.

Figure 8.22 shows the network configurator. The program looks and operates much like a Windows dialog box, including the tabs at the top to separate different categories of functions.

Figure 8.22: *Mandrake Linux Network Configurator.*

If you click Basic Host Information, the dialog box on the left in Figure 8.23 appears. You can't do anything on the Host Name tab but set the hostname; as you learned earlier for Linux setup, the hostname should include both the hostname and domain name. If you click the Adaptor 1 tab instead, though, you get the dialog box on the right in Figure 8.23, where you can set not only the hostname, but also how the TCP/IP address and netmask are defined (and what they are for static TCP/IP addresses), device driver, and NIC resources. You'll probably want to leave the Net device field alone unless you understand Linux devices well; leaving the I/O port and IRQ fields blank corresponds to probing the card during initial installation.

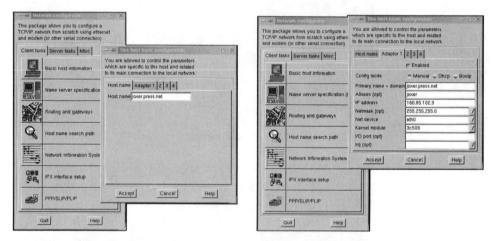

Figure 8.23: *Mandrake Linux Basic Host Information dialog box.*

Clicking the Name Server Specification button results in the dialog box shown in Figure 8.24, allowing you to examine and change the settings for the primary, secondary, and tertiary DNS. You can also enter the domain for your computer here; most desktop Linux machines need at most the primary domain name server address and the first search domain. You can ignore the entire dialog box if you use the Host Name Search Path dialog box to cause Linux to use only a hosts file.

Figure 8.25 shows the Routing and Gateways dialog box (the larger dialog box on the left). You set the default gateway by clicking on the Defaults button, resulting in the smaller dialog box on the right. You enter the TCP/IP address of the default gateway. You'll want to leave Enable Routing turned off (the button appears to stick out rather than be pushed in) for most desktop machines.

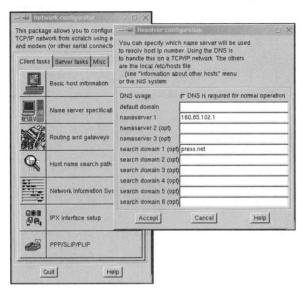

Figure 8.24: Mandrake Linux Name Server Specification dialog box.

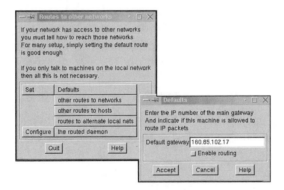

Figure 8.25: Mandrake Linux Routing and Gateways dialog box.

The Host Name Search Path dialog box lets you control which techniques Linux uses to convert computer names to TCP/IP addresses, and the order in which it uses them (see Figure 8.26). The computer we set up is connected to the Internet through our LAN, so we chose to use both a hosts file and a DNS (you can tell that's the option selected because the button appears pushed in). If the machine ran on a standalone LAN not connected to the Internet, you could choose to give each computer a hosts file and dispense with DNS altogether. You make the hosts file using the directions given in Example 8.5; store it in the /etc directory. You'll need root permission to store the file.

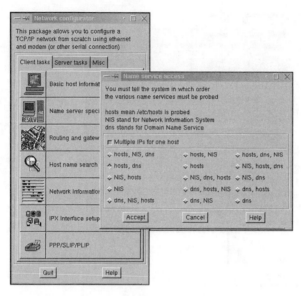

Figure 8.26: *Mandrake Linux Host Name Search dialog box.*

Figure 8.27 shows the IPX Interface Setup dialog box. IPX can be largely automatic with Linux, as it is in Windows; simply turn on the check box to enable IPX networking (it's turned off in the figure). Leave the other two autoconfiguration check boxes turned on.

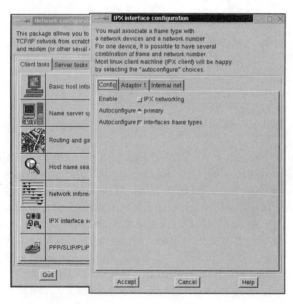

Figure 8.27: *Mandrake Linux IPX Interface Setup dialog box.*

The PPP/SLIP/PLIP dialog box sets up dial-up networking; you'll learn about that in Chapter 12, "Sharing an Internet Connection."

Summary

You've learned in this chapter how to add device drivers to Windows and how to pick your NIC device driver in Linux. You've learned how to add the layer 2 through 4 protocols to Windows and Linux, and how to add the upper-layer file sharing software. You've seen the details of Linux network installation and configuration.

What's Next

Using the information you now have, you're ready to progress to Chapter 9, where you'll learn how to configure file sharing and make sure only the people you want access your files.

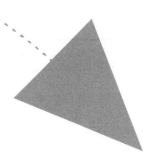

## 9

Sharing Fixed Drives and Setting Access Controls

In this chapter you will learn

- How to configure Windows and Linux file sharing

- What software to use for Windows and Linux file transfer

After you've completed the work in the last few chapters—installing your hardware, drivers, protocols, and application software—enabling file sharing can be the work of a few seconds. If you have a tiny, two-computer standalone network where you use both machines, the simplistic approach could well be all you need. You'll learn how to share files on all your computers in this chapter, along with how to configure a file server.

Having more than one or two people using your network, having untrained users who could accidentally damage the network setup, or having your network connected to the Internet—these all mean that you'll want to consider the security of your network. You'll learn how to limit what you share on a computer and in what ways users can access shared material.

The techniques you'll learn in this chapter apply to both fixed (internal) and removable drives including CD-ROM, DVD, and Zip. We've included a section at the end of the chapter to highlight concerns that you'll want to be aware of unique to removable media.

Configuring File Sharing

You learned in the last chapter to install Windows file and print sharing software as part of the software you work with in the Network control panel applet. You'll learn in this chapter how to configure the Samba software so you can share files among Linux machines or between Linux and Windows machines.

Whatever combination of operating systems and file-sharing protocols you use, you'll want to make sure you use a compatible set of operating system and protocol choices. Using the same choices on different machines running the same operating system always works; using NetBEUI and Windows file and print sharing running under Windows on all your machines is a workable combination. Table 9.1 shows your options when you're combining Linux and Windows. In summary, you can run SMB over TCP/IP using the software included with the two operating systems, and you can run NFS over TCP/IP using additional third-party software. IPX/SPX is available on Linux but not well supported.

Table 9.1: Combining Operating Systems and Protocols for File Sharing

	Windows					
	SMB			**NFS**		
	NetBEUI	**IPX/SPX**	**TCP/IP**	**NetBEUI**	**IPX/SPX**	**TCP/IP**
Linux						
SMB						
NetBEUI	N					
IPX/SPX		N				
TCP/IP			Y			
NFS						
NetBEUI				N		
IPX/SPX					N	
TCP/IP						*

* means additional software required

File sharing is a client/server relationship; the computer accessing the files is the client, whereas the one holding them is the server. You make connections from the client and control access permissions on the server.

Using either SMB or NFS, the difference between a peer network and a file server–based network is simply one of which computers in the network are configured to share files with others. Hybrid setups are common, but stereotypically if you configure some or all the users' computers to share files, you have a peer network, whereas if you configure only dedicated server computers to share files you have a file server–based network.

File sharing isn't your only option; you can readily configure both Windows and Linux for file transfer, where you have to copy the file from one computer to the other before using it, using the FTP protocol running over TCP/IP. Example 9.1 shows you the basics of how to pick between the two.

EXAMPLE

Example 9.1   Choosing Between File Sharing and File Transfer

File transfer is more desirable when you want other computers to have their own copies of files, but clumsy when you're trying to collaborate with others (see Chapter 13, "Collaboration and Multiplayer LAN Games"). Follow these steps:

1. Determine which kinds of files you'll share or transfer. Files on computers are categorically either programs or data; the decision between file sharing and file transfer depends on which sort of files you're interested in.

2. Program files themselves fall into two categories: files that—when run—install software, and files that are installed, executable software. Install programs and related files—the programs are often named setup.exe—are suitable for either file sharing or file transfer.

3. Executable programs are (conservatively) only suitable for file sharing, and then only if written to support networked installations. The problem is that programs tend to need configuration data stored on the local computer and components added to Windows, and those actions happen during the setup process. Simply executing the program from a shared drive or copying the program from one computer to another doesn't do that work, so the program isn't likely to run.

4. Data files are good candidates for both file sharing and file transfer. Read-only shared files are a good way to make sure people have access to the latest version of a standard document or report. Read/write shared files are the basis for collaboration with many people working on the same project. Transferred data files are the approach you should use to provide people with templates and other starting points for their work.

Windows 98

You should enable file sharing on the server first and then on all the clients that will access the files. Assuming you're using the Microsoft protocols (SMB) and installed File and Print Sharing for Microsoft clients (see Chapter 8, "Configuring Your System Software"), open the Windows Explorer on the server and look at the local drives (see Figure 9.1). We've annotated the figure to highlight all the local drives and to show what you see for both unshared and shared drives. The distinction in the window isn't much; Windows simply adds a small hand with a blue cuff under the drive icon. The icon probably reminds someone of a butler.

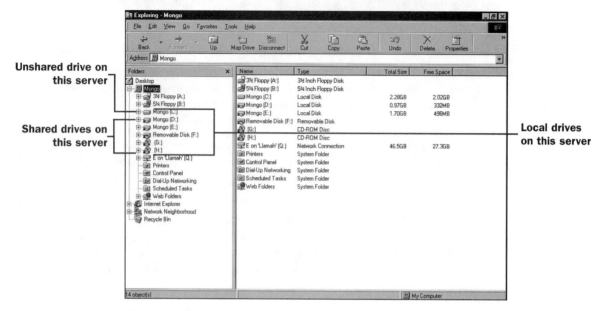

Unshared drive on this server

Shared drives on this server

Local drives on this server

Figure 9.1: Shared and unshared drives in Windows Explorer.

Example 9.2 shows how to turn on file sharing in Windows 98.

EXAMPLE

Example 9.2   Turning on File Sharing in Windows 98

The approach in the example works for any local disk drive (you can't provide access to what are already remote drives in Windows, partly because resharing the drive might violate security restrictions being enforced by the original server. Follow these steps:

1. Figure 9.2 shows how to open the Sharing dialog box for a disk drive. Right-click the item in Windows Explorer for the drive, and then left-click Sharing.

2. When you click Sharing, the dialog box in Figure 9.2 will appear. (The menu will go away; Figure 9.2 is a composite so you can see what happens.) The Not Shared button is selected in the figure, which is why the drive shows up in the Windows Explorer without the additional shared drive indicator.

3. Enable sharing for the drive by selecting Shared As in the dialog box. Windows then enables the sharing controls, resulting in the dialog box in Figure 9.3. For this example, we'll just leave the share name as C (which is also the drive letter for the local disk) and select full access.

Right-click the drive you want to share...

...and then left-click Sharing

The Sharing tab in the Properties dialog box lets you configure remote access

Figure 9.2: Opening the Windows sharing dialog box.

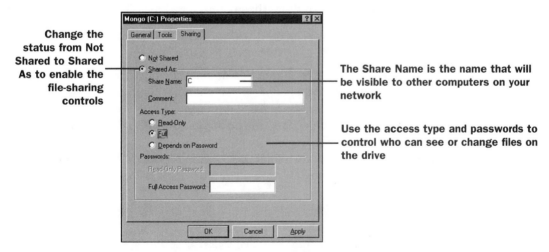

Change the status from Not Shared to Shared As to enable the file-sharing controls

The Share Name is the name that will be visible to other computers on your network

Use the access type and passwords to control who can see or change files on the drive

Figure 9.3: Enabling file sharing in Windows 98.

4. Click OK. After a few seconds, Windows Explorer should update the display to add the shared drive indicator.

The share name you apply need not be the same as the drive letter assigned to the local drive. It's far less confusing to people if the share names do match the local drive letter, but there's nothing to keep you from typing Suzy's House instead.

You'll complete the sharing process on each client computer. Don't expect that accessing a shared drive on one client computer will complete setup on all of them; each one needs the work done separately. You can access shared drives and files one of two ways in Windows, either by assigning a drive letter on the client machine that maps to the remote share or by navigating through the Network Neighborhood to what you want.

Example 9.3 shows how to assign a drive letter on a client machine to a remote shared drive in Windows 98.

EXAMPLE

Example 9.3 Assigning a Letter to a Shared Drive in Windows 98

The letter you assign is the one you'll use on the client; the server will continue to refer to the drive by the drive letter local to the server. You don't have to assign the same drive letter on each client referencing the remote drive, although it can be confusing to people if drive letter assignments are scattered all over. On our network, for instance, we keep an archive of data and files downloaded from the Internet on the E drive of one of our machines. Every client mapping a drive letter to that shared drive assigns Q, so no matter what computer someone uses (except the server), drive Q will get at the shared files. Follow these steps:

1. Open Windows Explorer and execute the command sequence Tools, Map Network Drive.

2. The Map Network Drive dialog box appears (see Figure 9.4). Pick the drive letter you want to assign on the client in the upper field, and then type a path to the shared drive on the server. Compose the path with two backslashes (\), the server name, another backslash, and the share name. In the figure you'll see that the path we entered—\\llamah\d—follows that model, because it points to the shared drive D on the server llamah.

Use this field to choose the drive letter you'll assign on the local machine to the remote drive on the server

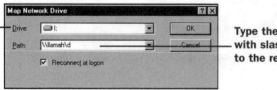

Type the computer name and share name, with slashes as shown, to define the path to the remote shared drive

Figure 9.4: Mapping a network drive in Windows 98.

3. Click OK and the new drive letter will show up in Windows Explorer. You can access remote files through the drive letter just as if they were on the local machine.

Don't simply assign the next available drive letter—for instance, if your hard disk is C and CD-ROM is D, it's a bad idea to use E for the first mapped network drive. You're better off to leave a few spare letters so if you add new drives to the computer sequence (which will extend the C, D, and so on) the letters assigned to the network drives won't have to move. It was common in NetWare networks to start assigning network drive letters at F just for this reason.

It's also a good idea to leave a block of a few letters for each computer you'll have serving files. You could reserve F through J for the first one, K through O for the next, and so on. You don't have to make the blocks five letters long, as we've suggested; simply be sure you leave enough for all the shared disks you'll want to access from the computer. Figure 9.5 shows how this approach can work. There are four servers in the figure, with a varying number of drives on each server. The drives are lettered from the C, D, E sequence locally on the servers. On a typical client, shown on the right, the drives are mapped to blocks of letters: F and G for the C and D drives on the first server, and so forth.

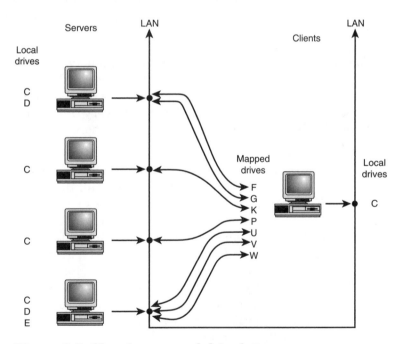

Figure 9.5: *Choosing mapped drive letters.*

Example 9.4 shows you how to use Windows Explorer or Network Neighborhood (they're really the same thing) to find a shared disk.

Example 9.4   Navigating to a Shared Drive and Shared File in Windows 98

Whether you use this example or Example 9.3 is mostly personal preference; they both get to the same place. Follow these steps:

1. Open Network Neighborhood by double-clicking the desktop icon, or open Windows Explorer and then left-click Network Neighborhood in the left pane.

2. Click the plus sign to the left of Network Neighborhood in the left pane to reveal the list of visible computers.

3. Similarly, click the plus sign next to a specific computer to expose the list of shared drives. Click a drive to show the available files in the right pane.

4. If you right-click the shared drive in the left pane, one of the choices you'll see in the pop-up menu is Map Network Drive. Select that and you'll get the Map Network Drive dialog box you saw in Figure 9.4. The dialog box will be a little different, though, in that the path will be filled in to point at the drive you clicked on and won't be changeable.

No matter which approach you use to map a network drive—that of Example 9.3 or of Example 9.4—the Reconnect at Login check box lets you specify that Windows should reestablish the connection between the drive letter and the shared drive on the server every time you restart the computer. The Reconnect at Login option takes more time when your computer starts.

If you want to transfer files rather than share them, your simplest approach is to install the TCP/IP protocol on all the relevant computers and run the File Transfer Protocol (FTP). Windows 98 has an FTP client built in, but it's difficult to use; there's no built-in Windows 98 FTP server. We recommend two programs to provide FTP capabilities on your computers: the WFTPD server available at `http://www.wftpd.com`, and the WS_FTP Limited Edition client available at `http://www.ipswitch.com`. You can download WFTPD directly from `http://www.wftpd.com/downloads.htm`; the WS_FTP LE download page is at `http://www.ipswitch.com/cgi/download_eval.pl?product=WL-100`. WFTPD is available on a trial basis with some operational restrictions; WS_FTP LE is available free of charge if you're a U.S. federal, state, or local government employee (government contractors must use WS_FTP Pro); a student, faculty member, or staff member of an educational institution; or a non-business home user (recreational use only).

Download the 32-bit version of WFTPD for installation on a Windows 98, NT 4, or 2000 system. When the download completes, run the downloaded setup program on the file transfer server. Example 9.5 shows how to install WinZip so you can handle the ZIP file containing WFTPD.

Example 9.5 Installing WFTPD Using WinZip

EXAMPLE

You'll need a program capable of opening ZIP files to do the installation; we recommend WinZip (download it at http://www.winzip.com). Next follow these steps:

1. Double-click the downloaded WFTPD setup file. WinZip opens and should look like the left part of Figure 9.6.

2. Click the Extract button and you'll get the dialog box shown on the right side of Figure 9.6.

Extract all the files to a directory, and then run wftpd.exe

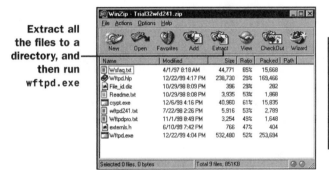
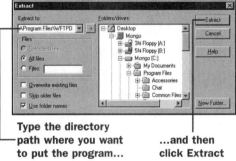

Type the directory path where you want to put the program...   **...and then click Extract**

Figure 9.6: Using WinZip to install WFTPD.

3. Fill in the directory path where you want to install the program (we used C:\Program Files\WFTPD in the figure) and then click Extract. Make sure you extract all the files using the All Files option in the middle-left of the dialog box.

4. Navigate with Windows Explorer to the directory where you extracted WFTPD (for example, C:\Program Files\WFTPD) and double-click the WFTPD icon. The program starts.

5. Click Security, General to open the General Security dialog box in Figure 9.7.

6. Click Allow Anonymous and on Allow Anonymous Uploads to permit access to the FTP server without establishing user accounts. This isn't a secure configuration; be sure to reconfigure your server when you learn more about FTP security later in this chapter.

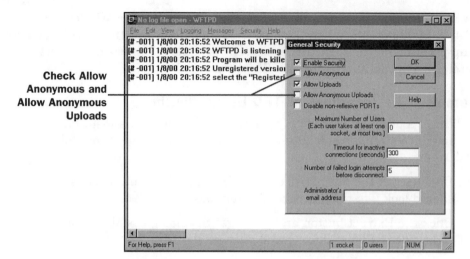

Check Allow Anonymous and Allow Anonymous Uploads

Figure 9.7: *Allowing anonymous FTP operation.*

With this installation configuration, you'll have to start WFTPD every time you restart the computer. You'll learn how to make WFTPD start automatically later in the chapter.

Once you have WFTPD set up, you're ready on the server side for file transfers, needing only to set up an FTP client to complete the job. Windows includes a primitive FTP client, but you can do better and (subject to license terms) do it for free using the WS_FTP LE client from Ipswitch Incorporated. Download the software using the form at http:// www.ipswitch.com/cgi/download_eval.pl?product=main. Fill in the required information, check off to download WS_FTP LE 5.06, and click Next. Continue to follow the instructions to download the software and install it onto your computer.

WS_FTP LE lets you configure the program to remember computers you'll be connecting to, calling each such configuration entry a *session*. (The program comes preconfigured with several sessions, including ones for several game manufacturers, Microsoft, and the US Internal Revenue Service forms download site.) Example 9.6 shows how to define a session for one of your local computers running an FTP server.

EXAMPLE

Example 9.6   Configuring a WS_FTP LE Session

The Session Properties dialog box, visible when the program starts or when you click the Connect button at the bottom of the window lets you define and edit session configurations (see Figure 9.8). You can also use the dialog box to pick one of the existing WS_FTP LE session definitions using the Profile Name drop down list on the General tab of the dialog box.

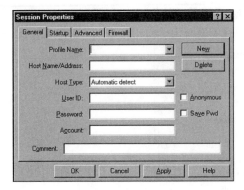

Figure 9.8: *WS_FTP LE Session Properties dialog box.*

If you're going to create your own session, follow these steps:

1. Begin creating a new session by clicking the New button visible in the upper-right corner of Figure 9.8. All the fields will clear out with the exception of the Host Type, which will show Automatic Detect.

2. Enter a name for the profile in the Profile Name field. The name could be the name of the computer you're connecting to, but could equally well be some word or phrase that reminds you of what the session is for. We entered *llamah* in this example because we're going to connect to a machine named llamah.

3. Enter the machine name in the Host Name/Address field. If you created a hosts file (see Chapter 8, "Configuring Your System Software"), you can use the name you put in there, otherwise for local machines you might have to use the numeric TCP/IP address of the machine.

4. Nearly all servers you'll work with support the Automatic Detect option for the Host Type field. If you can't make the client and server connect, try changing the value in Host Type to the specific operating system or FTP server you're using.

5. If you've configured the FTP server for anonymous access, as in the earlier example, check the Anonymous box; otherwise, fill in an authorized username and password in the User ID and Password fields. When you're finished, the dialog box will look similar to Figure 9.9.

6. Click OK; WS_FTP LE attempts to make a connection to the server. After it connects, you'll have two columns of directory listings, the one on the left for the local client and the one on the right for the remote server. You can double-click the folders (such as Accessories on the left or Outgoing on the right in Figure 9.9) to navigate around in the file systems. Double-click the up arrow at the top of either directory listing to move up a level in the directory tree.

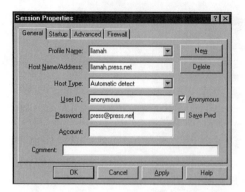

Figure 9.9: Completed WS_FTP LE Session Properties dialog box.

7. When you've found the file you want to transfer and its destination directory, select the file (you can select one, some, or all in a directory). Then either drag and drop the file into the destination, or click the appropriate arrow in the middle of the window. The file transfer will start, showing the progress dialog box you see in Figure 9.10. When the transfer finishes, the file has been copied as you instructed.

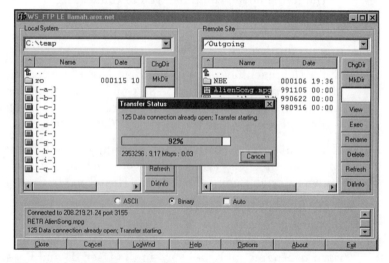

Figure 9.10: WS_FTP LE file transfer in progress.

Windows NT 4 and Windows 2000

With the exception of how security is handled (see the "FTP Access Controls and Security" section later in this chapter), both Windows NT 4 Workstation and Windows 2000 Professional handle shared drives and file transfer in the same way as Windows 98. You can use Windows Explorer to map drive letters to remote drives and to navigate across your network in nearly the same way as you learned to do for Windows 98 in the previous section. Example 9.7 shows how you share a disk drive under Windows 2000.

Example 9.7 Sharing a Disk Drive Using Windows 2000

Microsoft continues to move the graphical user interface of Windows 9x and Windows NT (most recently shipped as Windows 2000) closer together, so more and more of your knowledge from Windows 98 will apply as you migrate to the more stable Windows 2000. Follow these steps:

1. As with Windows 98, open Windows Explorer and right-click the drive you want to share. The Properties dialog box that appears looks different from the one for Windows 98 (see Figure 9.11). If the drive is not shared when you open the dialog box, the dialog box appears with a *default share*, which exists in lieu of a share you might define.

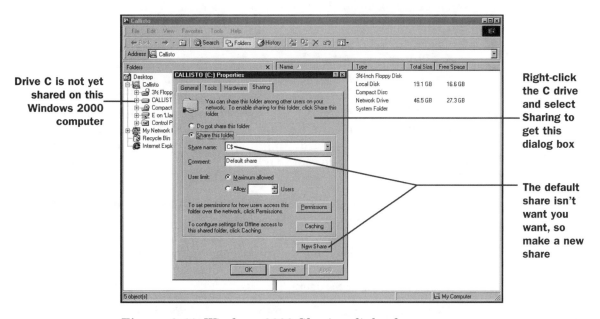

Figure 9.11: *Windows 2000 Sharing dialog box.*

2. Create a new share by clicking the New Share button in the lower-right corner of the dialog box. When you do, you'll bring up the New Share dialog box, shown in Figure 9.12. Fill in the name for the new share and click OK.

3. As with Windows 98, we recommend using the drive letter as the share name so you'll know what you're accessing from a remote computer.

4. Click OK and you'll see Windows Explorer add the indicator to the drive icon, showing it's a shared drive.

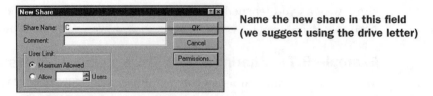

Figure 9.12: Windows 2000 new share dialog box.

The WFTPD FTP server installs on Windows NT 4 and Windows 2000 identically to how you learned to install it earlier for Windows 98. There's a built-in FTP server if you're running Windows NT 4 or Windows 2000 Server; under Windows 2000, look for it with the command sequence Start, Administrative Tools, Internet Services Manager. (Explaining how to install and operate the FTP server for Windows NT 4 or Windows 2000 Server is beyond the scope of this book; see a good book on Windows NT 4 or Windows 2000 Server.)

Linux Samba

Using what you're about to read in this section, you can use the Samba software package, included in most Linux distributions, to share files and printers with Windows 98, NT 4, and 2000 computers. After you have Samba configured and running, sharing files between Linux and Windows is simple and straightforward. Programs in most cases aren't compatible between Linux and Windows, though, so there are some limits on what's useful to do:

- **Data file sharing.** You can freely transfer data files between Linux and Windows computers. Many data file formats are common or almost common between programs running Linux and Windows, including graphics images, Web pages, and word processing documents, so data file sharing opens the door for collaboration among Linux and Windows users.

- **Program sharing.** There are no mechanisms for running Linux programs on Windows, and with one notable exception no mechanisms for running Windows programs on Linux. The one exception is the Wine project, which is an explicit attempt to develop software that allows Windows programs to run under Linux. You can find out more about Wine at http://www.winehq.com; for most people, it's enough to know that the only Microsoft Office application reported to run substantially correctly is Excel 97. Generally speaking, you're better off finding native Linux application software that does the job you need to do.

- **File serving.** You can freely use Linux machines as file servers for Windows clients or Windows machines for Linux clients.

The bigger issue you'll want to think about is that, for all its advantages, Linux is harder to install, configure, and maintain than Windows. Unlike the previous Windows-based sections, in which you learned to set up Windows file sharing using only graphical tools, some of the basic Samba configuration can only be done through text command lines. The Linux command line programs aren't the same as those you might remember from DOS, and there isn't room in this book for a tutorial on basic Linux operation. At best you'll have some learning to do; at worst, you might have to take some cryptic directions we'll give you on faith. If you're a novice with computers, you're probably going to have a tough time with Linux; we suggest beginners will be better off with Windows unless they have a local expert to help do the heavy lifting and furniture rearrangement.

You'll do the graphical tool-based part of Samba configuration through the Linux configurator, which you first saw in Chapter 8. Start the Linux KDE desktop running, leading to what you see in Figure 9.13. Of the icons on the left, left-clicking the one labeled Linuxconf starts the Linux configurator. (We've also used Figure 9.13 to point out the icon for the Linux command line window—shell—you'll need later in the Samba configuration process.)

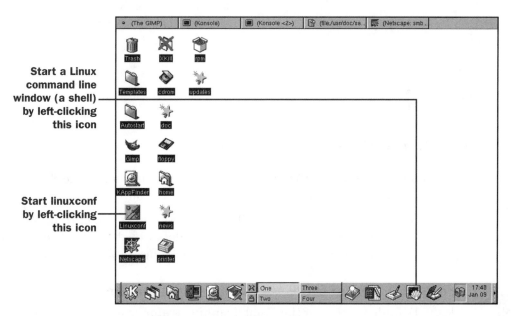

Figure 9.13: Initial Linux desktop.

If you're not logged in to Linux as the root user, linuxconf asks you for the root password when it starts. You'll also note from the bar at the top of Figure 9.13 that we had some programs running when we captured the image in the figure; the bar at the top of your screen will change to reflect what's running on your machine.

Example 9.8   Start the Samba Administrator

After linuxconf starts, you'll see the dialog box at the left of Figure 9.14. Follow the steps in Example 9.8 to open the Samba administrator, the graphical tool you'll use to configure the Samba software:

1. Make sure the Config tab in linuxconf is selected, so the Networking button is visible. Click the button.

Start the network configurator by left-clicking this icon

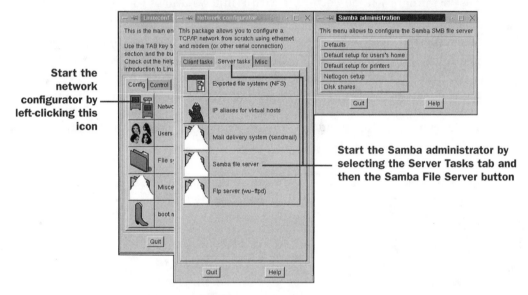

Start the Samba administrator by selecting the Server Tasks tab and then the Samba File Server button

Figure 9.14: Samba configuration administrator.

2. When the Network configurator dialog box appears, select the Server Tasks tab, and then click the Samba File Server button.

3. The Samba administrator dialog box appears, giving you buttons that lead to dialog boxes to set up system-wide defaults, defaults for each user, defaults for printers, network logon settings, and disk shares.

Example 9.9   Enter the Base Samba Configuration

Click the Defaults button in the Samba administrator to open the Share Setup dialog box (see Figure 9.15). Then click the Base Config tab. Example 9.9 shows you how to use this dialog box to enter the basic Samba configuration data.

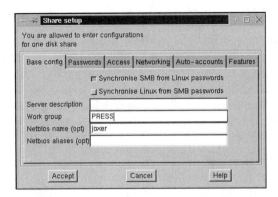

Figure 9.15: *Samba base configuration dialog box.*

Follow these steps:

1. Type any text you want in the Server description. What you type is the comment you see next to the server name in the Windows Explorer.

2. You learned in Chapter 8 to set the same workgroup name for all computers on your network. Use the Work Group field to define the workgroup name for Samba. We recommend using all uppercase letters, which should match what Windows did to the name you entered into the Windows machines.

3. Type the name for this computer, which should match the first part of the name you entered during Linux setup, into the Netbios Name (Opt) field. In Figure 9.15, you can see the name joxer; if the domain were press.net, the complete name entered during Linux setup would be joxer.press.net. You don't need the domain name for Samba, just the computer name.

4. Make sure the Synchronise SMB from Linux Passwords (alternative spelling and all) field is checked, although as we'll show you later you still have to coordinate passwords between Linux and Samba to make the SMB server work.

5. Click Accept.

Although Samba starts out setup for clear-text, unencrypted passwords, later builds of Windows 95, Windows 98 (all versions), Windows NT 4 (service pack 3 and later), and Windows 2000 require encrypted passwords be sent over the network by default. The two defaults are incompatible, so you still have some configuration to do.

Example 9.10   Enter Passwords Samba Configuration

Click the Defaults button in the Samba administrator once again to open the Share setup dialog box and on the Passwords tab to produce the dialog box shown in Figure 9.16. Work your way through Example 9.10 to learn how to use that dialog box to set up encrypted passwords in Samba. (It's possible to defeat Windows password encryption and use clear-text passwords, but we don't recommend it.) Follow these steps:

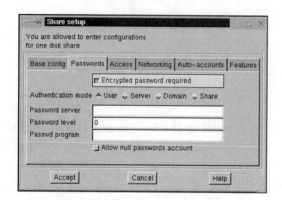

Figure 9.16: Samba password configuration dialog box.

1. The key configuration field in Figure 9.16 is the one labeled Encrypted Password Required; make sure it's enabled (the button will look pushed in).

2. Set the authentication mode to User, meaning that each computer accessing the Linux file server will require a user account and password on the Linux machine. Typically the account name will be the same as the network login name on the Windows machine.

3. You can leave all the other dialog fields alone. Click Accept to complete the example.

You're finished with the graphical part of the Samba setup. There are a lot more options you can exercise with Samba, but the defaults for those options are enough to enable basic operation.

Example 9.11   Exit the Linux Configurator and Activate Changes

Linux won't have altered the system configuration when you clicked the Accept button in the previous examples; it only records the changes for later. Follow the steps in Example 9.11 and Figure 9.17 to install your modifications into the running Linux system:

1. Click Quit in the Samba administration dialog box and then Quit in the Network configurator.

2. Click Quit in Linuxconf. When you do, you'll see the Status of the System dialog box shown in Figure 9.17. This is your chance to install the changes you've made, keep working on the configuration, or simply quit out of Linuxconf without making changes at this time (Linux will remember what you've done and make the changes available the next time you start Linuxconf).

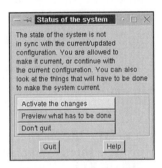

Figure 9.17: *Linux system status dialog box.*

3. Click the Activate the Changes button to install your changes or on Don't Quit to return to Linuxconf and work some more. Click Quit (without clicking Activate the changes) to exit Linuxconf and keep the system unchanged.

4. After you activate the changes, click Quit in the Status of the System dialog box to exit Linuxconf.

The graphical configuration you've done to this point corresponds to the setup you did in Windows using the Network control panel applet, setting the computer name and workgroup. The remainder of the work, corresponding to mapping drive letters and setting up drive shares in Windows, is text-based using Linux command lines. Start with Example 9.12 to gain access to shared Windows drives from Linux.

EXAMPLE

Example 9.12   Mount a Shared Windows Drive for Linux Access

Linux doesn't use drive letters as does Windows; no matter how the file system is spread across drives, it still looks like a single hierarchic tree starting at the root. The Linux notation for the root is /, similar to the Windows \ and used in the same way (including as a file separator in addition to the root indicator). When you access a Windows drive through the Linux file system, you have to tell Linux where in the tree the Windows drive connects. The process of establishing that connection is called *mounting* the remote file system; disconnecting the remote file system is called *unmounting*. Follow these steps:

1. Open a *console* (or *shell*) window using the shell window icon you saw in Figure 9.13. The commands you can run are different from those for Windows, but the window should have the familiar look of a prompt and a flashing cursor. On our machine our login account is press, and our default prompt is [press@joxer press]$. The press@joxer notation indicates the login account and on what computer the window is operating; the press notation indicates what directory is current. The lack of a leading root indicator means the current directory is underneath /home.

2. You must be logged in as root to mount or unmount file systems in Linux, so run the following command:

   su

   Linux will respond by asking you to type the root password; enter that followed by the Enter key. Your prompt should change to indicate you're now working as root; ours becomes [root@joxer press]#.

3. Linux provides a standard place in the file system hierarchy you'll normally use to connect in remote file systems, the /mnt directory. Move there with this command:

   cd /mnt

4. The process of connecting a remote file system is one of associating a directory name under /mnt with the root of the remote drive. If you have a Windows machine named fileserver with the C drive shared, for instance, you might create a directory under /mnt named fileserver and then mount the root of C there. The command sequence you'll use (assuming the remote Windows machine runs Windows 98 and no passwords are required by that machine) is as follows:

   mkdir fileserver
   smbmount //fileserver/c /mnt/fileserver

   Just press the Enter key when asked for a password. The mkdir command creates a directory named fileserver under /mnt in this example; the smbmount command actually makes the remote connection. Within the smbmount command, //fileserver/c is the remote machine and share name, whereas /mnt/fileserver is the complete path to the directory you want to map to the root of the remote disk.

5. Figure 9.18 shows what happens when you run the previous command sequence. We ran the Linux ls command after mounting the remote disk to show that the files on the Windows system were accessible.

Figure 9.18: Mounting a Windows shared drive in Linux.

6. After you complete the command sequence successfully, the remote Windows file system will be available to any program you run in any window on the Linux machine. The connection terminates when you log out of Linux or reboot the machine, although the directory you created under /mnt will remain. Because of that, you need only reexecute the cd and smbmount commands, skipping the mkdir.

You have some one-time setup tasks remaining before you can access files on a Linux machine from Windows. The problem you're going to solve is that the way you've configured Samba requires usernames and passwords from the Windows computer, and you don't yet have passwords for the Windows computer accounts established on the Linux machine. After you create user accounts in Linux for all the usernames you'll use from Windows, Example 9.13 shows you what to do to coordinate those accounts into Samba.

EXAMPLE

Example 9.13   Coordinate Passwords for Windows Access to Linux Files

Get ready to run the example by opening a shell window and gaining root access with the su command, as mentioned earlier. You'll run two commands in sequence once to do the initial Samba password setup and a third command once for each user account. When you're finished with the accounts, you'll run two more commands to restart the Samba server so it reloads the newly defined passwords. Follow these steps:

1. The initial two commands are these:

```
cat /etc/passwd | mksmbpasswd.sh > /etc/smbpasswd
chmod 600 /etc/smbpasswd
```

The first command, cat, creates a command file (/etc/smbpasswd), a script of Linux command lines. The second command, chmod, changes the permissions on the resulting file so it can be executed.

2. Run the /etc/smbpasswd command once for each existing Linux user account for which you want to have a Samba password. If you wanted to set the password for user press to be xxxxxxx, you'd use the following command:

```
smbpasswd press
```

3. Restart the server with these commands:

```
cd /etc/rc.d/init.d
./smb restart
```

Figure 9.19 shows the results when we followed the example on our Linux machine. We first used the ls command from the /home directory to identify all the accounts on the machine and carried out the commands including a password set for one account.

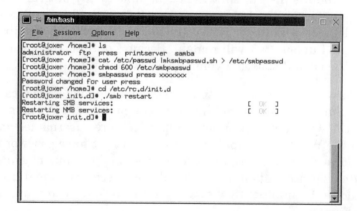

Figure 9.19: *Coordinating Linux and Samba passwords.*

After you complete the example, make sure you're logged in to a Windows machine with the username set to one of the ones you've defined to Linux (make sure you use the same uppercase/lowercase) and then go find the machine in Network Neighborhood. Give Windows the password you defined to Linux when the Windows dialog box pops up asking for a password, and you'll find the home directory for that Linux username is accessible.

Linux File Transfer

The best approach to file transfer using Linux is, as we described for
Windows, the File Transfer Protocol (FTP). Figure 9.20 shows how to set up
the FTP server. The server distinguishes between access permissions for
anonymous users and for known users; we've shown configurations for both
in the figure. You get to the FTP server configuration dialog box through
linuxconf and the network configurator, clicking the FTP Server
(WU-FTPD) button to bring up the configuration dialog box.

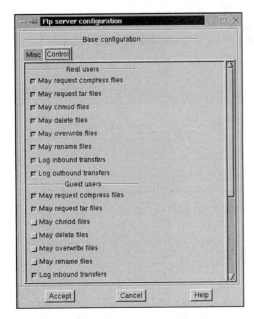

Figure 9.20: *Linux FTP server setup.*

Linux also comes with a built-in FTP client, gftp. Start the client using the
big K in the lower-left corner of the desktop and then select Gnome and X
Apps, Internet, gftp. Figure 9.21 shows the client connected to a computer;
the local file system is represented in the left pane, whereas the remote file
system is in the right.

Directory Organization, Access Controls, and Security

Give some thought to how you organize directories on machines you'll use
as file sharing or file transfer servers, because some forethought can make
your life enormously easier when you're trying to manage who can get at
what on the server.

With the exception of the root directory, directories exist inside other
directories. If you draw a picture of the nested directory structure, or look

at the view the two-pane Windows Explorer gives you in the left pane after you expand all the directories, you'll see that the directories on your computer form an upside-down tree. (Indeed, that's why the ultimate parent directory is called the root.)

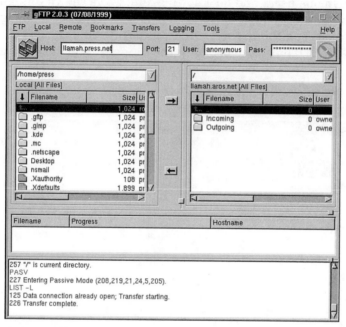

Figure 9.21: *Linux gftp FTP client.*

Both Windows and Linux let you set permissions on directories. Windows NT, Windows 2000, and Linux let you inherit permissions for a directory from the directories closer to the root or to set permissions on individual directories. Windows 98 only lets you set a permission that will be inherited by all lower-level (away from the root) directories; Windows 98 doesn't let you override parent permissions.

Those permission inheritance rules, and the simplicity of inheriting permissions rather than setting them individually on tens or hundreds of directories, require planning in directory layout to use effectively. For example, you might have a set of directories you want to make accessible while shutting off access to the rest of the disk. Follow the steps in Example 9.14 to achieve that goal.

EXAMPLE

Example 9.14   Restrict Access to Part of a Disk

The key to this example is that you aren't restricted to sharing entire disks; you can set up sharing on just a directory on the disk. Follow these steps:

1. Open Windows Explorer and create a directory—maybe called `public`—in the root of the disk that will be the parent of all the accessible directories.

2. Right-click the `public` directory in Windows Explorer, and then click Sharing in the resulting popup menu.

3. Give the directory a share name and permissions just as you learned to do earlier in this chapter for entire disks. Choose read-only access for this example.

4. Even if a parent directory is already shared with read-only permission, you can change the permission to read/write on a lower-level share. Just define a new share name for the lower-level directory and give it read/write access.

We constructed Example 9.14 carefully, using read-only access for the parent directory and read/write access selectively underneath it. Had we reversed the permission, using read/write access for the parent and read-only underneath, the read-only security would have been pointless. Figure 9.22 shows how misordered access permissions can subvert security. Accessing the `readonly` directory through the `readonly` share does limit remote computers' access properly, but accessing the public share on a remote machine gives read/write access to the public directory and everything underneath it, including the `readonly` directory.

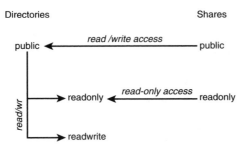

Figure 9.22: *Misordered file-sharing permissions.*

You can fix this problem, establishing secure access with the access pattern shown in Figure 9.22, using Windows NT 4 and Windows 2000. The technique involves using what those operating systems call permissions, but the process is beyond what we have space to cover here.

It's possible to control directory access under Windows 98 more selectively than simple read-only or read/write access controls on shares open to anyone on the network by using passwords. You have three options:

- You can let just those people knowing the one assigned password have read-only access (see Figure 9.23).

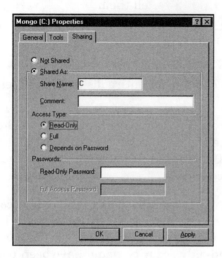

Figure 9.23: Read-only access.

- You can let those people have read/write access (see Figure 9.24).

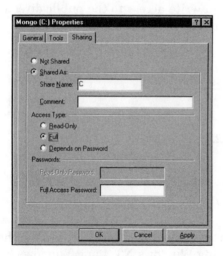

Figure 9.24: Read/write access.

- You can let people selectively have read-only or read/write access using the capabilities shown in Figure 9.25.

You control which form of access you're using with the Access type controls—choosing the Read Only, Full (read/write), or both, corresponding to dialog boxes in Figures 9.23, 9.24, and 9.25, respectively. If you choose

Depends on Password mode, make sure you use different passwords for read-only and read/write access, because you'll control what people can do by controlling which password you tell them.

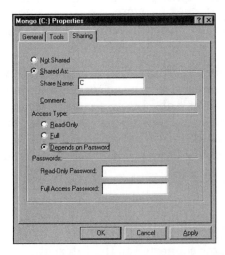

Figure 9.25: *Choose read-only or read/write access.*

Using the Samba configuration we described earlier, a Linux file server has a different and in some ways simpler security model than we've just described for Windows file sharing. (Linux has the same access capabilities as a Windows computer when used as a client accessing a Windows server.) Client computers accessing the Linux file server will have read/write access to the directory /home/*username* (replacing *username* with the actual account name), and to nowhere else. Using some of the other configuration settings in the Samba administrator, you can configure Samba to create a publicly accessible shared directory, or, because unique Windows 98 usernames aren't important on a small LAN, you can give several people the same username so they access the same shared area on the Linux file server. In essence, that last idea amounts to using usernames as project names, with the effect that everyone working on the same project accesses the same area on the Linux file server.

FTP Access Controls and Security

FTP servers implement three forms of access control and security:

- **Username access control.** Users can be required to provide a username and password known to the FTP server to access files, or the generic username anonymous can be enabled to permit unrestricted access. There's an Internet convention that people connecting to an FTP server permitting anonymous access use their email address as the password to identify themselves, but this convention isn't enforced by the software.

- **Root directory security.** Regardless of the username access controls imposed by the server, FTP servers can secure the files on the computer by restricting FTP client access to one specific directory plus all files and directories below that.

- **Network address restrictions.** Competent FTP servers let you specify the TCP/IP addresses to which the server will grant access. Address restrictions aren't absolutely secure for computers connected to the Internet, because it's possible for an attacker to confuse the server by *spoofing* the client address. Spoofing means the source address of the message is forged to be a legitimate address on your network, confusing the server software.

The WFTPD configuration you created when you followed the instructions earlier in this chapter is not at all secure, in that it permits anonymous read/write access to all files on the computer. You wouldn't want to use that configuration on a computer connected to the Internet.

All three features are available in WFTPD. Use the Security, Users/rights command to access the User / Rights Security Dialog where you can define usernames, passwords, and root directory security (WFTPD calls the user's root directory the home directory). Use the Security, Host/net command to access the Host Security Settings dialog box and define what TCP/IP addresses will be permitted access or excluded. Use the Security, General command to access the General Security dialog box with which you can turn all the security mechanisms on and off, enable or disable anonymous access, permit or deny file transfers from the client to the server (called uploads), and control other specific settings.

Sharing CD-ROM, CD-R & RW, DVD, and Zip

You're not restricted to creating shares on hard disks in your computers. You can share floppy drives, CD-ROM drives, CD-R and CD-RW recorders, DVD drives, and Zip drives. All these drives have *removable media*, meaning you can eject the disk media from the drive and take it elsewhere. You'll want to observe the following limitations when sharing removable media drives:

- **Complete operations before ejecting media.** It's possible to eject the media from the drive while someone on a remote computer is accessing the drive. If the user is writing files to the drive, the file being written will probably be corrupted. If a program is reading a file from the drive, the operation will fail; badly written programs might crash. Typically you'll solve these problems by either having shared removable media drives physically visible from the client computers or by using the drive for a fixed purpose, such as by leaving a street map CD-ROM in a drive for shared network use.

- **Program-specific restrictions.** Some programs are written to require that their CD-ROM disk be accessible from a CD-ROM drive on the local computer, not one shared across a network. Such programs simply aren't suitable for network sharing. The manufacturer might have a network version, or if sharing is important, you might have to find another program.

Software Licensing

File sharing and file transfer create wonderful opportunities for enhancing what you can do with your computers, but because they make copying easy, they come with responsibility too. The programs you buy invariably have licensing terms associated with them; some programs can be freely shared across a network, others might require you purchase additional licenses for each additional networked computer, and some impose rigid limits for use only on a single computer.

Your data is your own, but take the time to read the license terms that come with the software you want to share across the network.

Summary

In this chapter you learned the details of how to configure your Windows and Linux computers as file sharing servers and clients, and how to set up FTP servers and clients. You discovered that you can control who accesses what on your computers.

What's Next

The next chapter, "Network Backup," teaches you how to exploit your network to back up files to tape and other removable media.

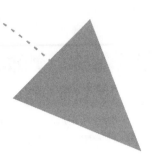

10

Network Backup

In this chapter you will learn

- What you must do before your computer crashes to save your data

- How to use networked file sharing to back up all your computers to a single tape drive

Computer backups—copies of your files that you can reload in case your computer crashes—are one of life's chores for computer users. Like mopping the floor and flossing your teeth, backing up your computer files is tedious, boring, and a good idea.

Who Needs to Back Up?

The problem that backups solve is that computers—and their users—are unreliable. Computers can crash and lose data; people make mistakes that can lose files or corrupt what's in them. If you have a backup of a lost or destroyed critical file, you can reload the backup and keep on working.

We advocate thinking about backups from a worst-case perspective: analyzing the effects of a complete crash after which all the data on your disk is lost. You can't predict when you'll need a copy of your work or how severe the problem you encounter will be, so a worst-case analysis guarantees that you won't be surprised. In that context, whether you should back up your computers depends on what you use them for and how painful it would be to have to reconstruct what you'd lose. Example 10.1 catalogs the steps you go through to restore your computer to operation after a crash in which you've lost everything.

EXAMPLE

Example 10.1   Resurrecting a Crashed Computer

Although the details of what you'll have to do after a complete crash depend on what was on the machine and how you backed up your files, the strategy is consistent:

1. Start by restoring the hardware to correct operation or verifying that it's working properly. Some crashes are completely due to software, but unless you're certain as to what happened, start by testing the hardware. We keep quality hardware diagnostic software around for that purpose—both AMIDiag by American Megatrends and QAPlus/FE by DiagSoft are good. Neither is for novices, though, so if the hardware tour in Chapter 6, "Picking and Installing Your LAN Adapters," was new or difficult for you, you'll probably want to refer hardware problems to an expert.

2. Assuming you've lost everything on the computer, your next goal is to get enough software running to start the restore component of your backup software. The best backup software can restore a full machine backup with no software operating on the computer's hard disk, but with some backup software you'll have to have Windows itself running. That requirement actually presents a serious problem, because to get Windows running you'll have to reformat the drive and install a new copy of Windows; after you do that, reloading the old copy of Windows on your backup is possible, but tricky. The backup program in Windows 98 Second Edition, which you'll learn about later in this chapter, includes the System Recovery utility to help you recover from a crashed disk without first installing Windows.

After you restore a full machine backup, all that's left is to restore or reconstruct any data files you changed after you made the backup.

3. If you backed up only your data and not Windows or your installed programs, your course of action is different than in step 2. You'll reformat the disk and reinstall Windows (including reconfiguring your network device drivers, protocols, clients and servers, connections, and shares), but then you'll reinstall each of your applications one by one from their original master CD-ROMs.

4. After you reload programs onto the computer in step 3, you'll reload data files. If you had backed up the data files, you'll reload from there; otherwise, they're gone and you'll start over whatever you were doing.

The value of a backup usually diminishes with time, because as you continue to work on the live version of the file, it becomes increasingly different from the backup. You therefore have to redo more work on the backup to catch it up to the current state of your file. Assuming you're backing up at all, you'll want to back up regularly to make sure your backups stay close to the work you're doing. You'll learn later in this chapter how to use different types of backups to speed up the process.

There is a subtlety in steps 3 and 4 of this example; for some people, backups can be unnecessary or trivial. For example, if you use your computer only for multiplayer games over a LAN or the Internet, it might not be worth the time to back up because it's simple to reload and reconfigure the game software after a crash. If all you use your computer for is to access the Web and balance your checkbook, it might not be worth backing up any more than the checkbook data, and your financial software probably has built-in tools for that. If you're using email, be sure to back up the message files, too—overall, if you're going to do a partial backup, be sure you know you have all the necessary files.

The Basics of Backup

The entire point of backup is to be able to recover from the unexpected loss of one or more files. You can't ever protect the primary files themselves—not on PCs, at least—so your only option is to have a copy. You have several choices for where to put the copy, each with advantages and disadvantages:

- **Back up to the same drive.** The simplest option, and one that many people use, is to copy critical data files somewhere else on the same drive as the primary files. (By same drive we mean *same drive letter*.) This option is easy because all you have to do is make a new directory for the backup files and do some simple copies; it's also the least effective because it protects only against loss or corruption of the individual data files. Any event that wipes out entire groups of files, such as a catastrophic software error or a disk drive failure, is likely to wipe out the backup files too.

- **Back up to another physical drive.** If you happen to have more than one physical drive in your computer, you can improve the chances your backup files survive by putting them on the other drive. It's unlikely that two disk drives would experience simultaneous hardware failures unless something extraordinary happens such as a direct lightning strike or the power supply blowing up, so having a copy on a different drive essentially guarantees your backups will be there after a hardware failure. It's also unlikely that a catastrophic software failure would take out both drives, so you're reasonably protected that way, too.

Don't mistake backing up to a different drive letter with backing up to a different physical drive. Most computers have only a single hard disk, but a surprising number of those have been partitioned into more than one drive letter. If there's only one disk, all the drive letters you have (ignoring floppy, CD-ROM, or Zip drives) are on the same physical disk. If the disk hardware fails more drastically than simply developing a few bad spots, you'll lose the data on *all* the drive letters.

Backing up to another physical drive has one other failing—your data is still resident inside the same computer. If the computer is stolen or destroyed (by fire, flood, tornado, hurricane, small children, or so on), you've lost your data. You can back up the drives from one computer to a shared drive on another (we do this often as a fast temporary backup of work we're doing, for example), but the best solution is one of the next two.

- **Back up to removable media.** Your most secure backup option is to write the backup files to some medium you can remove from the computer and store separately. Barring failure of the backup software itself, coincidental destruction of the media, or corruption of the data before you write the backup, removable media guarantee that you'll be able to recover your data. If you want the ultimate in protection, you'll keep backup media far enough away from the computer to survive disasters. (Companies often do this, storing backups of critical data in vaults miles or cities away from the computers themselves.)

The disadvantage of removable media is cost, because you'll need both a drive to write the media and the media itself. You can choose from Zip drives (and similar, higher-capacity drives), read/write CD-ROM drives (called *CD-RW* drives), or tape drives; no matter which you choose, if you have to buy new hardware, you'll spend somewhere in the vicinity of $250–350 by the time you buy the drive and a number of high capacity blank media.

- **Back up to a shared removable media drive across a network.**
  Using your network to share a Zip, CD-RW, or tape drive is nearly an ideal answer. You get the benefits of removable media without significant added expense for each computer. The only disadvantage is that backups can be somewhat slower across a network (depending on the network speed and loading). If you have a 10Mbps network, you'll probably see little loss of speed to a tape drive capable of 35MB per minute (because the tape is averaging only 4.7Mbps). If you're using a 1Mbps telephone-line network, though, backups will take far longer than if the drive were on the same machine as the disks you're backing up.

The rest of this chapter regards that last alternative: backing up to a shared removable media drive across a network. You'll learn how the backup process splits across machines on your LAN, what to watch out for, and how to set up the backup software.

Backing Up Through Shared Drives

The most common model for network backup is to use file sharing to make the backed-up files accessible to the computer hosting the removable media drive (see Figure 10.1). Backup software on that computer accesses the shared files as a file-sharing client, reading the files across the network and writing them out to the removable media drive.

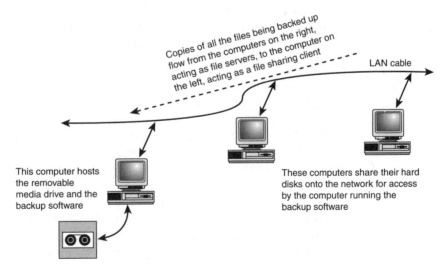

Figure 10.1: Using file sharing for network backup.

The disadvantage of this approach is that the backup is controlled from the one machine, not by users at their individual machines. If users want to control the backups from their own machines, you need to coordinate the backup so that the correct removable media is available in the drive. It's possible to solve these difficulties, but usually only with complex, expensive backup software.

Mapped Drives Versus Network Neighborhood

You learned how to access shared files through both mapped drive letters and the Network Neighborhood in Chapter 9, "Sharing Fixed Drives and Setting Access Controls," and saw that for most purposes the two are equivalent.

However, backup software (running on the computer with the removable media drive) is one of the more common exceptions to that equivalence. Not all backup software permits access to files you're backing up through the Network Neighborhood, demanding instead that you map a drive letter and navigate to the files through that. There's no significant difference in functionality with that restriction, but if you're going to save backup jobs for later use incorporating mapped drive letters, you'll have to be sure the same drive mapping exists when you run the job as when you created it. (The easiest way to make sure that's true is to create permanent drive mappings that survive a reboot, and then leave them in existence.)

Locked Files

Unless you spend enough money to get a very fast tape drive, complete machine backups are likely to take hours. Durations like that mean you either back up overnight while the computer is idle, or you'll have to back up while people work. If you do the latter, you'll have to solve the problem of what to do about *locked files*.

A locked file is one that's already in use and subject to modification by some other program than the one requesting access. Such competing file accesses occur when two people attempt to modify the same shared document, but also occur when a backup program tries to copy a file to tape that some person is simultaneously using. Backup programs usually attempt to request file access in a way that minimizes the chances of a locked file problem, but ultimately if the software can't access the file, it can't write the file to tape. Backup software is smart enough that it doesn't abandon the backup job when that happens; it skips the file and continues. You'll get an error message in the log for the backup job if that happens. If the skipped file is critical, you should make a temporary copy of it somewhere until it's successfully picked up by a backup operation.

Software Configuration and Use

We're going to explain how to configure and use Microsoft Backup, and specifically the version included in Windows 98. Versions of Microsoft Backup are included in Windows 95, Windows NT4, and Windows 2000; the versions in Windows 95 and Windows 2000 are similar to what we'll describe here.

Figure 10.2 shows the initial view of Microsoft Backup you'd see from the perspective of a computer being used to back up files on other computers accessible over a network. The first things to notice in the figure are that you're looking at the Backup tab and that the bulk of the view comprises two panes that look almost identical to those in the two-pane view of Windows Explorer.

These two panes operate just like the two-pane Windows Explorer with the addition of checkboxes to select and deselect items for inclusion in the backup

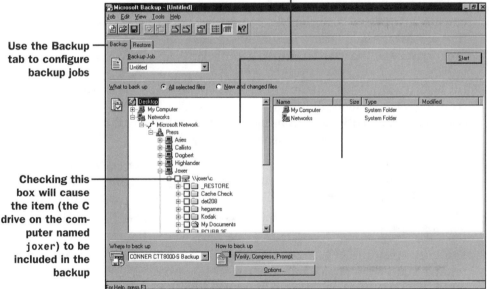

Use the Backup tab to configure backup jobs

Checking this box will cause the item (the C drive on the computer named joxer) to be included in the backup

Figure 10.2: *Microsoft Backup opening view.*

There's a key addition to the panes in Figure 10.2; every item you can select for inclusion in the backup job has a checkbox next to it. If the item will be completely backed up, a black check appears in the box. If the item will be partially backed up (because some subsidiary items are selected and some are not), the check will be gray, and if no items will be backed up, the box will be white with no check mark.

If you look at the left-hand pane in Figure 10.2, you can see we've scrolled down inside the Networks top-level item to expand Microsoft Network and the Press workgroup. Doing that exposed several computers on the LAN. We then expanded one of them (joxer) to reveal the shared C drive and the top-level directories on the drive. Checkboxes appear starting at the level of the shared C drive. To back up the entire C drive on joxer, all we'd have to do would be to check off the drive and push the Start button in the upper-right corner of the figure. If we wanted to back up files from several computers onto the same tape, we'd have simply expanded the items for those computers and checked off more shared drives.

Full, Differential, and Incremental Backups

The most straightforward type of backup is to write out every file on the disk as part of the backup job. Doing this guarantees that you have all the files you need (subject to the locked files problem) and that all the files are consistent with one another. Backups of this sort are called *full backups*.

However, the rapid increase in disk drive size for even entry-level machines—10GB is seemingly the smallest drive anyone uses now—and the corresponding increase in the size of applications—popular games have broken the 2GB barrier for a full installation—create a large mass of data to be written to tape for a full backup. Suppose you back up to tape. A typical high-performance consumer-quality tape drive can achieve net data transfer rates of about 35MBps. If you actually have 10GB to write to tape (which is admittedly more than most people will have), the backup is going to take nearly five hours and span at least two tapes.

A full backup taking that long is impractical to run very often for most people; the duration is so long you'd want to run it overnight, but the need to change tapes partway through requires someone be present to do the tape swap (and it's *really* boring sitting around in the middle of the night waiting for tapes to fill).

You're completely right if you're thinking it's pointless to keep copying files to tape that haven't changed since the last backup. Windows keeps track of which files need to be backed up due to changes with a per-file indicator called the *archive flag*; backup software developers have exploited that capability to implement two standard backup types besides full backups:

- **Differential backup.** After you back up all the files on disk, the archive flag is clear for every file. Every file you create or modify after that point gets its archive flag set. If after some time, you back up all the files with archive flags set, you'll end up with a much smaller backup job that, if restored after the corresponding full backup, updates the files to their current state. The differential backup operation leaves the archive flags alone, unchanged, so every differential backup job you write is a complete image of the changes that occurred since the full backup.

- **Incremental backup.** An incremental backup is nearly the same as a differential backup, also writing only files with their archive flag set, but with one key difference: After the incremental backup completes, the backup software clears all the archive flags. The next incremental backup therefore takes as its starting point not the last full backup, but the last incremental backup. To restore all the current files on the computer, you have to restore the full backup plus all the incremental backups *in order*.

Both differential and incremental backups have the problem that they have no mechanism to note and remove deleted files. Because of that, if you have to reconstruct a machine from a series of full and differential or incremental backups, you'll find files on the re-created disk you'd previously deleted. Fortunately, resurrecting deleted files is reasonably benign—it's a good trade in return for greatly reduced backup times.

Creating Backup Configurations

You're likely to find that you have several backup jobs you run over and over. If you're at all selective about what you back up—perhaps you exclude the Windows temporary files directory (\windows\temp) or perhaps you exclude directories you know have only program installation files—you have to configure the backup software each time to include the files you want and exclude those you don't. That process is not only tedious, it's error prone and, if you exclude important files, it's error prone in a way you might not discover until you go to restore from your backup and find out files you need are missing. By then, it's far too late to correct the error.

Every worthwhile backup program, including Microsoft Backup, has a way to define and save backup job configurations. After you've defined a job (and verified the definition is correct!), you simply start that job running. You need do no further configuration, increasing the reliability of the backup process.

Figure 10.3 shows how you start creating a backup job. Select either All Selected Files or New and Changed Files to make the job perform a full or incremental backup, respectively. (You can also specify a differential backup, but you have to use the Options button at the bottom of the window.)

Navigate to the first computer and disk you want to back up, and check off the drive. Expand the view in the left pane underneath the drive by clicking the plus sign and you'll see that all the underlying directories are checked off. Click the drive so its contents appear in the right-hand pane and you'll see all its directories and files are checked. You can deselect items by clicking on a check mark to remove it.

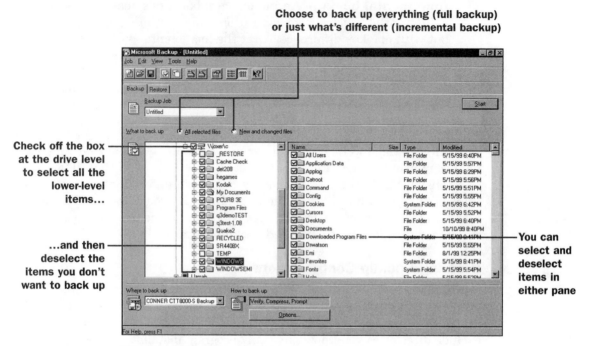

Choose to back up everything (full backup) or just what's different (incremental backup)

Check off the box at the drive level to select all the lower-level items...

...and then deselect the items you don't want to back up

You can select and deselect items in either pane

Figure 10.3: *Microsoft Backup file selection.*

Continue to navigate across computers, drives, directories, and files until you've set up the complete selection pattern you want and use the Job, Save command to save the job definition to disk. Any time after that you want to run the job, just start Microsoft Backup, run the Job, Open command to load the job, and click Start.

Figure 10.4 shows how you can use the Options dialog box (click the Options button or use the Job, Options command to open the dialog box) to further tune what you want the job to do. Perhaps most important is the setting on the General tab that requires the backup program to verify the contents of the tape against the originals on disk after the backup completes. That independent check doubles the time the complete operation requires but gives you the assurance that the data on tape can be read and is a faithful copy of the originals.

The other tab you'll want to look at is the Type tab, which allows you to specify whether the backup will be a full, differential, or incremental operation.

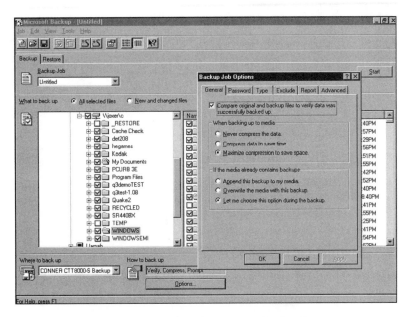

Figure 10.4: *Microsoft Backup options dialog box.*

Summary

Backing up the files on your computer can save you when (not if) your computer crashes. Using a good, high-performance tape drive on one machine to back up files on computers across your network lets you have the benefits of using the right hardware for the job without the expense of buying a tape drive for every machine you own. Configuring your backup software to match your backup needs saves time and, because you write out less data, saves tape.

One last point. Trust no backup system until you've tested it by performing a restore and comparing the results with the original files. Even if that seems absurd to you, do it; we've known too many people who failed to heed that warning and discovered their backups were catastrophically flawed in some obscure way.

What's Next

Network backup is perhaps the simplest network application besides file sharing. In the next chapter you'll learn about the most popular reason to have a network after file sharing—printer sharing.

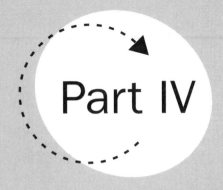

Part IV

Using Your Network

## 11

Sharing Printers and Fax

In this chapter you will learn

- How to configure Windows for print sharing
- Ways to eliminate the attached computer to support printer sharing
- How to set up for fax sharing on your LAN

Sharing a printer and, to some extent, a fax is one of the most popular reasons to put in a LAN. In the case of a two-machine LAN, the cost you avoid by sharing a printer instead of buying a second one can pay for all the LAN equipment you need. That argument extends to the third, fourth, and later computers, of course, but it's almost impossible to imagine that many computers in the same area each with its own printer and no LAN.

Given what you learned in Chapter 8, "Configuring Your System Software," basic printer sharing is no more difficult to set up than file sharing. You'll want some additional capabilities from your network printers beyond the simple ability to print—capabilities that fall into the category of remote printer management. You'll learn to configure printer sharing in this chapter, to ensure that the printer drivers your client computers need are available, and what to expect from remote management software when you buy a printer.

Remote fax is, in practice, nearly identical to remote printing because you end up commanding your application software to print to the remote fax device across your LAN. You'll learn about the Symantec WinFax software in this chapter, focusing specifically on how to set it up and configure it for remote access.

Finally, you're not constrained to use a full-scale computer as a print server. Small, low-cost print server devices are now available that let you put a printer anywhere you need one on your network and have it accessible from all your network computers. You'll learn what one of the best available, the Intel InBusiness Print Station, can do and how to use it.

Setting Up Sharing

Print sharing is much like file sharing: You'll have a server computer with an attached printer and one or more client computers. You can have more than one print server on your network; just follow what you learn in this chapter for each server.

The first step is always to connect the printer to the server and configure the operating system to work with the local printer. Until you do that, there's no hope any network printer access will be possible.

Next, set up the file and printer sharing software. If you need a reminder on how to do that, go back and read Chapter 8, particularly the section "Adding Applications and Clients." You'll quickly be able to tell whether you've done that under Windows; open the Printers folder and right-click the printer you want to share. If you don't see a Sharing menu item in the resulting popup menu, you either don't have file and printer sharing installed at all, or you installed the file sharing but not the printer sharing. If you do find a problem, Example 11.1 shows you how to fix the configuration.

EXAMPLE

Example 11.1 Correcting the Windows File and Printer Sharing Setup

Assuming you've done the usual checks that all the networked computers share a common protocol, there are only a few things that could go wrong and prevent the Sharing menu item from appearing. Follow these steps:

1. Open the Network control panel applet (Start, Settings, Control Panel, Network) and look for File and Printer Sharing for Microsoft Networks in the list of installed networking components.

2. Click the button labeled File and Print Sharing and verify that the check box for print sharing is selected. If not, check the appropriate boxes, which are available for both file and print sharing.

3. File and printer sharing for Microsoft Networks should now be in the list of installed networking components if it wasn't previously. Click OK. Windows might ask for the installation CD-ROM and should then ask to reboot.

After you confirm the file and printer sharing software is running, open Windows Explorer and navigate to the Printers folder. (Alternatively, you can step through Start, Settings, Printers to get the same result.) The right pane will list the printers installed on this computer. The printer sharing indicator is the same as for shared disks: a small blue hand appears under the printer icon.

Right-click the printer icon, and then left-click the Sharing item in the resulting popup menu. Figure 11.1 shows the popup menu with the Sharing item highlighted.

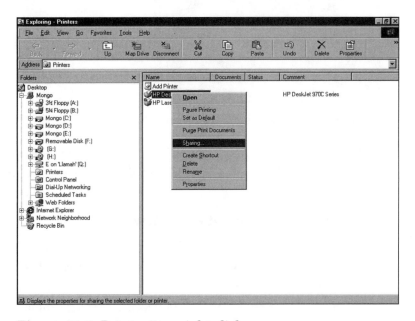

Figure 11.1: *Printer item right-click popup menu.*

Figure 11.2 shows the dialog box that appears after you click the Sharing menu item. The dialog box is similar to the file sharing control dialog box (see Figure 9.3 in Chapter 9, "Sharing Fixed Drives and Setting Access Controls"), with the exception that the print sharing dialog box is simpler; you can set only an access password because read-only or read/write controls don't make sense for printers.

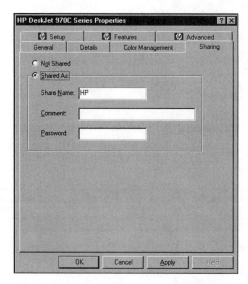

Figure 11.2: *Printer sharing control dialog box.*

Follow Example 11.2 to use the printer sharing control dialog box to set up sharing on a local printer, making it available to other computers on your network.

EXAMPLE

Example 11.2   Sharing a Windows Printer

The basic printer sharing setup is very simple:

1. Click the Shared As button, which enables the fields for Share Name, Comment, and Password.

2. Change the Share Name field if you want; we prefer short, direct names that are easy to remember and identify the device in basic terms.

3. Fill in the Comment field with a description of the printer. We most often fill in the manufacturer and model number, making it easier to know what drivers you need to load on a remote machine.

4. Specify an access control password in the Password field. The only common use we've seen for access passwords on printers has been to limit use of printers for which paper or ink supplies were very expensive.

5. Click OK. Windows adds the sharing indicator in the Windows Explorer window; no reboot should be required.

After you set up printer sharing, move over to another computer you want to access the printer as a client and follow the steps in Example 11.3.

EXAMPLE

Example 11.3   Setting Up a Print Sharing Client

The network browsing features in Windows make it simple to locate a print server; there's no need to remember and type the detailed path to the printer:

1. Open Windows Explorer and navigate to the Printers folder (or, follow Start, Settings, Printers). Double-click Add Printer; in Windows 98 and Windows 2000, that starts the Add Printer Wizard.

2. Click the Next button, select Network printer, and click Next again.

3. In Windows 98, the following dialog box offers a Browse button you can use to find and select printers on network printer servers (see Figure 11.3). Using Windows 2000, you simply leave the path to the network printer blank and click Next, leading to the Browse for Printer dialog box shown in Figure 11.4.

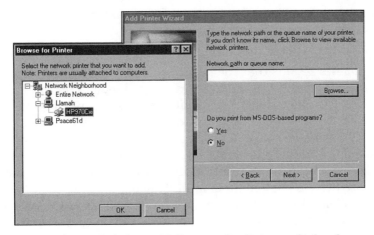

Figure 11.3: Windows 98 Browse for Printer dialog box.

4. In Windows 98, select the printer you want to access and choose whether MS-DOS programs should be able to use the printer and then click OK. For Windows 2000, click Next, make the MS-DOS selection and click Next again.

5. In many cases, Windows will now have to ask you to pick the printer make and model from a list so it can install the appropriate printer driver. Make the appropriate selection (see the following section on providing drivers for some suggestions on how to make this easy) and finish the wizard steps, selecting whether this printer will become the default printer.

6. Click Finish to complete the installation.

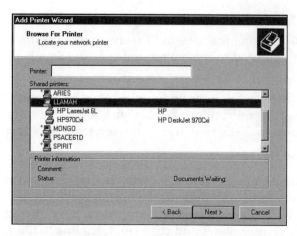

Figure 11.4: *Windows 2000 Browse for Printer dialog box.*

Print a test page to the newly installed printer to make sure the drivers and network are working properly.

One of the subtle differences between Windows 98, Windows NT 4, and Windows 2000 is that the latter two will actually let you define sharing for network client printer access, whereas Windows 98 will not. It might seem absurd to make a network client printer setup itself be shared, but we've found it useful for helping older operating systems access printers for which they'd otherwise lack network support. For example, older beta versions of Windows 2000 we tested lacked support for the network protocols to access the Intel InBusiness Print Station we'll discuss later in this chapter. Until those drivers showed up in later versions of the operating system (and in the released version), we relayed printing from the Windows 2000 computers through a Windows NT 4 machine and on to the print station.

Providing Drivers

You have to install the corresponding printer drivers on every Windows machine accessing a printer, whether the machine's a client or server. If the drivers are available built into Windows itself, they'll show up in the list of printer manufacturers and models, and so there's nothing special you need to do. If not, such as if the printer was released after Microsoft finalized that version of Windows, you'll have to install the drivers shipped with the printer on every computer.

It's a nuisance to have to carry the CD-ROM around to each computer needing access, particularly because you might not want to set up all the network clients at the same time. Instead, it's useful to create a directory on one of your computers acting as a file server containing the driver installation files. Follow the steps in Example 11.4 to set up the shared driver installation files.

Example 11.4 Making Printer Driver Installation Files Readily Accessible Using File Sharing

The only new aspect of what you'll do in this example is figuring out which files you need to copy to the server from the CD-ROM; everything else is the same as you learned in Chapter 9. Follow these steps:

1. Go to the computer you'll use as the printer driver file server. Open Windows Explorer in the two-pane view (right-click My Computer and select Explore).

2. Select the drive you want to hold the driver installation files (most likely C) in the left pane and right-click in any empty spot of the right pane and select New, Folder. Give the folder a name such as *Printer Drivers* and press Enter.

3. Double-click the Printer Drivers folder to open it and make another folder inside Printer Drivers to hold the drivers for the specific printer. We used drivers for the HP DeskJet 970 Series printers in this example, so we called the folder HP970.

4. Set Windows Explorer to View All Files to make sure you copy all the files off the CD-ROM (some driver files are commonly "hidden" and won't copy if View All Files isn't enabled). In Windows Explorer for Windows 98, use the command Tools, Folder Options, View, Hidden Files, Show All Files. In Windows Explorer for Windows 2000, use the command Tools, Folder Options, View, Hidden files and Folders, Show Hidden Files and Folders.

5. Insert the driver CD-ROM in the drive and select the CD-ROM in the left pane of Windows Explorer (simply close the installation program if it starts up automatically during this process).

6. Select everything on the CD-ROM by pressing Ctrl+A and drag and drop the files with the mouse from the right pane to the driver files folder you created on your disk.

You might be able to reduce the volume of files you store on disk by selecting just the driver files on CD-ROM and omitting other software and supplementary material on the CD-ROM, but because every installation disk is different, there's no way to provide a general guideline. Another option, though, is to visit the printer manufacturer's Web site—for example, on the HP Web site http://www.hp.com, we clicked HP Services and Support, HP DeskJet Printers, HP DeskJet900 Series, and finally HP DeskJet 970 Cxi

Printer to reach the page `http://www.hp.com/cposupport/prodhome/` `hpdeskjet918369.html`. Clicking there on Downloads and Driver brought us to a page with drivers for all supported operating systems. Clicking the entry under Microsoft Windows 98 for HP DeskJet 970C Series Printer Driver FOR HOME USERS-USB CONNECTION downloaded a file with just the drivers, which we then expanded into the file server directory we'd created.

Don't forget to make sure the driver directory is shared so client computers can access it.

Remote Management

Printers require a certain amount of care and feeding—even if the printer's out of sight, you'd like to know whether it requires more paper, has run out of ink, is jammed, or otherwise needs attention. Most consumer-grade printers don't support remote management well. For those that do have support, what you'll get varies from the simple—the HP 970C driver properties shown in Figure 11.5 can simply clean the print cartridges, but reports no status remotely—to the comprehensive—the HP JetAdmin services you'd use with the HP Color LaserJet 4500DN printer give you comprehensive status and control.

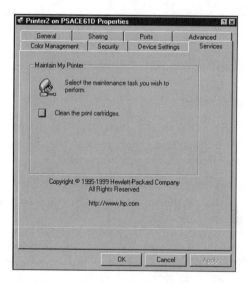

Figure 11.5: *Windows 2000 HP DeskJet 970C Driver Remote Services.*

Figure 11.6 shows the JetAdmin status dialog box for the HP Color LaserJet 4500DN printer, including notification that one of the drums is nearly exhausted. The lesson to learn from Figures 11.5 and 11.6 is that you'll want to research to find out how comprehensive the remote network status and maintenance support is for a printer's drivers before you make a purchase. Remote management doesn't come for free—the HP Color LaserJet 4500DN printer, for example, is a $3,500 (street price) unit.

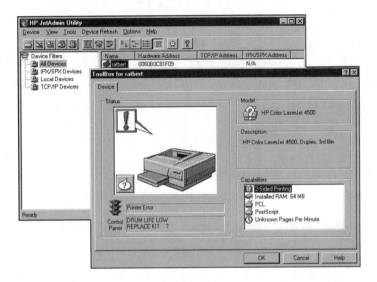

Figure 11.6: *HP JetAdmin status dialog box for the HP Color LaserJet 4500DN printer.*

Intel InBusiness Print Station

It's often inconvenient to have a network printer tied to a computer; remote users create foot traffic and disruptions around the computer, making it undesirable to use as a place to work, and the computer takes a relatively large amount of space. Printers such as the HP Color LaserJet 4500DN printer will connect directly to your LAN, but they're usually expensive.

Your option, instead of tying a computer to a printer, is to use what's called a *print server*, which is a small, dedicated-function box designed to connect printers to networks. Figure 11.7 shows the front of the Intel InBusiness Print Station, a compact, low-cost network print server capable of supporting two printers using standard parallel port connections between the print server and the printers. Controls on the front of the Print Station include a power switch and a switch to cause every connected printer to print a test page; indicators include a status LED and a LAN activity LED.

Figure 11.8 shows the rear view of the Print Station. The two connectors are the parallel-port connectors for the standard cables to the printers; the opening in the middle provides access to switches that control the network data rate. The default network data rate setting is to automatically sense 10 or 100 Mbps operation, so in nearly all cases you can leave the switches alone.

Figure 11.7: *Intel InBusiness Print Station front view.*

Figure 11.8: *Intel InBusiness Print Station rear view.*

Figure 11.9 shows the side view, including the LAN and power connections.

Installing the Print Station is simple: Cable your printers and LAN to the box and hook up the power supply. Turn on the printers and then the Print Station.

You use the Print Station software included on the CD-ROM to set up and configure the server. Figure 11.10 shows the software in operation, with HP LaserJet 6L and DeskJet 970Cxi printers connected. When you first install the Print Station and the software, the printer types will be unknown; click the line for the correct port, and then click Add Printer. You'll install a printer driver much as you do for Windows normally using the Add Printer Wizard dialog boxes that appear.

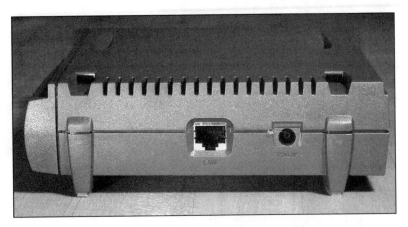

Figure 11.9: *Intel InBusiness Print Station side view.*

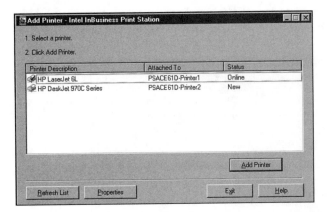

Figure 11.10: *Intel InBusiness Print Station software listing available printers.*

After you install drivers, you can click the line for the printer, and then click Properties. Doing that leads to the Properties dialog box, which lets you get information and set up the Print Station (see Figure 11.11). The server implements all three common transport protocols, NetBEUI, Novell, and TCP/IP. The TCP/IP tab (shown selected in Figure 11.11) lets you configure the server's TCP/IP address. The figure shows the server configured to obtain a TCP/IP address automatically from a DHCP server on your LAN (see Chapter 7, "Network Software—Protocol Stacks and Applications"). If you're assigning TCP/IP addresses manually, you'll change the selection to Specify an IP Address and fill in the IP Address, Subnet Mask, and Default Gateway fields. The three fields are essentially the same as you learned about in Chapters 7 and 8.

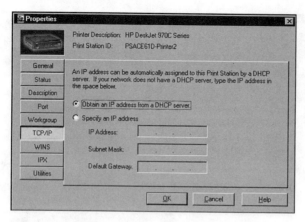

Figure 11.11: *Intel InBusiness Print Station TCP/IP configuration.*

You'll also want to set the workgroup to match your LAN setup so the browse functions work; use the Workgroup tab for that (see Figure 11.12).

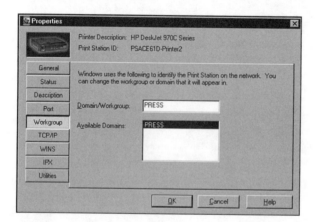

Figure 11.12: *Intel InBusiness Print Station workgroup configuration.*

The rest of the default settings for the Print Station should work on most any network.

If you're using Windows 98 Second Edition or Windows 2000, you don't have to install the Print Station software to use the printers because those operating systems include network protocol drivers compatible with the Print Station. All you should have to do is browse for a network printer in the Add Printer wizard, looking for the name of the server you'll find on the sticker on its bottom or in the port listing in the Intel software (ours is named PSACE61D, and there seems to be no way to change that name).

Networked Fax

You'll need third-party software to be able to fax across your network, sharing the modem on the fax server. We've used Symantec WinFax Pro version 9 in the examples that follow.

After it's set up, networked fax is essentially identical to networked printing—you simply select the fax driver as the printer you're using in an application and print to it.

You'll need to install WinFax Pro (or whatever equivalent software you pick) on both the server and client computers to make networked faxing work, and you'll need TCP/IP running on your network. Configure the server first following the steps in Example 11.5 so the clients can find it when you configure them.

EXAMPLE

Example 11.5   Configure WinFax Pro as a Fax Server

WinFax Pro makes server configuration simple, requiring only that you state the computer should act as a fax server and make a few choices about how the program should behave. Follow these steps:

1. Open the Fax Sharing Host Properties dialog box using the Tools, Setup, Program Setup command; then select Fax Sharing Host and click Properties.

2. Step 1 will result in the Fax Sharing Host Properties dialog box appearing (see Figure 11.13). Check the Use this WinFax Station as a WinFax Host option.

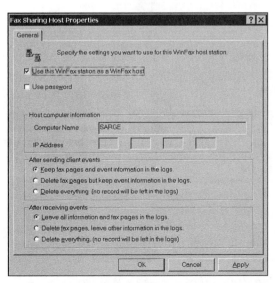

Figure 11.13: WinFax Pro Fax Sharing Host Properties dialog box.

3. Decide what behavior you want the program to have after sending client faxes and after receiving.

4. Click OK in the Fax Sharing Host Properties dialog box and on Close in the Program Setup dialog box.

Example 11.6 shows you how to do the corresponding operation on the client computers.

EXAMPLE

Example 11.6   Configure WinFax Pro as a Fax Client

Setting up WinFax Pro to work as a fax client is every bit as simple as setting it up as a host, and after you're finished you can use the WinFax programs and print to the fax device.

You'll need to have installed WinFax on the host computer and then on the client machine before starting this example. Follow these steps:

1. Open the Modem and Other Fax Device Properties dialog box by using the Tools, Setup, Program Setup command, selecting Fax Sharing Client, and clicking on Properties. (You get the same result by selecting Modem and Other Fax Devices instead of Fax Sharing Client; presumably they're both there to make choices more obvious.)

2. Check off the WinFax Pro Fax Sharing option on port WinFax to make the client connection active, as shown in Figure 11.14. If this is the first time you've configured the port, you'll see the warning that you need to configure the program that's visible at the front of Figure 11.14.

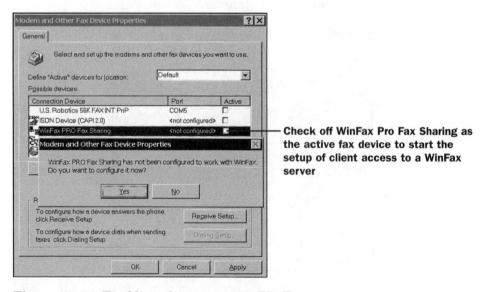

Figure 11.14: Enabling client access in WinFax.

3. Click the Browse button to get a list of the computers on your LAN and select the WinFax host computer. The WinFax software apparently isn't smart enough to winnow the list down to just the computers set up as WinFax hosts, so you'll have to pick the right computer manually (see Figure 11.15).

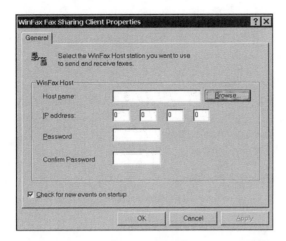

Figure 11.15: WinFax Fax Sharing Client Properties dialog box.

4. Click OK to return to the Modem and Other Fax Device Properties dialog box; then click OK again and Close to finish all the open dialog boxes.

Summary

You learned in this chapter how to configure Windows to share a printer attached to one of your computers across your LAN and how to configure your other computers to access the shared printer. You learned that you can substitute a small, dedicated device, a print server, for the computer attached to the computer, saving space and eliminating foot traffic from around the computers. Finally, you learned that sharing a fax modem is a capability built into fax software such as WinFax Pro, and learned the steps to configure that software for fax sharing.

What's Next

The Internet is the largest network in existence, with millions of connected computers and a wide variety of available services. In the next chapter, you'll learn the basic ways to share Internet access through a modem across your LAN, including the software and the configurations you need.

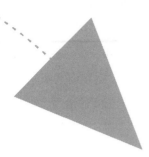

## 12

Sharing an Internet Connection

In this chapter you will learn

- How TCP/IP supports modem sharing
- How to configure Windows and Linux for modem sharing

Searching the Web with the AltaVista search engine for the phrase "information at your fingertips" results in a list of over 10,000 Web pages. Not in the same league as searching for "Albert Einstein" (over 72,000 pages) or "DVD" (over 1.6 million pages), but apparently an idea that has significance for a reasonably large number of people.

When we think of the phrase "information at your fingertips" we think of being able to ask questions and get immediate answers. Not of having to trek to the library, not of having to ask our friends in industry or at universities, but of having the answers available *right now*, no matter when we ask, no matter what we ask. The Internet, and the Web in particular, is approaching being able to meet that requirement. An amazing range of information is available on the Web and is accessible through some reasonably effective search engines.

Despite that, people are driven by habit and by convenience. Our experience is that people who have to turn on the computer, wait for it to start, dial up an Internet connection, and *then* ask a question won't do it most of the time. Conversely, people we know who leave their computers on all the time, and who have arranged for those computers to either be connected to the Internet all the time or to automatically and invisibly connect on demand use the Web all the time. When the time and thought costs of reaching for information are near zero, people's habits change.

We're not about to argue that everyone on Earth should turn into a slave of their computer screens, frantically reaching for keyboards with the most trivial question. We do suggest that the value of ready access to information in the world is increasing and that with a relatively small amount of effort you can make the Internet simultaneously accessible to everyone on your LAN.

What you do with that capability is up to you.

Shared Internet Access Through a Modem

Figure 12.1 shows the idea of using modem sharing to access the Internet. All computers are configured for TCP/IP; one particular computer on the LAN has a modem and is set up to dial to an Internet service provider (ISP), which in turn routes traffic from that computer to the Internet. The computer with the modem itself works as a router too, relaying traffic from the rest of the LAN out over the modem.

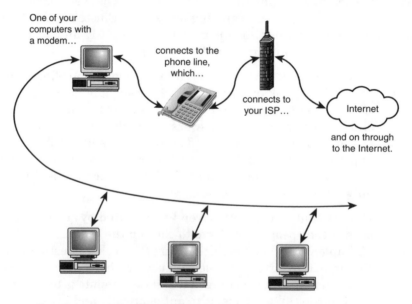

One of your computers with a modem...

connects to the phone line, which...

connects to your ISP...

Internet

and on through to the Internet.

Your other computers each connect to the LAN, and through that to the modem, phone line, ISP, and Internet.

Figure 12.1: *Sharing a modem enables Internet access from the LAN.*

With your understanding of TCP/IP and routing from Chapter 3, "Understanding and Evaluating Network Services," you should realize that routing is all it takes to share an Internet connection—TCP/IP is inherently designed to be relayed from one computer to another. The details of TCP/IP addressing make modem sharing a little complicated, though.

TCP/IP Routing and Proxies

Let's start by looking at the situation for one computer dialing into an ISP. Your ISP most likely uses the PPP protocol over the modem connection between your computer and the ISP's LAN, assigning your computer a TCP/IP address when the connection is made and freeing that address when the connection drops.

Now consider the situation of Figure 12.1 where you want to route many computers through that one modem connection. Each computer connection on the LAN needs a unique TCP/IP address. You can't reuse the TCP/IP address your ISP assigned to the dialup computer, because it's already being used to identify the connection out from the modem—indeed, you need a TCP/IP address for the LAN interface on the computer with the modem in addition to the TCP/IP address for the modem itself.

The question, then, and the source of what complexity there is in connecting LANs to the Internet, is where to get the TCP/IP addresses for the computers on the LAN.

There are two possible answers for getting TCP/IP addresses:

- **Static TCP/IP addresses.** Your ISP might offer to assign your LAN a block of TCP/IP addresses. You then assign one of those addresses to each of your computers, either manually or by programming the addresses into a DHCP server (see Chapter 7, "Network Software— Protocol Stacks and Applications"). Assigning you a block of addresses is a service most people don't require, so some ISPs don't offer it and those that do commonly charge at least a setup fee.

- **Private TCP/IP addresses.** You can assign addresses yourself from the defined private TCP/IP address blocks you learned about in Chapter 7, without any action by your ISP.

The trouble with private TCP/IP addresses, though, is that they're impermissible on the Internet—you can't send messages from computers using private addresses out to the Internet without some trickery.

Network Address Translation

The trickery you need to permit your LAN to use private TCP/IP addresses is called *Network Address Translation*, or *NAT*. NAT software running on the computer with the modem routes network traffic from your LAN out onto the Internet, changing the addresses in each message from the private TCP/IP address of the LAN computer to the single TCP/IP address of the modem.

Don't rush past that last sentence. What NAT does is to transform *all* the private TCP/IP addresses on your LAN into the *single* TCP/IP address for the modem. It's easy to see ways that could work for message traffic going out from your LAN to the Internet—just substitute the modem's address, for example—but how incoming messages get to the right computer is more complicated.

The answer to how NAT works lies in a closer look at TCP/IP addresses. In addition to the numeric address that uniquely identifies each computer, complete TCP/IP addresses include a *port number*, which identifies the specific program running on that computer that's the destination for the message. There are standard port numbers reserved for well-known services. Table 12.1 shows some of the most common application-level TCP/IP services and the corresponding port number.

Table 12.1: Common Application-Level TCP/IP Services and Ports

Service	Port Number
FTP	21
Telnet	23
SMTP (email servers)	25
HTTP	80
POP3 (email clients)	110

When a message arrives addressed to a specific computer and to port 21 on that computer, the protocol software knows to relay that message to the FTP software running on the computer. If there's no FTP software running and attached to the port, an error occurs.

Although the well-known port numbers are small, below 1024 or so, TCP/IP permits port numbers in the tens of thousands. Those larger port numbers are called *transient port numbers*, meaning they're open for use by programs as required.

NAT exploits the transient port numbers to work its magic, switching the source address on outbound messages from private TCP/IP addresses and well-known port numbers to the modem's TCP/IP address and a transient port number. NAT keeps a table of what it does, so when a message comes back in from the Internet to the modem's address and a transient port number NAT has used, NAT knows to relay the message onto the LAN using the right private address and port number.

The NAT mechanism works well for clients but is unsuitable for servers because clients on the Internet trying to access a machine on the private LAN have no way to construct an address NAT will see as needing to be relayed onto the LAN; a message originating on the LAN has to occur first, which is an action of a client and not a server. For the same reason, you'll never find a computer behind a NAT relay listed in a Domain Name Server—the computers are essentially invisible.

The inability of computers on the Internet to initiate conversations with the mostly invisible computers on a LAN behind a NAT relay helps secure those LAN computers against attack. The computers are still vulnerable to attacks from servers they contact, but are protected from random attacks from unknown computers.

Network Proxies

NAT relays are one example of network services called *proxies*. NAT intercepts messages addressed to *all* TCP/IP ports—even outgoing transient ones such as port 26000 used by Quake, for example—to provide a transparent network level service well below the application program level.

Another example of a proxy is the Web server proxy offered by most good Internet service providers. The value of Web server proxies is that many page requests into the Internet are for the same page, such as the Netscape or Microsoft portal sites (http://www.netscape.com and http://www.msn.com, respectively). Web server proxies keep local copies of the pages they return to requesting client computers and can recognize when later requests are for a cached page. When that happens, the proxy invisibly responds to the client from its local copy, speeding access and reducing overall Internet traffic.

Although the idea of having smart lower protocol level agents—proxies—is a very powerful one, proxies sometimes introduce problems because they might inadvertently affect Internet traffic in ways that unmodified network operation would not. For example, in the case of NAT, some Internet Relay Chat (IRC) servers now require that the originating computer have a name that can be looked up in a DNS from its numeric address. Because computers linked to the Internet via NAT *cannot* have a DNS entry, they fail this test and are rejected by those servers.

The problems proxies can cause aren't arcane issues of concern only to network wizards, because you'll find NAT operating in some very important places:

- **Home telephone networking.** You saw in Chapter 4, "Picking Your LAN Cable Technology and Speed," that the simplicity of installing telephone line networking gives it advantages over most other LAN technologies for use in homes. Home users aren't likely to want to deal with the complexities of routers and static TCP/IP addresses, so NAT and DHCP are the ideal technologies to combine with the home telephone line networking hardware. Users plug in the network hardware, install the drivers, install software on the computer—which turns out to be the NAT application—and they're done.

- **Digital Subscriber Line (DSL, ADSL, and others) and cable modems.** The telephone and cable companies have more than their share of failings, including failing to deploy high-speed Internet service widely for decades despite good available technology. One decision some of them managed to get right, though, is to support using NAT to connect more than one computer to DSL and cable modem services. External modem hardware that you use to connect to DSL or cable modem service nearly always includes router, NAT, and DHCP services, making computer connections as easy as plugging in computers configured for TCP/IP and DHCP.

  Not that the telephone and cable companies are being entirely altruistic with their decision—the presence of NAT in the path between your computers and the Internet means you won't be running a server on their network using the available bandwidth. You'll pay extra for that.

Windows

The one essential lesson of the last few pages is that you'll want to use NAT software to share your Internet modem connection. Because most desktop computers run Windows, NAT and similar software have been available for Windows for years. You'll learn in this section about the NAT software recently added to Windows (you'll need Windows 98 Second Edition). You might come across other software with home networking kits, or you can download programs such as WinGate (`http://www.wingate.com`) or SyGate (`http://www.sygate.com`) directly from the Internet.

Example 12.1 shows you how to add the Internet Connection Sharing (ICS) software to your Windows 98 Second Edition configuration. ICS isn't part of the standard Windows installation, so plan on having to add it.

EXAMPLE

Example 12.1   Installing Internet Connection Sharing

Internet Connection Sharing is a new component in Windows 98 starting with Windows 98 Second Edition. As you learned in Chapter 8, "Configuring Your System Software," Windows 98 Second Edition is shown as build 2222 A in the General tab of the System control panel applet. If you're running an older build of Windows 98 or Windows 95, you'll have to upgrade to get ICS. You'll need the complete upgrade version, not the lower-cost bug fix update, because the latter does not include ICS. All the steps in this example assume you have Windows 98 Second Edition installed. Carry out these steps on the computer hosting the modem:

1. Open the Add/Remove Programs control panel applet (Start, Settings, Control Panel, Add/Remove Programs) and then select the Windows Setup tab.

2. Scroll the list down and select Internet Tools.

3. Click Details. Internet Connection Sharing will be the entry at the top of the list in the resulting Internet Tools dialog box (see Figure 12.2). Check the box to select ICS and click OK.

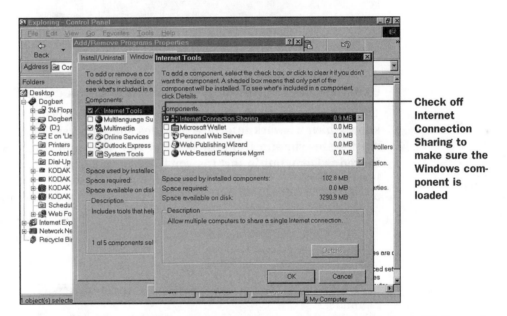

Figure 12.2: Installing Internet Connection Sharing in Windows 98 Second Edition.

4. Click OK to close the Add/Remove Programs dialog box.

Windows will likely request the installation CD-ROM and load some files; when it's finished, the Internet Connection Sharing Wizard will start (see Figure 12.3).

Follow the steps in Example 12.2 to work through the ICS Wizard and configure the program.

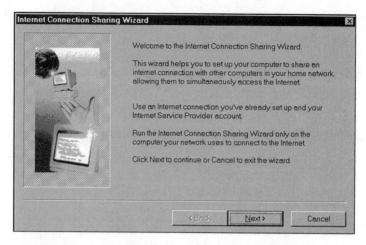

Figure 12.3: *Internet Connection Sharing Wizard.*

Example 12.2   Running the Internet Connection Sharing Wizard

The ICS Wizard's role is to give your system the information it needs to know which network interface provides shared access to the Internet. We've written this chapter from the point of view that that interface will be a shared modem, but in fact (as you'll see in this example), the shared Internet interface can equally be another LAN. We've omitted some of the unimportant screens in this example, focusing only on the important steps:

1. From the opening screen shown in Figure 12.3, click Next to get to the dialog box in Figure 12.4, where you'll identify the shared Internet interface.

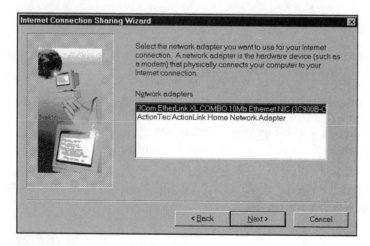

Figure 12.4: *Internet Connection Sharing Wizard Internet connection selection.*

2. Every machine qualified to run ICS will have two network interfaces: the shared Internet access point, and the LAN using private TCP/IP addresses. You can see a 3Com network interface card (NIC) and an ActionTec home telephone network adapter listed in Figure 12.4; a more typical listing would include a modem and a home telephone network adapter.

It's worth noting that, even though the ActionTec card comes with its own NAT software, we've nevertheless chosen to use ICS. We installed the ActionTec device drivers, but omitted installation of their application software.

3. Select the network interface in the dialog box that connects this computer to the Internet. In Figure 12.4, that interface is the 3Com NIC; in computers with a modem you want to share, that interface will be the modem.

4. Click Next. The ICS Wizard will display a dialog box allowing you to create a Client Configuration Disk (see Figure 12.5); you really don't need the client disk and can skip the client disk steps.

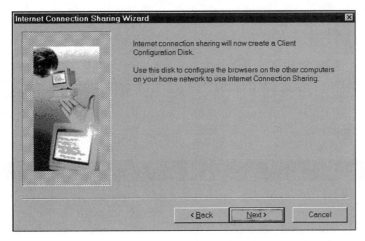

Figure 12.5: Internet Connection Sharing Wizard client disk creation.

5. Finish off the ICS Wizard and allow Windows to reboot when it asks. After the reboot finishes, open the Network control panel applet (Start, Settings, Control Panel, Network); you should see that it's changed to something like what's shown in Figure 12.6. You might have to scroll the list to see what's shown in Figure 12.6, and the protocols in the list might be different depending on what protocols you have installed.

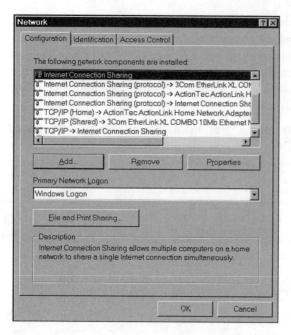

Figure 12.6: *The Network control panel following creation of a Client Configuration Disk.*

After you install it, ICS runs all the time whenever the computer is powered on. Modifications ICS makes to the normal operation of Windows allows dialup access to the configured ISP without a confirmation dialog box, so there's no need for someone to be present at the machine hosting the modem.

Linux

You have two tasks to accomplish to set up a Linux computer to act as the NAT relay and share access to an attached modem: First, you have to make the modem dial your ISP in the first place and, second, you have to set up NAT. Those two steps are also part of Windows ICS setup, of course, but the dialup setup is very straightforward in Windows. That's not always been true in Linux—earlier versions required some pretty arcane steps to make PPP dialup networking work—so first we want to steer you in the right direction with Example 12.3.

Example 12.3   Set Up Linux PPP Dialup Internet Access

Although once the restricted province of wizards, Linux PPP setup is now relatively easy thanks to a graphical setup interface tied into the same

EXAMPLE

Linuxconf program you used in Chapter 8 to access the configuration tools for the Samba file-sharing software. Follow these steps:

1. Start Linuxconf, entering the root password if requested and then click Networking. You'll get the Network configurator, as in Chapter 8, in response; click at the bottom on PPP/SLIP/PLIP to get the PPP/SLIP/PLIP configurator.

2. Click Add, and then select a PPP connection. Click Accept to get the PPP interface dialog box shown in the bottom right of Figure 12.7.

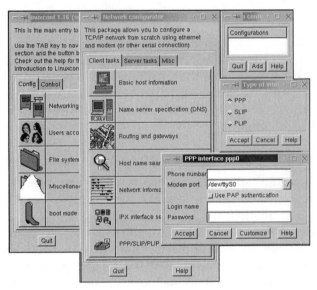

Figure 12.7: *Linux PPP setup.*

3. The PPP interface configuration dialog box makes setting up dialup networking in Linux nearly as simple as doing the same job in Windows. The dialog box lets you enter the same information as Windows requires: the ISP dialup telephone number, login name, and password. Unlike Windows, though, Linux requires you to identify the modem by naming the serial interface device acting as the modem I/O port and allows you to enable or disable logins using the Password Authentication Protocol (PAP; plan on checking off the Use PAP authentication box).

   Linux represents all devices in the file system, and locates all device file system entries in the /dev directory. Serial ports are named ttyS0 through ttyS3, so the entire path becomes /dev/ttyS0 through /dev/ttyS3. These devices correspond to the DOS devices COM1 through COM4, respectively, so if your modem is on what DOS or Windows would call COM1, set the Linux PPP modem port to /dev/ttyS0.

Some Linux systems create a device /dev/modem linked to one of the serial ports.

4. After you enter all the parameters, click Accept. You can exercise finer control over PPP via the Customize dialog box (click the Customize button), but in most case the defaults work. After you click Accept, the new configuration shows up in the PPP/SLIP/PLIP dialog box; clicking on an entry in that dialog box brings up the same dialog box as Customize would have.

Test your PPP configuration by opening the Customize dialog box and clicking Connect. Your modem should dial out to your ISP and connect your computer to the Internet.

After you have PPP working and tested and have verified that the Ethernet connection is working from that machine out to your LAN, you can configure Network Address Translation to link your LAN out through your modem to the Internet. Follow the steps in Example 12.4 to make Linux NAT work.

Example 12.4 Set Up Linux Network Address Translation

There are specific software components—the same ones that let Linux function as a router—you need in your Linux system for NAT to work. That statement is equivalent to saying the Linux kernel must have IP routing support compiled in. Mandrake Linux 6.1—the version we're using—does; you can check whether other distributions do at http://members.home.net/ ipmasq/ipmasq-HOWTO-1.81-7.html#MASQ-supported-Distributions. It appears most newer distributions have the necessary support already compiled in; you might need to update your version if it lacks support. After you've verified that the right components are available, you can enable them:

1. You might have assigned the LAN addresses on your network without thought to later enabling NAT. You'll want to ensure that the network interface card on the machine to run NAT (and on the computers making up the rest of the LAN, for that matter) has a private address (for example, 192.168.0.1).

2. Linux initializes itself as it starts by carrying out commands from a series of script files. The file rc.local is the right place to insert initialization unique to a specific computer, so add the following lines into the /etc/rc.d/rc.local file, which will load the NAT modules and enable NAT automatically after each reboot. NAT is commonly called IP Masquerade or IPMASQ in Linux:

```
#rc.firewall script - Start IPMASQ and the firewall
/etc/rc.d/rc.firewall
```

The first line is a comment; the second line says to go run the configuration script in the file /etc/rc.d/rc.firewall.

3. Next, create the /etc/rc.d/rc.firewall file. The following simple version is abridged from the *Linux IP Masquerade HOWTO* by Ambrose Au and David Ranch; you can find the entire document at http:// linuxdoc.org/HOWTO/IP-Masquerade-HOWTO.html. We've interspersed comments in between the lines of code (which itself includes comments preceded by the pound sign character). You'll only want to put the code lines in your file.

```
#!/bin/sh
```

Like Windows, Linux uses a *command interpreter* or *command shell* to process command lines from the command prompt or in a script file. /bin/sh is one of the several command shells in Linux; putting this line at the start of the file ensures the right command shell is used to interpret the remainder of the file.

```
# Load all required IP MASQ modules
#
#   NOTE:  Only load the IP MASQ modules you need.


# Needed to initially load modules
#
/sbin/depmod -a
```

Linux NAT (IPMASQ) isn't a single, monolithic structure; you have to specify what you want in stages. This command starts up the IPMASQ module load sequence, and has to be the first thing you do.

```
# Supports the proper masquerading of FTP file transfers using the PORT
# method
#
/sbin/modprobe ip_masq_ftp
```

IPMASQ is less automatic than other NAT software; you have to explicitly configure it for some of the protocols you might use, especially if those protocols by default use what would normally be transient port numbers. We've left out essentially all the protocol-specific initializations; with this configuration, you should still be able to run Web browsers, FTP, and some other standard applications.

```
#CRITICAL: Enable IP forwarding since it is disabled by default since
echo "1" > /proc/sys/net/ipv4/ip_forward
```

Type the previous line very carefully. The character in quotes after the word echo is the number one, not the letter L.

```
# MASQ timeouts
#
#   2 hrs timeout for TCP session timeouts
```

```
#  10 sec timeout for traffic after the TCP/IP "FIN" packet is received
#  160 sec timeout for UDP traffic (Important for MASQ'ed ICQ users)
#
/sbin/ipchains -M -S 7200 10 160
```

Network traffic doesn't always terminate cleanly, and you don't want your NAT relay to accumulate dead connections indefinitely. These timeouts tell NAT when it's okay to discard inactive connections.

```
# Enable simple IP forwarding and Masquerading
#
#  NOTE:   The following is an example for an internal LAN address in the
#          192.168.0.x network with a 255.255.255.0 or a "24" bit subnet
#          mask.
#
#          Please change this network number and subnet mask to match your
#          internal LAN setup
#
/sbin/ipchains -P forward DENY
/sbin/ipchains -A forward -s 192.168.0.0/24 -j MASQ
```

The last two lines actually make IP forwarding and masquerading start operation when they're processed by the command interpreter. Be sure to change the network address in the last line to match what you've implemented on your LAN, remembering that the address you enter here has to be the subnet address without a host number (refer back to Chapter 7 if you're unsure what all that means).

After you're finished editing the /etc/rc.d/rc.firewall file, save it out and flag it as an executable script with the command line:

```
chmod 700 /etc/rc.d/rc.firewall
```

In addition to options to let specific protocols work with IP Masquerading (including Quake, CU-SeeMe, and others), there are options in the HOWTO document at http://linuxdoc.org/HOWTO/IP-Masquerade-HOWTO.html that help simplify operation with DHCP services on your NAT server. There are also some good recommendations on things to do after NAT is running to further secure your system.

Summary

You discovered in this chapter that the fundamental capabilities built into TCP/IP inherently support sharing a modem from your LAN and that all you need is software to relay TCP/IP messages between LAN and modem. The software doing that implements a function called Network Address Translation (NAT). A simple, automatic version of NAT for Windows is Internet Connection Sharing (ICS); a more powerful but more difficult software package for Linux is IPMASQ (IP Masquerading).

What's Next

Now that your LAN is running and securely attached to the Internet, it's time to put it to work playing games! Oh, right, and doing solid collaborative work too.

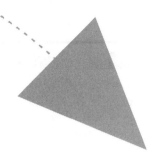

Collaboration and
Multiplayer LAN Games

In this chapter you will learn

- How your LAN can help people work on the same project

- What the different approaches are to multiplayer gaming and how to use them

You learned ways to share computer resources across your network in the preceding chapters. You'll learn about how people can work and play together across a LAN in this chapter. You could accurately describe collaboration and multiplayer gaming as sharing people across your network, but people are going to think you're weird if you start to talk like that.

Collaboration

We define *collaboration* as the collective work of individuals toward a common objective. We're specifically targeting collaborative work; we'll cover the collaborative and competitive sides of multiplayer gaming later in the chapter.

People share information among themselves when they collaborate. They write documents—email, text, graphics, or whatnot—to capture ideas and images, pass the documents around to communicate ideas and products, and mark up documents from others to respond with new ideas and suggestions. Eventually the process terminates in some work product (along with the history of exchanged information leading to that point).

At the level of activities on a computer, people collaborate by using tools to create, review, and edit content in files. Using the file sharing and transfer mechanisms you learned about earlier in this book, plus conventional office automation tools, here are the techniques you have to work with:

- **Collect and compile files, and then review on paper.** The traditional approach to large documents is to break the work down, assign out sections, collect the results, and edit the composite.

- **Circulate files.** For smaller works, such as position papers or brochures, it's common to circulate the document to reviewers, having each mark it up using tools to leave revision marks.

- **Edit files in a shared file area.** You can use either the collect-and-compile or the circulation approach with shared files, having each author and reviewer directly access the live document on a file server.

Collect and Compile Files, and then Review on Paper

Suppose you're working on a large project, such as a proposal or report to a customer, where the end product will have to be between 100 and 200 pages and include both drawings and photographs. Assuming your timelines are such that it's impossible for one person to write the entire thing, you'll need to have several people collaborate and to coordinate their work.

Many proposal development courses and workshops teach that you should approach this problem in steps:

1. Outline the document.

2. Storyboard each section, which means writing down the sections' key messages and a sketch of the central graphics.

3. Review the outline and storyboards.

4. Develop each section independently.

5. Collect and integrate each section into a master document.

6. Distribute the master document for review and comment; collect reviews and edit into the master. Repeat until done.

Let's suppose you're using common office automation tools, such as Microsoft Office or Corel WordPerfect, along with a collection of drawing, illustration, and photo editing tools. Table 13.1 shows that you have several practical options at each step for helping people collaborate.

Table 13.1: Collaboration File Size and Transport Options

Step	File Size (KB)	Transport Options
Outline	10–50	Email, file sharing, file transfer, paper
Storyboard	10–100	Email, file sharing, file transfer, paper
Section Review	10–100	Email, file sharing, file transfer, paper
Develop and Integrate	1,000–30,000	File sharing, file transfer
Review Cycle Integrate	10,000–150,000	File sharing, file transfer, paper

Table 13.1 reflects the relatively large files a project like this can create—files for publication-quality photographs can be huge—and suggests that as files get bigger email becomes impractical. The size of the files we created for this book can help calibrate what you'll see; files for individual chapters, including drawings and photographs, are as large as 37MB, whereas the complete set of files for the book, including separate files for the text, drawings, and photographs, is nearly 600MB.

This section helps you analyze your options based on reviewing paper in the final steps; the next two extend that baseline to apply file-transfer and file-sharing techniques.

Every collaboration approach you use has to solve two crucial problems:

- **Consistent format and style.** Any professional result looks and reads as if it were written by one person. The presentation has to speak with a single, consistent voice and has to remain visually consistent. If not, readers get confused and miss the key messages.

- **Current versions and version control.** People working on the project have to stay up to date with changes made to the integrated document because there's little point in reviewing and editing material that's already been changed by someone else.

A lot of details go into achieving a consistent format and style. Most small offices can't afford to have a dedicated production and page layout department, leading many to fall into the trap of asking each author to follow the final formatting guidelines. People's word processing skills vary wildly, but it's a good general assumption that most people aren't at all good at formatting. Instead, you'll want to have a ruthlessly simple author's format, including perhaps no elements besides headings, text paragraphs, bulleted paragraphs, and numbered paragraphs. Using that approach lets the people doing final edit and formatting concentrate on getting the wording and look they want without the nuisance of first removing inappropriate formatting added by authors.

Successfully implementing that first bullet point requires divorcing people from their natural pride of ownership and inclination to tweak material they've developed. Successful collaboration *requires* clear, positive control of who owns every bit of material at all times, and after an author turns over a section, she doesn't own it any longer—the editor does.

The positive control requirement is part of the basis for the second bullet point. Aside from the fact that it's often pointless to review old material, an editor who loses version control will at best have a lot of extra work to do and at worst might fail to deliver the product on time.

The paper approach to solving the control problem (see Figure 13.1) is to never let anyone but the current document owner access the corresponding file. You can do that by keeping it on the individual's computer, or you can do it by keeping the document in an access-restricted area on a file server. When it's time to start a new review cycle, you make enough paper copies of the printed version to hand out, let people mark up the paper, and collect all the copies. The editor (or stuckee, as the case might be) then slogs through all the comments, incorporating the ones that matter, and starts the review cycle again.

Paper review is a lot of work for the editors but isn't as awkward as it sounds. It doesn't make the most of your network, though, so let's turn to some more network-centric approaches.

Circulate Files

The review-and-edit cycle is the leverage point for improving the collaboration process because the original authoring work is more likely to be done by individuals. The most direct way to exploit your network for collaboration during review-and-edit is to transfer files from one reviewer to the next, as shown in Figure 13.2.

The review-and-edit cycle consists of a series of file transfers, first when the editor transfers a copy of the master document file to the first reviewer, and then when each reviewer in turn transfers the marked-up file to the next person in line. Everyone in the cycle has to work with revision marks turned on in the document, so the editor knows what's different. The editor finally receives the document back from the last reviewer, works over each change, and makes the result the new master file.

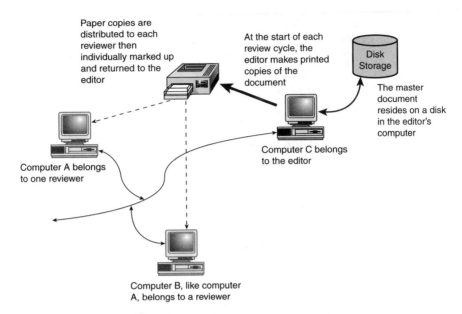

Figure 13.1: *Using paper copies for the review-and-edit cycle.*

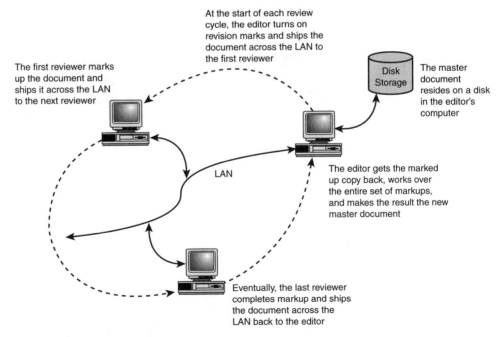

Figure 13.2: *Using file transfer for the review-and-edit cycle.*

Sequentially transferring the file from one person to the next solves the problem of makings sure each person works on the most current version of the file, and (because the editor retains the final decision of what goes in the new master) maintains control of the final product. The problem with this approach is that it seemingly takes forever—while one person works, all the rest are idle. If that one person is busy with something else, the entire process stalls.

Edit in a Shared File Area

Rearranging the order in which people review the document reduces the time required to circulate a file but doesn't solve the inherent problem that only one person can work at a time. Using file sharing eliminates the document routing problem because everyone can get at the file at any time (see Figure 13.3). The office automation tools and operating systems themselves provide the necessary file access coordination, similar to what you learned about locked files in Chapter 10, "Network Backup."

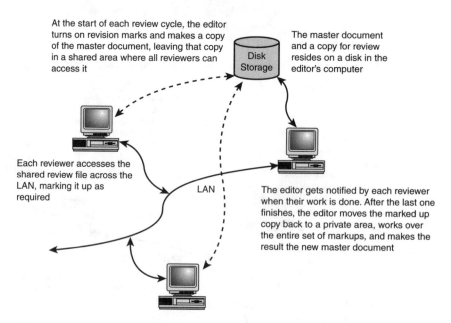

Figure 13.3: Using file sharing for the review-and-edit cycle.

The requirement to lock a file while someone edits it means you have to take special steps to keep standard one-at-a-time editing from slowing the review process. Microsoft Word and other office automation tools provide a feature Word calls master documents, which simply means that you can divide a complete document into multiple subsidiary files that are combined by the master document. If reviewers edit the subsidiary files, several reviewers can work at once. In practice, though, we've found master documents to be unreliable and won't use them.

Microsoft Office 2000 Server Extensions

The recent release of Microsoft Office 2000 includes a number of features directly targeted at collaboration. Perhaps the most powerful, but least known, are the discussion features—capabilities to let multiple people comment on a document at the same time.

Implementing document discussions requires the Microsoft Office 2000 Server Extensions (OSE) running on a Windows NT Server with Internet Information Server, and in fact installing and configuring OSE is difficult to get right. If you decide to use OSE, you might want to consider using an Internet service provider such as Interland (http://www.interland.com) that provides OSE services, especially if the people you want to collaborate with are geographically dispersed without access to your private LAN. After you get OSE running, you can convert your review-and-edit cycles to the model shown in Figure 13.4; everyone can comment on the same document at once, and you can maintain a bulletin board of notices and discussions distinct from individual documents.

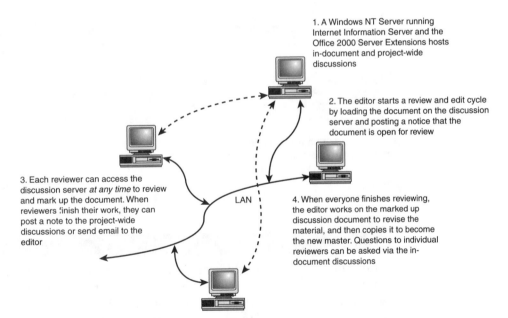

Figure 13.4: Using Microsoft Office 2000 Server Extensions for the review-and-edit cycle.

Facilities such as those provided by the Microsoft Office 2000 Server Extensions significantly enhance the ways in which you can use your network for collaboration. Figure 13.5 shows the beginning of the manuscript file for Chapter 12. The bottom pane in the windows permits adding general discussion items, whereas in the top pane you can highlight and annotate specific parts of the text.

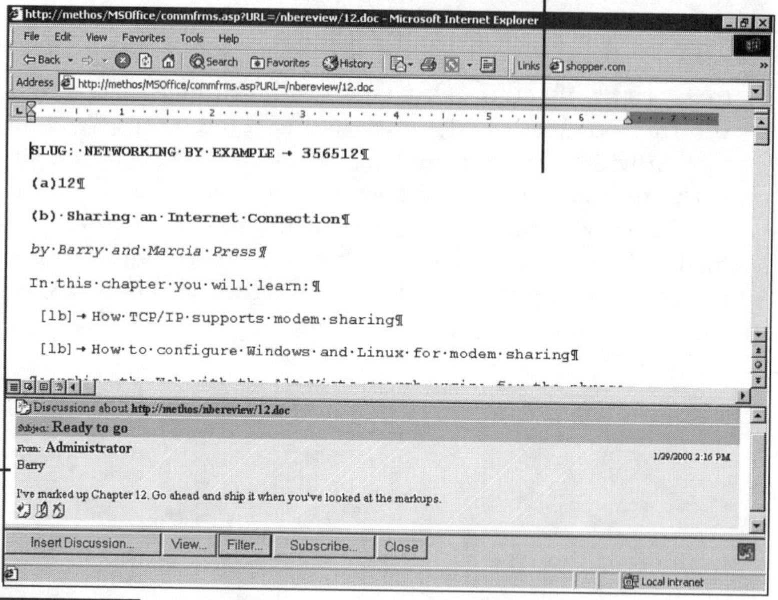

You can annotate specific words, phrases, or paragraphs in the document test from this pane as well as add general discussion items below

Discussions within a document let multiple reviewers comment on the document simultaneously

Figure 13.5: *Collaboration from within Microsoft Word.*

Games

Multiplayer games are different from collaboration as we've defined it—rather than work toward finishing a product, the multiplayer gamer either works or competes with others to progress within the game. Computer games typically operate in a *single-player* mode, in which the player competes against the computer, or in *multiplayer* mode. There are several different kinds of multiplayer games:

- **Competitive against other players.** More than a few classic board games have been adapted to multiplayer competition on computers, and it's reasonable to think of competitive multiplayer computer games as the next generation of board games. The games you can play competitively on computers have evolved far beyond what is possible in a board game, but the underlying model remains accurate—the computer provides an environment in which people play against each other.

- **Cooperative against the computer.** Single-player computer games differ from board games in that the computer program operates as the player's opponent. A natural extension of this idea is to have a multi-player team play cooperatively against the computer.

- **Competitive against other teams.** Combine the idea of computer-hosted competition and team play and you have competition not among individuals but between teams.

Unlike dedicated game consoles such as the Sega Dreamcast or Sony PlayStation, which often host several players on one machine, multiplayer computer games nearly always require one computer per player, interconnecting all the computers with a LAN or over the Internet.

Game Protocols

The earliest multiplayer games, including the groundbreaking game *Doom* from what is now id Software, were released before the Internet became as popular as it now and typically supported only the IPX protocol over a network or a serial connection using either direct connection or modems. Fast action games such as Doom, or the more recent Quake series, use unreliable datagram protocols (such as those provided by IPX and the TCP/IP equivalent, UDP; see Chapter 7, "Network Software—Protocol Stacks and Applications") because they can't afford the delays that might occur while a reliable delivery protocol attempts to retry a failed transmission. The games arrange to send all the necessary information in each message, so losing a single message isn't catastrophic.

Today, reflecting the explosive growth of the Internet, multiplayer games all support TCP/IP (still using UDP); some retain IPX support for LAN play on networks not supporting TCP/IP.

Typical Game Setup

Games use two different approaches to implement multiplayer operation:

- **Peer-to-peer networking.** The earliest multiplayer games were developed in a time when far fewer computers were networked together, and their communications model was more basic than now. It was common for the early multiplayer games either to operate on a dedicated serial connection with only two computers playing, or to literally broadcast their traffic over a LAN to enable all interested computers to participate. Two factors made these early games targets for swift rejection by network administrators: the LAN traffic and the computer processing required for computers not playing to reject the broadcast traffic.

- **Client/server networking.** Virtually all multiplayer games made now use some form of client/server operation, even if a single computer doubles as both a client, playing the game, and as the server hosting a number of clients. Starting a multiplayer game has become a little more complicated in the process, but the added complexity has made possible both Internet-hosted games and tools to help find servers and opponents.

There are two common ways game clients and servers are distributed. Using one player's client as a server is shown in Figure 13.6: All three machines work as clients; one of the three also works as a server to host the game. The combined client/server model is common for small numbers of people playing across a LAN or across the Internet.

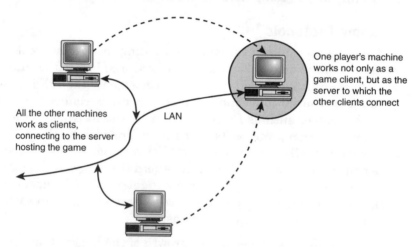

One player's machine works not only as a game client, but as the server to which the other clients connect

All the other machines work as clients, connecting to the server hosting the game

LAN

Figure 13.6: Using one player's client as a server.

The alternative to combining the client and server on one machine is to use one machine as a dedicated server, with no client running (see Figure 13.7). Four machines are required to host three players, but the response-time advantage for the player with the client on the server (as in Figure 13.6) goes away.

We're going to use two games to illustrate how to set up multiplayer games—DarkStone, written by Delphine Software International and published by Gathering of Developers, and Quake III Arena, written by id Software and published by Activision. Both games run under Windows 9x and Windows 2000; a version of Quake III Arena is available for Linux.

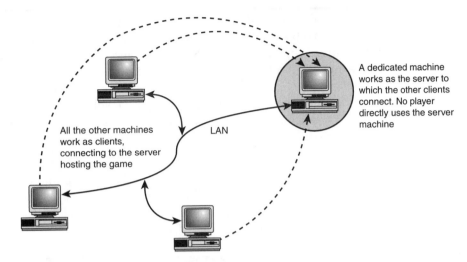

Figure 13.7: *Using a dedicated server.*

DarkStone is a role playing game (RPG), in which players explore a world while on a quest. Players gain skills and abilities as they gain experience and make decisions that determine the course of the game. DarkStone players can either cooperate or compete. DarkStone operates strictly with a combined client/server multiplayer model.

Quake III Arena is the reduction to the multiplayer essence of the earlier Quake and Quake II first-person shooter games in which players or teams of players compete for survival against each other. Quake III Arena supports either combined client/server operation or games hosted on a dedicated server.

Competitive and timing advantages aside, dedicated servers offer the opportunity to host far more players in the game. The client software, which is responsible for generating the detailed images and smooth onscreen animation characteristic of games today, requires a lot of computer power to run, so moving the client away from the server leaves much more processing power available to run the server software.

Server Setup

DarkStone is simple to set up for multiplayer, requiring that you make only a few specific selections as you start a game. Example 13.1 shows how you start a DarkStone server and how clients on other machines join the game.

EXAMPLE 13.1   RUNNING MULTIPLAYER DARKSTONE

Like seemingly every other game using accelerated 3D graphics today, you'll need a 3D accelerated video adapter in your computer, and you might

EXAMPLE

need to update the adapter drivers to the latest ones from the card manu-facturer's Web site. The computers we used for the next few examples used video cards with an nVidia TNT2 Ultra accelerator, for example, so we made sure we had the latest drivers from the nVidia Web site at http://www.nvidia.com. We also installed the latest DarkStone game patches; get them from the Gathering of Developers Web site at http://www.godgames.com, following the links for DarkStone, Files, DarkStone US Patch. Now follow these steps:

1. Start DarkStone. After the opening graphics finish (you can bypass them by pressing the Esc key), you'll see the game main menu as on the left in Figure 13.8. Click New Game (the top menu item; we've positioned the sword mouse cursor next to it) to get the New Game menu on the right of Figure 13.8.

Figure 13.8: Starting DarkStone multiplayer.

2. Click Multiplayer from the New Game menu, which indicates to the game you'll be playing a network game, and you'll reach the character selection screen. If you're playing for the first time, you'll need to cre-ate a character using the button near the lower-left corner; otherwise, you can choose from the existing ones or create another character. We've chosen an existing player we named Ngai; after you pick the character, click OK at the bottom center of the screen to reach the menu shown at the right of Figure 13.9 in which you'll pick a network protocol.

3. You can use either IPX or TCP/IP to support DarkStone on a LAN; if you're playing on the Internet, you'll have to choose TCP/IP. After you pick the protocol, you'll advance to the screen shown on the left in Figure 13.10, where you'll decide whether you're starting a server on your machine (in addition to the running client) or connecting a client to an existing server. Pick Create a Session to start a server; pick Join a Session to connect to an existing one. Choosing Create a Session

leads to the screen on the right in Figure 13.10, in which you specify the difficulty of the game you're starting. The characters we were using didn't have enough experience to start an Expert, Master, or Hero game, so the only choice open to us was Novice.

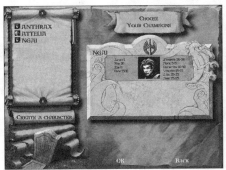

Figure 13.9: *Picking a character and network protocol.*

Figure 13.10: *Starting a multiplayer session.*

4. Once you complete step 3, the game has enough information to start the client and server, leading to the opening screen in Figure 13.11. You'll want your partners to join your game before you set off, though, so continue on with step 5.

5. If, back on the left side of Figure 13.10 in step 3, you'd chosen Join a Session, you'd next have seen the screen on the left in Figure 13.12, where you tell the game the location of the server. We picked TCP/IP earlier, so here we've entered the name of a TCP/IP host (joxer.press.net in the figure). Click OK and the client joins the game, as on the right in Figure 13.12. Both computers in the game now see both characters onscreen, and when a character moves or acts, the result is visible on both computers.

Figure 13.11: The started DarkStone server.

Figure 13.12: Joining a game on a running server.

6. Multiplayer games, because they implement their own protocols on top of the IPX or TCP/IP transport, usually offer in-game features besides letting each player see the entire game. In Figure 13.13, for instance, we've clicked the message icon in the bottom-right corner of the screen and then typed a message that will appear on each player's screen. Different games offer different multiplayer features, so be sure to (gasp) read the manual.

Quake III Arena is similar to DarkStone for operations using a combined client and server on a single computer; only the menu structures really differ. Example 13.2 gives you the corresponding startup instructions.

Figure 13.13: *Sending a message to the other players.*

EXAMPLE

EXAMPLE 13.2   RUNNING MULTIPLAYER QUAKE III ARENA

This example starts with the Quake III Arena (Q3A) equivalent to the instructions you saw for DarkStone in Example 13.1. After that, though, you'll learn how to use the built-in server browser to find Q3A games on the Internet. Follow these steps:

1. The left image in Figure 13.14 shows the initial Q3A menu following the opening cinematics. Click Multiplayer to get the Arena Servers menu on the right in Figure 13.14. The list at the top contains game options; for now, leave the Servers option set to Local to restrict the scan to your LAN.

Figure 13.14: *Quake III Arena multiplayer server initial startup.*

2. You're setting up the server at this point, so click the Create button at the bottom of the Arena Servers menu. When you do, you'll move to the Game Server menu on the left in Figure 13.15. Pick a map from the four shown and click Next to move to the second Game Server menu (see the right image in Figure 13.15).

Figure 13.15: Completing Quake III Arena multiplayer server startup.

3. Set any game parameters you want on the second Game Server screen, click Fight to transport your player into the Arena, and wait for the other players to join (see Figure 13.16).

Figure 13.16: Opening Quake III Arena screen.

4. On a second machine, click Multiplayer as before. Because there's now a running server, there will be a server list as shown on the left in Figure 13.17. Wander around until you find the player hosted on the same computer as the server; that player will then see you as shown in Figure 13.17 on the right.

Figure 13.17: Multiplayer view in Quake III Arena.

5. Q3A isn't about looking at the pretty buildings, though; it's about destroying your opponent, and if you're not fast the victim will be you. That's what happened in Figure 13.18—the second player into the game fired a rocket at the player on the server.

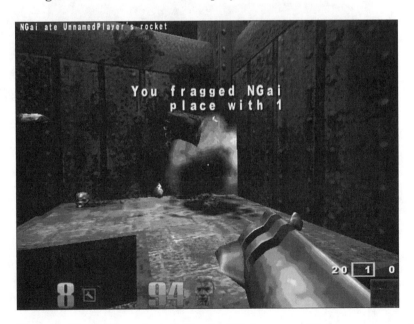

Figure 13.18: Completing Quake III Arena multiplayer server startup.

6. If you leave this arena (press Esc, and choose Leave Arena), you can go back into Multiplayer and click the Servers item in the Arena Servers screen. You have several choices for how to find servers; Figure 13.19 shows a list of servers available on the Mplayer multi-player gaming service (http://www.mplayer.com) at the instant we took the screen shot. There are other Internet sites hosting multiplayer gaming, of which one of the largest is the Microsoft MSN Gaming Zone (http://www.zone.com). Not all services host all games, and some games (such as Interstate 76) have servers operated by the publisher just for that game.

Figure 13.19: Finding Quake III Arena multiplayer servers on the Internet.

7. Your best choice is to sort the list of servers by lowest ping time (round-trip delay from you to the server and back) because you'll play best on the lowest ping server. Pick the server you want, and then click Fight in the lower-right corner to join the Arena.

Internet Access, Speed, and Latency

Victory in action games such as Quake III Arena—sometimes called *twitch* games—depends on fast reflexes and good aim. Everything's moving in the game world based on the messages your client sends to and receives from the server.

The dependency of what you see onscreen on message traffic to and from the server means that your reaction times are crucially dependent on how long those messages spend in transit. The measure of that time interval is the *latency* in your Internet connection and not, surprisingly to some people, its speed. The biggest factors determining latency will be the kind of modem you have (DSL and cable modems are often best, followed by ISDN, V.90 modems, and V.34 modems) and how your messages are routed across the Internet. Latencies are generally in the 10–400 millisecond range, too big to be significantly affected by the specifics of your LAN design.

However—you knew this was coming—there's one important caveat that gaming places on LAN design. If you're sharing your Internet access via your LAN, as we recommend, traffic from other computers across the modem can drastically raise the ping time from you to the server. Enough competing traffic from other computers (including other computers playing games) and your latency can get so high that your game becomes unplayable. There's no good fix for that problem except to get a higher-speed connection that's less subject to contention from the traffic on your LAN.

Summary

Collaboration and multiplayer gaming, diverse as they are, are two of the most compelling things you'll ever do with a network. One gives you unprecedented power to combine the work of many people; the other delivers entertainment impossible by any other means.

The intense involvement of people in collaborative and multiplayer applications means you have to pay more attention to how well the applications fit what people are doing and (perhaps more importantly) how they do it. You'll have to choose collaboration software that fits how your people work—email versus document markup, for example—and games that suit how people want to play.

What's Next

With this chapter, you've completed the key applications of your network that this book has to teach you. In the next part of the book, you'll learn how to improve the capabilities of your network beyond the basics. The next chapter starts that topic by examining how to improve your network's connection to the Internet.

Part V

Getting the Most from Your Network

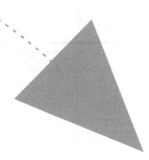

## 14

Advanced Internet Access

In this chapter you will learn

- How to configure your LAN with a router to enhance service
- About threats to your LAN and approaches to countering them

Although tying your LAN to the Internet using the techniques you learned in Chapter 12, "Sharing an Internet Connection," works well, it's not the best you can do. In this chapter, you'll learn advanced ways to connect your LAN to the Internet; these methods eliminate the requirement for one of your computers to remain connected and they defend your computers from attack via the Internet. You'll also learn how to use dedicated communications computers—routers—to limit the places on the Internet accessible from your network.

Routers and High-Speed Internet Access

Chapter 7, "Network Software—Protocol Stacks and Applications," teaches you that layer 3 of the TCP/IP protocol, the network layer, is responsible for transporting messages from one computer to another, independent of the distance or the number of intervening computers. The ability of the TCP/IP network protocol layer to do that underpins the Internet's capability to span the globe and host millions of computers.

You can use the operations in Figure 14.1 to exploit the organization and compactness of the TCP/IP protocol stack and avoid having to dedicate an entire computer to routing messages between your LAN and the Internet. Following the numbered sequence of notes in the figure, you can see that messages start in application software and enter the protocol stack, flowing down to lower layers and out the physical layer onto the Ethernet LAN. A router on the LAN (which could equally well be another computer running Internet Connection Sharing; see Chapter 12) receives the message but doesn't need to run it all the way up the protocol stack into the upper layers. Instead, the network layer in the router detects that the message simply needs to be forwarded out another physical port and sends it back down the protocol stack to that port. The process continues to the server, which finally passes the message all the way up the stack to the server application software.

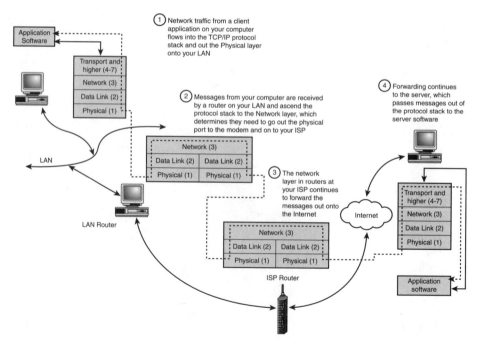

Figure 14.1: Protocol stacks in computers and routers.

Because a router only needs to support protocol processing up through layer three, and because it doesn't need to run application programs, the normal resources of a full-scale computer, such as a monitor, keyboard, and disk, are not required. All that's really required are a processor, memory, flash memory (the same as what holds a PC basic input/output system, or BIOS, when the power's off), and two or more network interfaces. A small router can therefore be a lot less expensive than a complete PC and, because it can run simpler software than Windows or Linux, will be more reliable.

The relatively high data rates for Internet access now available in some areas make conventional modem packaging and serial port connections inadequate, so many companies now offer products combining some form of high-speed modem with a small router. Having a router attached between your LAN and the Internet simplifies connecting multiple computers to the Internet, because the router hides the details of connecting to your Internet service provider (ISP), and makes Internet access equivalent to all other network access on your LAN.

The resulting simple, transparent network interface should make users on your LAN more likely to use the Internet, which increases the importance of a fast Internet connection. Aside from connections up to 53Kbps available on 50–80% of the telephone lines in North America using a V.90 ("56Kbps") modem, you have three reasonable choices for faster Internet access:

- Digital Subscriber Line (DSL)
- Cable modems
- Integrated Services Digital Network (ISDN)

We've intentionally omitted the satellite-based Internet access technology from this list because of its high cost and often severely limited performance.

Digital Subscriber Line

Digital Subscriber Line (DSL) is an interesting technology available from your telephone company and (in some areas) from competitive service providers who use the wires installed by the telephone company. Assuming DSL is available in your area and to your location—those are very different requirements—you can get rates from around 256Kbps up to over 1Mbps. DSL is generally relatively inexpensive—under $100 per month in many areas for flat-rate access—and can operate on the same telephone lines as your regular telephone.

DSL (and cable television modems) has the characteristic that it's always connected to the Internet—there's no dialup or tear-down process required.

Don't underestimate the value of being able to run DSL on your normal telephone line, because that means there are a lot of "don't" advantages to DSL:

- **Don't order another telephone line.** DSL operating on the same incoming telephone line as your regular service means you don't have to order a second telephone line, so you don't have to pay the monthly expense of a second line, and you don't have to worry about having RJ-11 jacks installed for that second line. In older buildings, or in areas where there aren't spare lines available to connect to your building, the ability to use an existing line could be the difference between getting service and not.

- **Don't fight over who gets to use the telephone.** Not only can DSL use your existing telephone line, you can use the telephone for incoming and outgoing voice calls while DSL is in operation. Strictly speaking, you could use a modem on the same line as the DSL service, but with your LAN and a router it's hard to see why you'd do that.

- **Don't fight for modem bandwidth.** DSL is 5–20 times faster than even the fastest V.90 modems, fast enough that several people can view Web pages, download files, and play games at the same time.

- **Don't worry about shared media security.** Because both DSL and cable modems are always on and connected, other people on the same network segment can see your computer just as if they were on your LAN. Unlike cable modems, DSL uses a private, dedicated wire between you and the telephone company switch. You'll still have to cope with security threats from the Internet itself, but there are no users on your telephone connection besides you to go rooting about on your LAN.

- **Don't worry about reduced bandwidth on a shared connection.** Because you're the only user on your DSL telephone connection, you always get the full bandwidth connection available on the line. The Internet itself might not supply or accept data at the speed your line permits, but you won't be contending with others on the line.

Our preference for high-speed Internet access is *whatever you can get*, because the telephone companies and cable television operators have for the most part been slow to roll out service, hyping what's available far beyond reality. If you have a choice, though, we recommend DSL.

Cable Modems

Cable modems exploit another of the wires commonly coming into homes and buildings, the cable television connection. Cable TV connections are always coaxial cable, which in principle lets the cable TV operator support a far larger frequency range over the cable than the telephone company can use on its simpler twisted-pair wires.

Cable television operators make most of their money delivering television broadcasts to viewers, though, so those that do support cable modems invariably choose to devote only a small fraction of the available bandwidth—typically the equivalent of one TV channel—to Internet access. Far worse, though, and the reason most people can't get cable modem service, is that nearly all cable TV networks are one way, designed to bring signals from the cable operator's facilities, called the *headend*, to you. Until the operator upgrades the network for two-way traffic, a very expensive proposition, the only options are to provide no service or to provide service using your telephone line and a modem for the return path back to the headend. Most operators simply choose not to provide service.

Cable modem technology has another unavoidable problem diagrammed in Figure 14.2: Each coaxial cable running from the ugly green boxes to homes is shared among hundreds or even thousands of homes. The cable acts like a single LAN segment, carrying TCP/IP broadcast and normal messages everywhere along the segment. Because broadcast messages are the foundation of Network Neighborhood browsing in Windows, people on cable television networks don't necessarily even need network sniffer tools to find other computers; they might be able to simply use the tools built into Windows and Linux.

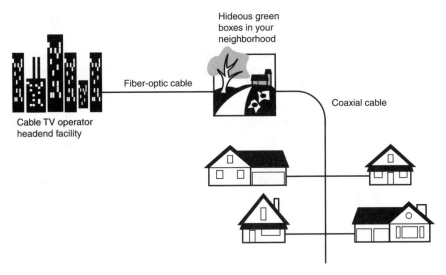

Figure 14.2: *Cable television media sharing.*

The visibility of computers on a shared cable television network segment is potentially dangerous. If you set up file sharing on your computers and make it available through TCP/IP, your disks are potentially visible to everyone on the same segment, protected at most by a password.

We use words such as *potentially* in the last paragraph because some cable television modem system build in safeguards to close this security hole. Not all do, though, so be sure to use the NetBEUI technique you learned in Example 7.2 of Chapter 7 to keep your disks invisible outside your LAN if you don't use any of the more-advanced security approaches in this chapter.

Integrated Services Digital Network

Integrated Services Digital Network (ISDN), a service available in cities nearly everywhere in North America from the telephone companies, is the oldest technology for fast connections to the Internet; it is literally decades old, and offers connections at speeds up to 128Kbps each way. Only incompetent marketing and support by the telephone companies, and in many areas fantastically high pricing, kept ISDN from being widely adopted. The technology is (finally) available in most areas, with a good selection of inexpensive equipment available.

Think of an ISDN line as a pair of telephone lines bundled together, each capable of running at 64Kbps. Each line has its own telephone number and is capable of independent operation. The two telephone numbers (called the *D channels*) connect over the usual copper telephone lines, but you can't use your conventional modem on an ISDN line—you need an ISDN modem. You *can* use conventional equipment to access the two D-channel telephone circuits with the right ISDN equipment (Figure 14.3 shows how that works), because many ISDN modems provide RJ-11 analog connections on the back that translate inside the modem to the digital signals that go across the ISDN circuit. When a telephone wants to use one of the ISDN telephone numbers, that circuit is disconnected from the data port and devoted to the telephone connection. When the telephone hangs up, the circuit can be used again for data.

ISDN connections, because they operate more like telephone lines than DSL or cable modems, require dialup processing. In some areas service is metered by the minute, whereas in other areas you can get inexpensive flat-rate ISDN service. If you can get flat-rate service, you can afford to leave the connection live all the time.

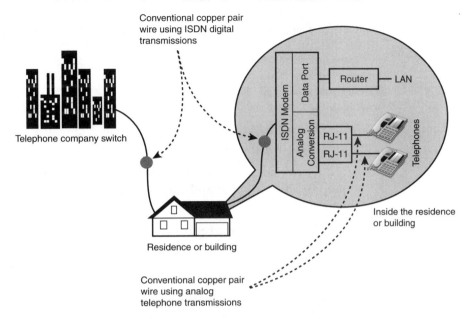

Figure 14.3: Connecting analog equipment to ISDN service.

Security

The Internet is often called *cyberspace* to both distinguish and compare it from the real-world space we live in. There are unfortunate parallels in cyberspace to the evils in the real world, so you need to be concerned about attacks on your computers from the Internet.

What you *do not* have to do, though, is run around like Chicken Little, fearing everything. You're going to learn in this section how to organize your thinking so you can create defenses and analyze attacks.

For example, one of the most common threats to computers—and not just ones running Windows—is that of computer viruses. Our email inbox is constantly flooded with panicked messages of doom from the latest virus. Here's a typical one:

```
Subject: FW: Serious Virus Warning

VIRUS WARNING a new Virus - WOBBLER is on the loose.  It will arrive on email
titled "How to Give a Cat a Colonic".  IBM and AOL have announced that it is
very powerful, more so than Melissa.  There is no remedy. It will eat all your
information on the hard drive and also destroys Netscape Navigator and Microsoft
Internet Explorer.
```

```
Do not open anything with this title and please pass this message on to all your
contacts and anyone who uses your email facility. Not many people seem to know
about this yet so propagate it as fast as possible. This information was
announced yesterday morning by IBM.  Please share it with everyone in your
address book so that the spreading of the virus may be stopped.  This is a very
 dangerous Virus and there is no remedy for it at this time.  Please practice
cautionary measures and forward this to all your online friends A.S.A.P.
```

As with most email virus warnings we receive, this is a hoax, which you can immediately see in several ways:

- **No legitimate authorities.** Although several organizations and companies actively track and warn about viruses, neither IBM nor AOL do so.

- **Credible-sounding technobabble.** The message includes the text `... very powerful, more so than Melissa. There is no remedy. It will eat all your information on the hard drive and also destroys Netscape Navigator and Microsoft Internet Explorer` making the virus sound dangerous and the warning credible. There's no information there though—nothing about how it is like the (real) Melissa virus, nothing about the damage it does to the two Web browsers, and no explanation of the apparent conflict between `eat all your information on the hard drive` and `destroys Netscape Navigator and Microsoft Internet Explorer`—how can the browsers survive if the drive has been wiped?

- **Classic virus hoax format.** The United States Department of Energy maintains the Computer Incident Advisory Capability (CIAC) with the mission of providing technical assistance and information to Department of Energy (DOE) sites faced with computer security incidents. They maintain an excellent public Web site at `http://www.ciac.org`. One area on the site (at `http://www.ciac.org/ciac/CIACHoaxes.html`) is a list of many of the hoaxes circulating on the Internet. On the CIAC site is the history of perhaps the original chain letter virus hoax, the Good Times Virus. You can find the details at `http://www.ciac.org/ciac/CIACHoaxes.html#goodtimes`. If you compare the original Good Times chain letter to the one listed here, you'll quickly see that the one here follows the classic hoax format.

What you want to learn from this is how complete the analogy between the Internet and the real world is; there are many good people in both and enough losers to make both the Internet and the real world places to be careful.

As in the real world, though, attacks and threats on the Internet don't just occur randomly; they happen in predictable ways. We suggest you use the same layered network protocol stack model you learned in Chapter 7 to analyze Internet security. Figure 14.4 shows what we mean; different levels in the seven-layer model are vulnerable to attack in different ways, all of which can be dangerous if successful. Most of the attacks you'll hear about in the media occur at the application layer, going after Web servers and browsers and the information they have access to, but application layer attacks on open file shares are also common.

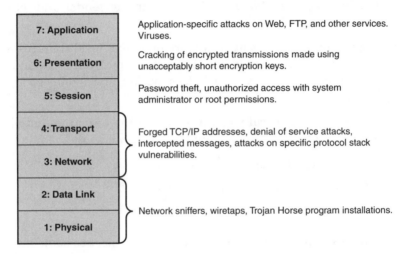

Figure 14.4: *Security vulnerabilities against the seven-layer model.*

It's ridiculous to think an array of defenses against many specific threats is worthwhile, because like the Maginot Line, the defense fails the first time an unanticipated threat shows up. The same insight that lets you understand attacks in terms of how they operate against the seven-layer model, however, also lets you deploy defenses against entire classes of threats at once. Two main approaches have proven extremely valuable:

- **Packet Filters.** You can examine traffic at the network layer, looking at the source and destination addresses. The filter can disallow traffic to or from specific addresses or address ranges and can disallow traffic with suspect address patterns.

- **Firewalls.** You can also examine traffic as high as the application layer, checking ports in message addresses or even checking the internal content of specific application messages. Traffic that fails any of those tests can be rejected.

The next three sections teach you the different ways to implement both packet filters and firewalls.

Router Packet Filters

Recall from Chapter 7 that TCP/IP addresses are composed of both a machine address and, within the machine, a port number identifying the program to handle the message. The combined address/port information is available in every TCP/IP message with the exception of broadcasts and some messages exchanged while a TCP/IP address is being assigned via the DHCP protocol and is available for both the sender and receiver of the message.

Packet filters, operating at a more primitive level than firewalls, tend to look at the TCP/IP addresses but not the port numbers and not the internal content of messages. Nevertheless, packet filters offer good security tools to help protect your network.

Packet filters generally operate using a top-to-bottom list of rules. For example, a typical rule set might be the following:

1. Permit all outgoing traffic.

2. Deny new incoming connections.

3. Accept everything else.

This is a somewhat secure setup, since (subject to some attacks) it rejects unsolicited connection attempts from the Internet to your computers. It explicitly protects against unauthorized access to shared drives and files, since it blocks incoming traffic using TCP. A filter using this pattern does have one significant impact on users, in that it breaks the normal operation between FTP clients and servers, which requires the server to initiate a connection when starting a transfer. Essentially all FTP software today supports the *PASV* mode, which is a workaround designed just for this problem. By setting the client to request PASV mode exchanges with the server, you cause all connections to be initiated by the client so you can use this filter.

The common application of a filter such as this is to deploy it in a router connecting your computer to the Internet (see Figure 14.5). By placing the filter between the LAN and the Internet, you're guaranteed all Internet traffic goes through the filter.

If your packet filter software is capable enough to examine the subnet of the source address based on which physical port delivers the message to the router, you can set up rules to avoid spoofed TCP/IP addresses, as described in the text in Figure 14.5. The idea behind spoofing is for messages from the Internet to appear to have originated from your LAN; the spoofing filter prevents this by rejecting messages coming on a port with impossible source addresses. The antispoofing filter is an important part of protecting machines on your network on which you've installed filters to limit particular services to machines on your subnet. For instance, suppose you've installed the Samba software on a Linux machine as a file server. You can configure Linux to reject all network traffic originating outside your subnet, preventing computers on the Internet from seeing the file server. If an attacker could pretend to be on your LAN, that safeguard would be bypassed. Defeat that attack with the antispoofing filter.

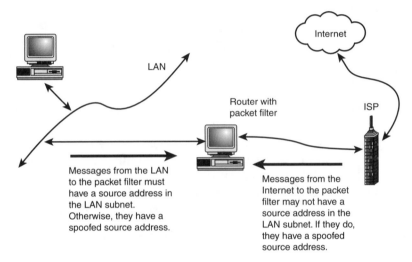

Figure 14.5: Packet filter deployment.

Packet filters are good, but they aren't bulletproof. They generally don't protect against attacks using the UDP protocol; because there's no formal connection opening with UDP as there is with TCP, the filter can't reject the opening message. Packet filters also might not protect against lower-level attacks, such as intentionally malformed ping messages, often called the "Ping of Death." Technically, the messages involved are Internet Control Message Protocol (ICMP) *echo* requests, but the common term is ping.

Standalone Firewalls

Examining more information than a packet filter enables firewall software to exercise a finer degree of control over what moves between your LAN and the Internet. Figure 14.6 shows an abbreviated form of the TCP/IP packet headers, illustrating the difference between packet filters and firewalls by highlighting what parts of a TCP/IP packet are examined. The firewall has all the information available to the packet filter—the source and destination TCP/IP address—but also can examine the source and destination port numbers and the content of the packet data.

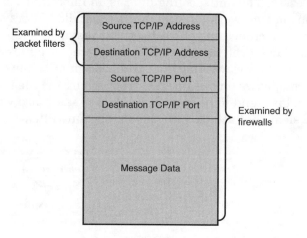

Figure 14.6: Packet filter and firewall information sources.

The port and packet data information gives a firewall far more power than the simpler packet filter, because the additional information gives the firewall the ability to look all the way up the protocol stack to the application layers. Using that information, a firewall can, in addition to controlling access to and from specific host addresses, do the following:

- Allow or disallow specific application services such as FTP or Web pages

- Allow or disallow access to services based on the content of the information being transferred

Combinations of these functions are possible too, such as allowing incoming FTP access from the Internet only to a specific, designated server.

The ability to screen traffic based on message content makes it possible to create filters for objectionable content, such as sites inappropriate for minors. (Note that it's very hard to define rules for that filtering, which is why there are companies whose business is to sell lists of sites you might want to filter for various reasons, along with filter software to act based on those lists.) Content screening also makes possible defenses against specific attacks by looking for telltale signatures in the incoming attacking packets. When the firewall detects those signatures, it discards the packets and logs the events.

The most direct implementation of a firewall uses the same architecture shown in Figure 14.5 but sites a firewall between the LAN and the ISP rather than a packet filter. This is the most secure application of a single firewall, because it protects all the computers behind the firewall.

There's a problem with the Figure 14.5 architecture, in that it provides no good place to locate publicly accessible servers. You don't want servers out on the Internet in front of the firewall, where they're unprotected, but you don't want them behind the firewall either, because you have to create holes in the firewall protection to permit access to the servers.

A variant of Figure 14.5, shown in Figure 14.7, is a good answer to this problem. The firewall router in Figure 14.7 has three ports, rather than the two on the packet filter in Figure 14.5. The third port connects to another LAN typically called the demilitarized zone (DMZ). The idea is that the computers in the DMZ are less secure than those back on the secure LAN, but in return those computers are accessible from the Internet. You put Web and FTP servers in the DMZ, keeping all other computers back on the secure LAN. The rules in the firewall prevent incoming traffic to the secure LAN, allowing only outgoing connections.

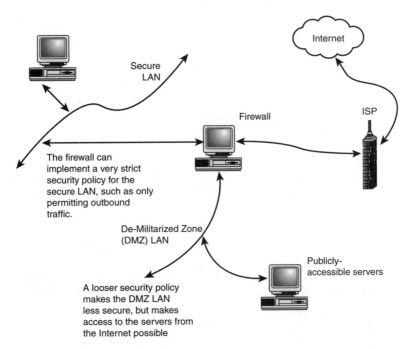

Figure 14.7: *Demilitarized zone (DMZ) used with a firewall.*

Even though the DMZ LAN is less secure, you would still want to restrict what can be done there. You'd want to use antispoofing filters, limit the allowable ports to those used by the servers on the LAN, and disallow access from known attacking sites.

You can extend the idea of segmenting your LANs for security, protecting each segment with a firewall and a different set of security rules. Just remember that firewalls themselves aren't a guarantee of security—you have to be disciplined about examining the firewall logs for suspicious events, and you have to be vigilant about discovering and applying software security patches. Most patches apply to operating systems or server software; besides the software manufacturers themselves, a good source for information about security patches and threats is the SANS Institute at http://www.sans.org.

On-Computer Firewalls

Don't interpret the figures in this chapter as meaning you're defenseless if you don't have a standalone router or firewall between your LAN and the Internet. Even if you use a product such as Internet Connection Sharing to let one of your computers tie a modem to your LAN, you can still improve your network security.

Start by analyzing the threats:

- The PC hosting the modem, ICS, and the network interface card (NIC) is vulnerable to attacks at all levels (refer to Figure 14.4).

- The LAN itself is reasonably protected from attack by the Network Address Translation (NAT) function built into ICS; the LAN uses private addresses not routable on the Internet itself. Threats from servers back to client software are possible, as is access to content you might choose to block in some circumstances.

The biggest threat is to the PC directly connected to the Internet; the answer is either to install a packet filter or firewall product directly on that computer or to have your ISP install packet filter or firewall protection for your access. The latter isn't widely available from ISPs; a more readily available solution is a PC-hosted solution such as Network ICE BlackICE Defender, which you'll learn about in the next section.

Sample Access and Firewall Products

This section covers typical products you can use with your LAN to route between the LAN and the Internet and to implement firewall protection for your network. This isn't a comprehensive list of products in either category; it's a description of specific products. We strongly believe in sticking with companies whose products work well and shunning those whose products give trouble; this list reflects products of companies we buy from.

3Com 56K and ISDN LAN Modems

Although you've learned two ways to connect a LAN to the Internet in this book—through a computer and through a router—we strongly prefer the router approach because it avoids the complexity of maintaining router and NAT functionality under Windows or Linux, and it works no matter which computers are switched on or busy.

3Com markets a dependable, inexpensive pair of routers designed just for this purpose in its OfficeConnect line of products: the 3Com 56K and ISDN LAN Modems. Both include a router, four-port 10Base-T hub, and a modem; the two differ only in the nature of the included modem. Figures 14.8 and 14.9 show the front and back view of the version with a 56Kbps modem; the ISDN LAN Modem differs only in that the lights on the front are slightly different and the connectors at the back include one for the incoming ISDN line. The RJ-11 analog telephone jacks are still there on the ISDN LAN Modem—you can plug telephone or fax devices into the two analog connectors for access to either of the telephone lines through the ISDN circuit.

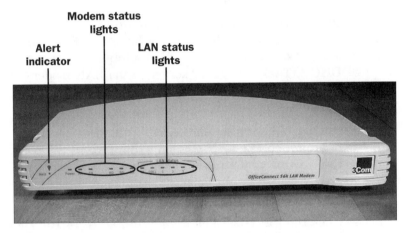

Figure 14.8: 3Com 56K LAN Modem front view.

Perhaps the most interesting characteristic of these products is that you're not paying much more for the router than you would for an equivalent-quality modem and hub—for example, we've seen the 56K LAN Modem available on the Internet for under $240.

Installation of the LAN modems is very simple. After you wire up the telephone line, power, and LAN connections, you follow the steps in Example 14.1.

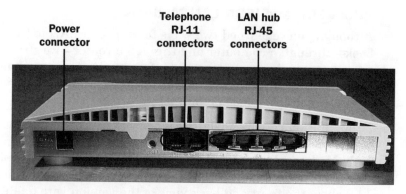

Figure 14.9: 3Com 56K LAN Modem rear view.

Example 14.1 Configuring a 3Com 56K LAN Modem

To configure a LAN modem, follow these steps:

1. Turn on the LAN modem.

2. Identify the PC you'll use to configure the LAN modem. Check its network configuration to be sure it has TCP/IP installed and that the TCP/IP stack is configured to obtain its address automatically via DHCP. (There's a DCHP server in the LAN modem.) If not, check back to Chapter 8, "Configuring Your System Software," to learn how to do the necessary reconfiguration.

3. Open a Web browser on the PC. No matter what Web address you try to browse to, the LAN modem will intercept the request and give you the starting configuration page shown in Figure 14.10. The defaults are most likely right for most settings in the LAN modem; what you need to configure is the setup defining your ISP.

4. Click the ISP Wizard on the left of Figure 14.10 to get to the screen shown in Figure 14.11 where you'll tell the LAN modem the name and dialing parameters for your ISP. What you fill in for the ISP name is irrelevant except as identification to you (you can set up multiple ISP profiles). Most homes won't have a Dial Out Prefix setting; offices using switchboards commonly require you to dial 9 or some other digit for a local call. (Of course, office telephone lines routed through a switchboard aren't likely to complete a V.90 telephone call, either; they'll fall back to V.34 operation at 24–33.6 Kbps.)

5. Finish filling in the form. The string *70 is common to turn off call waiting. Enter an area code in the telephone number if you need one to dial your ISP. The User ID and Password fields are the same as the account name and password information you give Windows or Linux

for dialup connections. Most ISPs won't require you to explicitly enter the DNS address; if you need to specify an address, your ISP should have given it to you. Click Continue when you're finished.

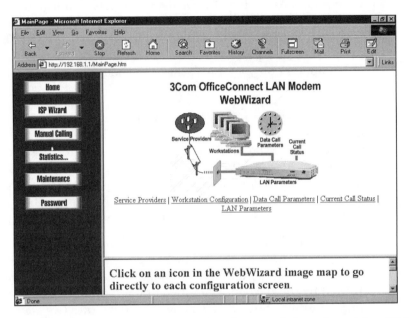

Figure 14.10: *3Com 56K LAN Modem initial configuration Web page.*

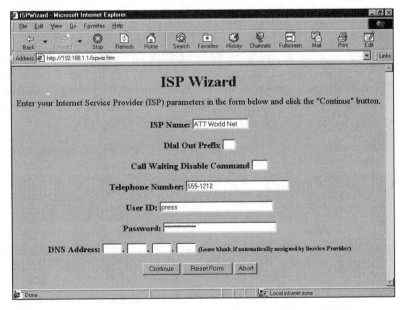

Figure 14.11: *3Com 56K LAN Modem ISP Wizard Web page.*

6. After you've done that, the LAN modem should be operational. Close and reopen the Web browser (you might have to click the Refresh button, too) and you should see traffic on the LAN and hear the modem dial out. As soon as the modem connects and logs in to your ISP, you should start to receive the data for your Web home page on that computer, indicating the connection is established and in place. If you've checked and possibly corrected the protocol stack settings for the other computers on your LAN, they too should have complete Internet access.

Many people want to know how quickly their calls send data and other characteristics known to the LAN modem. To get ready to do that, or to reconfigure the LAN modem if required, enter the address http://192.168.1.1 into your Web browser. That's the address the LAN modem assigns to itself by default, so accessing that address in a Web browser opens a conversation with the Web server in the LAN modem. You'll see the page in Figure 14.10 when you do.

Click Current Call Status on the right of the opening page and you'll see the page in Figure 14.12. The most significant information in Figure 14.12 is the first line—the Connect Message—which shows the information returned by the modem when it completed connecting the call. The initial number in the string, 26400, shows the data rate (we connected through lines incapable of supporting V.90 connections); the remaining terms indicate automatic error correction (ARQ), the line signaling in use (V.34), the data link protocol (LAPM), and modem-level data compression (V.42bis).

The rest of the information on the page is straightforward—the IP address in use is the IP address assigned for the current call to the modem by the ISP; the DNS addresses were provided via the PPP protocol when the modem made the connection; the Data call options note that the PPP protocol and PAP authentication are in use, with no PPP-level compression active. The word *octets* is synonymous with *byte*.

You can review and change the way the modem manages the telephone line, too, using the Web page in Figure 14.13.

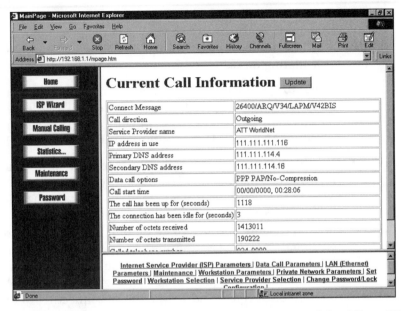

Figure 14.12: *Current Call Information screen of the 3Com 56K LAN Modem ISP Wizard Web page.*

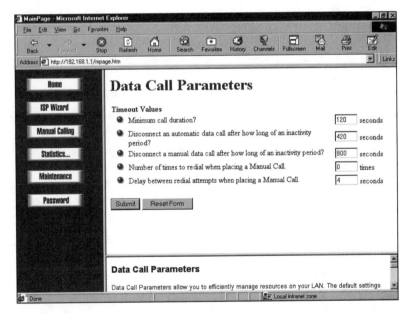

Figure 14.13: *Data Call Parameters screen of the 3Com 56K LAN Modem ISP Wizard Web page.*

You'll mostly use automatic data calls, reflecting the fact that the modem will dial out automatically when some computer on your LAN tries to send a message out to the Internet. Here's what the call parameters related to automatic dialing do:

- **Minimum call duration.** You can control how long a call has to be active before the inactivity timer starts. You'd at least want this time to be as long as it takes to log in with your ISP; setting it to the default of 120 seconds (two minutes) should work in most cases.

- **Disconnect an automatic call after how long of an inactivity period?** The modem has no direct way to know when you're finished using the Internet, so it uses this timer instead. The idea is that if you don't send or receive any messages for as long as this timer states, there's probably nothing going on and it's reasonable to hang up the telephone line. Your computers won't know that's happened; if you send a message after the telephone line drops, all you'll notice (unless you hear the dial sequence) is that there's a longer delay (while the line connects) before the server you're connecting to responds.

Even though the defaults are likely what you want, the LAN modems are highly configurable to adapt to almost any requirement. You can control what ISP a given workstation can use, and you can prevent specific workstations from accessing the Internet. You can turn the NAT function off, using static TCP/IP addresses, and you can control specific modem functions such as the speaker volume and use and dialing parameter string.

3Com OfficeConnect Internet Firewall

The LAN modems you learned about in the last section don't include packet filters or firewalls. If you want that sort of security for your Internet connection, you might want to look at a product such as the 3Com OfficeConnect Internet Firewall. You can implement the same functions with a properly configured Linux system acting as both router and firewall; the Internet Firewall has the advantage that it's far simpler to set up.

The Internet Firewall uses RJ-45 10Base-T connections for all its interfaces. Versions are available with two ports, one for the LAN and one for the modem, or with three ports, one for the LAN, one for a DMZ, and one for the modem. Figure 14.14 shows the two models; the one on the left is the two-port model 25, whereas the one on the right is the three-port model DMZ.

Figure 14.14: *3Com OfficeConnect Internet Firewall model 25 and model DMZ. (Photo courtesy 3Com Corporation)*

Both models of the OfficeConnect Internet Firewall provide a broad set of security features through tools to simplify firewall configuration:

- Deny incoming connection attempts from the Internet.

- Examine packet contents and connection state to block denial of service, spoofing, and other network-layer attacks.

- Block or screen Web data to guard against attacks via Java or Active X technology.

- Log all security-flagged events.

- Alert the network administrator to an ongoing attack.

- Permit Web access only to specific sites, or deny access to a list of sites. Controlled access sites can be defined by a list developed and maintained by a third party.

- Hide a LAN behind a NAT translation layer. An embedded DHCP server simplifies configuring workstations on the LAN.

The firewall configuration process is via an embedded Web server, so (as with the LAN modems) you can configure the firewall through a Web browser, with no special software required.

Network ICE BlackICE Defender

As powerful as the 3Com OfficeConnect Internet Firewall is, it's relatively expensive, with (in early 2000) a street price a little under $500 for the model 25 and a little over $1,000 for the model DMZ. That's inexpensive protection for offices and small businesses but quite possibly too expensive for homes and home offices. You have an alternative if that description applies to you, which is that you can protect your computers using firewall

software such as BlackICE Defender from Network ICE Corporation
(http://www.networkice.com/Products/BlackICE/blackice%20defender.htm).
As Figure 14.15 shows, you have two options for how you deploy the product, depending on whether you connect to the Internet through a modem on
a PC or through a modem in an external router. The LAN on the left in the
figure uses an external router such as in the 3Com LAN Modem for the
Internet connection. Because the LAN Modem gives each computer direct
access to the Internet, the only protection inherently available to each computer is that of the NAT layer, and there's no protection whatsoever if you
choose to use routable static TCP/IP addresses on your LAN. If you want
firewall-class protection, you need to put a firewall on each computer.

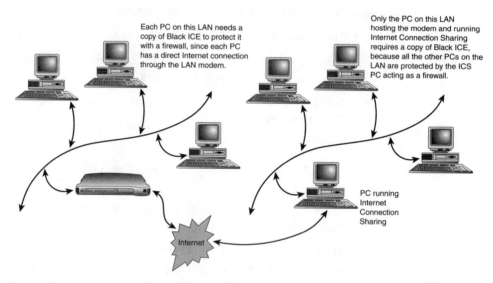

Each PC on this LAN needs a
copy of Black ICE to protect it
with a firewall, since each PC
has a direct Internet connection
through the LAN modem.

Only the PC on this LAN
hosting the modem and running
Internet Connection Sharing
requires a copy of Black ICE,
because all the other PCs on the
LAN are protected by the ICS
PC acting as a firewall.

PC running
Internet
Connection
Sharing

Internet

Figure 14.15: Network ICE Corporation BlackICE Defender deployment.

The LAN on the right uses Internet Connection Sharing on a PC rather
than a standalone router, giving you a less expensive option for firewall
protection—firewall software such as BlackICE running on the PC. Figure
14.16 shows a listing of detected intrusions on a PC immediately after
installing BlackICE. The top item (showing the intruder as 0.0.0.0) is an
artifact of the installation, but the second one is a detected scan of the computer.

Double-clicking the intruder, or clicking the Attacks tab, gives the display
in Figure 14.17, showing the intruder's attack used the WhatsUp program,
a network diagnostic tool you'll learn about in Chapter 17, "Troubleshooting
Network Problems." WhatsUp isn't an attack per se, but it can be used to
scan for open TCP/IP ports and reveal information about a target computer.

BlackICE lets you know the scan occurred and logs information about the source of the intrusion including the originating TCP/IP address, which can be used to track down the individual with the help of your ISP.

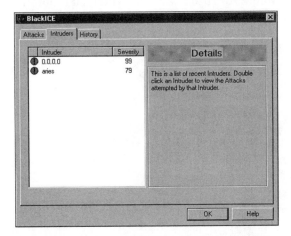

Figure 14.16: *BlackICE intruders list.*

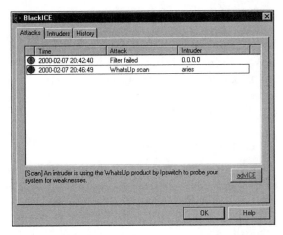

Figure 14.17: *BlackICE attack detail.*

BlackICE also provides a graphical display of your network's recent history of attacks and network traffic (see Figure 14.18). You can select the time-frame for the display, ranging from 90 minutes to as much as 90 days, using the Interval selections at the upper left. The top graph shows the times when suspicious or critical intrusions were detected, whereas the lower one shows the level of network traffic. High levels of network traffic unrelated to activities of users on your network could correspond to an attempted denial of service attack, attempting to render your LAN useless or cut off from the Internet by flooding the LAN and its Internet connection with higher levels of traffic than the equipment can handle. Unless you have a very high speed connection to the Internet, your Internet connection has a lower possible data rate than your LAN, so a denial of service attack would only succeed in preventing Internet access.

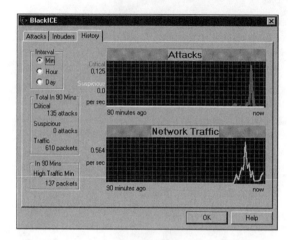

Figure 14.18: BlackICE history display.

BlackICE is highly configurable to tailor it to your LAN and the security threat you face. LANs using a dialup connection and NAT, for example, aren't as at risk as those using a permanent connection and static routable TCP/IP addresses; you'd want to set up tighter security for the latter case. Follow the steps in Example 14.2 to configure BlackICE.

EXAMPLE

Example 14.2   Configuring BlackICE

As you read this example, keep in mind that BlackICE is really a toolkit you can configure to meet your needs. For example, you'll see in the example how to configure BlackICE to trust the computers on your LAN. Combine that with the setting that lets BlackICE block access to the file sharing ports on the PC and you have a way to use TCP/IP for file sharing (very convenient if you have computers running Windows NT, Windows 2000, or Linux) without letting your disks be vulnerable to attack from the Internet. Follow these steps:

1. Open the BlackICE configuration dialog box by right-clicking the BlackICE icon in the Windows taskbar, and then selecting the Configure BlackICE choice in the resulting pop-up menu. When you do, the BlackICE Configuration dialog box opens showing the Back Trace tab (see Figure 14.19).

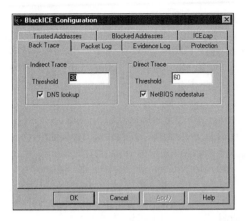

Figure 14.19: BlackICE back trace configuration dialog box.

2. The Back Trace tab lets you configure how BlackICE responds when it detects an intrusion. Indirect tracing means BlackICE is to find out what it can about an intruder without using methods that could be detected as a back trace by the intruder; direct tracing uses methods that can be detected if the intruder has defenses running. Because the direct back trace can potentially be detected, the default setup sets it for a higher severity attack threshold than for indirect traces.

3. The next tab in the dialog box, Packet Log, lets you record to a file *every* packet seen on the network by the computer (see Figure 14.20). You'd enable the packet log function only if your computer is actively under attack, because the log file will get *very* large *very* quickly, and because the logging operation is likely to slow down your computer noticeably.

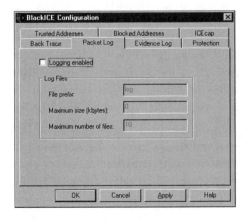

Figure 14.20: BlackICE packet log configuration dialog box.

4. The Evidence Log tab lets you control where and how BlackICE records evidence gathered in response to an intrusion (see Figure 14.21). The information is written to a file if you enable evidence logging. The default file prefix, evd%d, creates files with names starting with evd001, evd002, and so on, up to the maximum number of files specified in the dialog box. When it reaches that limit (evd032 for the configuration in the figure) it starts over again, wrapping around to a prefix of evd001 in this example. Evidence files have an extension of .enc. The maximum size controls how big a single file is permitted to be; the maximum number of seconds (86,400 seconds, or 24 hours, by default) a single file can span. Evidence files aren't directly readable; you need a program such as the Windows NT 4 Server Network Monitor to open and decode the file.

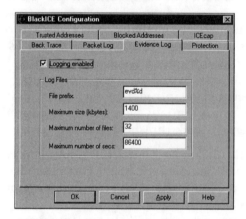

Figure 14.21: *BlackICE evidence log configuration dialog box.*

5. You can control how rigorously BlackICE protects your computer using the Protection tab in the configuration dialog box (see Figure 14.22). Setting the security to Trusting blocks essentially nothing other than file sharing, and permits even that on your subnet (see Chapter 7 for more information about subnets). If you check the box at the bottom of the dialog box to allow Internet file sharing, BlackICE is essentially disabled.

Cautious security blocks inbound activity on any of the normal ports—the ones with predefined functions. Transient ports are not blocked, so FTP should work without any changes.

The Nervous security level blocks inbound activity on all TCP ports and predefined UDP ports. You'll have to reconfigure your FTP client to use PASV mode if you set the security level to Nervous or Paranoid.

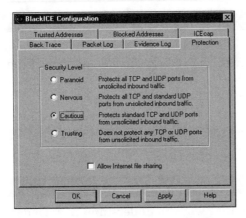

Figure 14.22: BlackICE protection level configuration dialog box.

The Paranoid security level blocks all inbound connections. Some Internet applications are likely to no longer work properly, but your computer is as secure as BlackICE can make it.

6. Finally, BlackICE lets you specify TCP/IP addresses the program should trust, allowing any operation, and reports addresses that have been blocked, allowing no operations. Use the Trusted Addresses and Blocked Addresses tabs, respectively, for those functions (see Figure 14.23). You use the Add and Delete buttons in the Trusted Addresses dialog box to manage the list, entering the TCP/IP address of computers you want to be trusted in the Add button dialog box. The Blocked Addresses list reflects computers BlackICE has detected as attempting to intrude into your system and blocked; computers only get added to the list if auto-blocking is turned on.

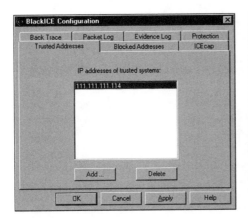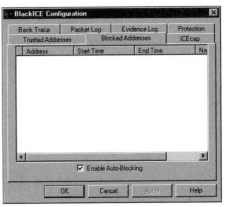

Figure 14.23: BlackICE trusted and blocked address configuration dialog boxes.

Summary

You've learned in this chapter how to use a router to simplify connection of your LAN to the Internet and reduce the dependence of connected computers on the computer hosting a modem. You've learned how to think about attacks on your network and computers in terms of the seven-layer model and what kinds of tools you can use to counter those attacks. You've looked at the key characteristics of typical router and security products and learned about how to choose among them.

What's Next

The next chapter examines ways to understand how loaded your network is and teaches you strategies you can use to improve performance. The chapter after that shows you specific products you can use to implement those strategies.

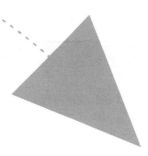

## 15

Evaluating Network Performance

In this chapter you will learn

- To understand the impact of different traffic loads on your LAN's performance

- What your existing network hardware and freely available software can do to help measure and analyze network loading

- How you can change your LAN structure to improve performance

You learned a rule of thumb for estimating in Chapter 4, "Picking Your LAN Cable Technology and Speed": You're likely to get no more than 80% of the signaling rate of your LAN in delivered performance. If you're not careful, though, you'll get far less. In this chapter, you're going to look at network performance again with an eye to what determines the actual performance, how you can evaluate whether you're getting the performance you should, and what the possible approaches are to improving the performance of a slow network.

The bases for a better understanding of network performance are also in Chapter 4; the two-key performance measures on your LAN are latency and jitter, and the key determinant of how bad latency and jitter get in your network is the collision rate on your network cable.

Understanding Network Performance

Let's do some thought experiments to understand what distinguishes a
LAN running at top speed from one crumbling under its load. Example 15.1
is the first experiment, helping you set a baseline for the most your network is capable of.

EXAMPLE

Example 15.1 Performance of Two Computers on a LAN with One-Way Traffic

These thought experiments range from the highest performance possible
from a LAN to the lowest:

1. Imagine two computers networked together using the UDP protocol to
   send data from one to the other. UDP requires no return acknowledgements, so the traffic on the LAN is completely one way. You could
   approximate this experiment using Microsoft NetMeeting to send
   audio and video data from one computer to the other, sending no
   return audio or video.

2. After you start transmission, the sending computer looks to transmit
   every time it creates a packet. Because there's no other traffic on the
   LAN, the sending computer transmits immediately, with minimum
   latency and minimum jitter. Collisions don't occur, because no other
   computer is transmitting. The network achieves its highest possible
   performance.

The key to performance in Example 15.1 is the absence of traffic on the
LAN, leading to no jitter, latency, or collisions.

Example 15.2 changes the experiment somewhat, adding return traffic from
the receiving computer.

EXAMPLE

Example 15.2 Performance of Two Computers on a LAN with Limited Two-Way Traffic

In this experiment, we'll add a little additional traffic to the LAN—just
enough to confirm packets are getting through reliably:

1. Imagine two computers networked together again, but in this experiment we'll use the TCP protocol to send data from one computer to the
   other. TCP connections require approximately 10% of the data transmission rate to send back acknowledgements, so if you're sending at a
   full 10Mbps, the return traffic will be approximately 1Mbps.

2. You can perform this experiment and measure network performance
   by copying a very large file from one computer to another, timing the
   copy while there's no other activity on the LAN. The acknowledgement

packets are short compared to the data transmission packets, and there aren't all that many of them, so the chances of a collision or of the computer sending the file seeing other network traffic are fairly low. You lose a little network performance, primarily due to collisions. If you actually run this experiment using two fast computers through a hub that indicates collisions with a light on the front, you'll see that collisions do in fact happen.

Performance went down somewhat in Example 15.2 because of collisions on the LAN. You'll see in Example 15.3 how increasing collisions reduces performance.

EXAMPLE

Example 15.3   Performance of Two Computers on a LAN with Symmetric Two-Way Traffic

The next step up from Example 15.2 is to make the traffic between the two computers symmetric, transferring data both ways between two computers at the same time:

1. Construct the third experiment again with two computers on a LAN, but this time transfer a large file both ways, with both transfers going on simultaneously. You could run the experiment by having one person at each computer start a transfer.

2. While the file transfers run, there are both data transfer and acknowledgement messages being sent from both computers. They are both actively contending for access to the shared media at the same time, so there's a significant probability of both latency and collision in transmission. If you run the experiment and calculate the total data transmission rate, you'll find it's significantly less than that in Example 15.2.

You're seeing increasing contention for access to the LAN as the thought experiments progress, which is causing sharply reduced performance. The final experiment, Example 15.4, illustrates that the situation can be even worse than Example 15.3 suggested.

EXAMPLE

Example 15.4   Performance of Many Computers on a LAN with *N*-Way Traffic

Instead of just two computers, let's extend the situation to many computers all active on the same LAN at once:

1. Be it from Dell, Micron, IBM, or some other company, haul out your favorite computer catalog and imagine ordering several hundred computers. Get some LAN hubs with a lot of ports while you're at it, and

chain the hubs together so you have enough ports for all the computers. Wire it all up, pay the electric bill, and start the computers running.

2. On each computer, create a test file that's several gigabytes large so transfers last long enough to get the experiment running and then launch the experiment by starting file transfers from every computer to every other computer (this will take a lot of people!). If you were to measure network performance while the transfers are finally all running, you'd find most of the network bandwidth going to collisions and error recovery; very little data would get through. The network is overloaded and delivering very little performance.

Except for the degree of loading, which we intentionally made extreme in Example 15.4, many real-world LANs resemble what we described in the experiment: Too many computers strung together on the same shared media segment, with people sitting idle and grumbling about how badly the network performs.

Assessing Your Network Load

Figuring out where and how bad the load is in your network doesn't have to be a science project for small LANs; sometimes all you need is a little thought.

Start the assessment with the network map you learned to maintain in Chapter 5, "Installing Your LAN Wiring," paying close attention to the network activities you noted each computer would perform. Update the map if it has been a while since you created it, and watch how each computer is being used to make sure your prediction was correct.

Next, see what you can learn from indicators on the network hardware. There are typically two sorts of indicators to look at:

- **Hub indicators.** Many hubs have LEDs on the front to indicate both activity on individual ports and packet collisions. The Intel InBusiness 8-Port 10/100 Fast Hub has both: the LEDs marked 1–8 flicker to indicate traffic on each port (and change color to reflect whether the port is operating at 10 or 100Mbps), whereas the two LEDs at the left side light to indicate packet collisions at 10 or 100Mbps, respectively (see Figure 15.1).

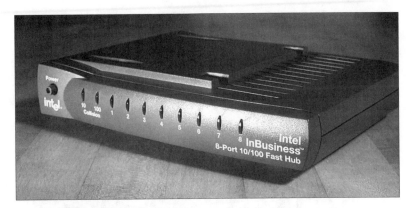

Figure 15.1: *Intel InBusiness 8-Port 10/100 Fast Hub.*

Other hubs organize the lights differently. The 3Com OfficeConnect Dual Speed Hub 8, for example, offers (left-to-right) alert and power lights, packet collision lights, port status lights, and a sliding bar of lights at the right to indicate overall LAN loading (see Figure 15.2).

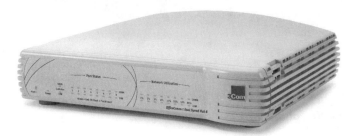

Figure 15.2: *3Com OfficeConnect Dual Speed Hub 8 (photo courtesy 3Com Corporation).*

- **Network Interface Card (NIC) indicators.** There are typically at least two LEDs on the face plate of internal NICs. On the 3Com 3C905C-TX-M, for example, the link integrity lights show that the NIC is properly receiving a signal from the hub and at what speed (see Figure 15.3). The link integrity light remains off until the device driver installs, after which it turns yellow to indicate link traffic of either speed.

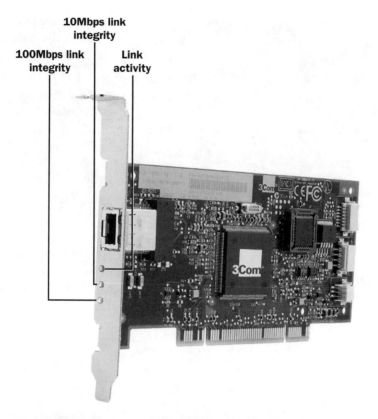

Figure 15.3: *3Com 3C905C-TX-M Network Interface Card indicator LEDs (photo courtesy 3Com Corporation).*

There are differences in how different hub manufacturers implement load indicator lights (such as the sliding scale lights on the 3Com OfficeConnect Dual Speed Hub 8) and differences in how you would interpret different levels of activity in the lights. The collision lights are better defined, since there's a clear meaning to collision, but even those lights can vary in what rate of collisions cause noticeable brightness in the light. Despite that, there is value for rough load assessment in both types of lights. Suppose your network consists of one or more hubs chained together, with computers connected to the hubs. Under those circumstances, you can draw the following conclusions. Some of these also relate to troubleshooting, which you'll learn more about in Chapter 17, "Troubleshooting Network Problems":

- **Backbone connectivity.** The chain of one or more hubs forming your network is called the network *backbone*. The interconnected hubs form a single LAN segment, so the indicator lights on all the hubs should respond the same (particularly if all the hubs are the same model). If you see a difference in the hubs at one end of the network versus the ones at the other end, you've got a cable problem or other hardware issue.

- **Light or heavy loading.** Simplistically, a lightly loaded network will perform near optimally, whereas a heavily loaded network is going to limit performance. If the performance indicators are constantly on at high levels (or flickering in a sustained way, depending on your hub), you can expect to start to see collisions. Even before collisions become visible, though, you may start to see some performance degradation as the network load goes up because the individual computers will be waiting for access to the shared media segment.

- **Light or heavy collision rate.** After the loading on your LAN becomes noticeable, you'll start to see collisions on the hub indicators. Look at how regularly collisions occur; if there's just an infrequent flicker, the LAN is operating normally. If the collisions are constant, your LAN is probably overloaded and is definitely not giving you the best performance possible.

The activity light on each NIC gives you much the same insight as the activity lights on the hubs; if there's always heavy activity on the LAN, you're likely to be seeing a lot of collisions.

Evaluation Tools

Recall from Chapter 7, "Network Software—Protocol Stacks and Applications," that TCP/IP addresses are decomposed into a subnet number and a host or node number, and that there are two reserved host addresses in each block of TCP/IP addresses. Of those two, one (with the host number set to zero) is the network number; the other (with the host number set to its maximum value in the block) is the *broadcast address*. Messages sent to the broadcast address are received and processed by every computer on the LAN segment. The need to process broadcast messages results in a requirement for normal computers to handle messages sent to two TCP/IP addresses, the address of the computer and the subnet broadcast address.

It's possible to set up computers that operate differently, though, receiving and processing all messages on the LAN regardless of the actual destination TCP/IP address. You can do that by changing the setup of the network interface card with the appropriate software. NICs set up that way are said to be in *promiscuous mode*; computers running software that puts the NIC into promiscuous mode often do so to monitor and decode LAN traffic. Computers watching LAN traffic are commonly known as *sniffers*.

More elaborate versions of sniffers can see and report packets on the LAN that are "broken"—packets that are the victims of collisions or otherwise malformed when received. Those more-capable sniffers require specialized network hardware; both computer-based and dedicated sniffers can display the traffic on the LAN and give you some insight into the traffic patterns.

Aside from the Network Monitor sniffer software and Performance Monitor network statistics available in Windows NT Server and Windows 2000 Server, capable sniffer software for Windows (such as the Sniffer Portable Analysis Suite from Network Associates; see `http://www.sniffer.com/asp_set/products/tnv/pas.asp`) is expensive. Linux users have a clear advantage over Windows users in that regard, with a relatively large number of sniffer tools available for free (see `http://www.freshmeat.com/search.php3?link=&mode=appindex&query=sniffer`, and in particular `http://ksniffer.veracity.nu`).

Ksniffer can't reveal the collision rate on your LAN, but it can tell you the data rate it sees on your LAN. Ksniffer is capable of operating the NIC in promiscuous mode, so by experimenting with different loading—controlling what's going on at each computer—you can find out what load each application presents and can discover at what point performance starts to decline because of excessive traffic.

Figure 15.4 shows the general interface statistics from Ksniffer. The network activity being reported in the figure is a transfer of a large number of relatively large files from a Windows 2000 server to a Windows 98 client over a 10Base-T LAN. The transfer rate—a little over 3.6Mbps—suggests there's performance penalty due to the TCP acknowledgement packets being sent back from the client to the server, since the transfer rate is only 36% of the signaling rate on the LAN.

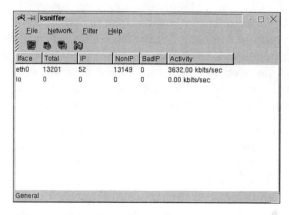

Figure 15.4: Ksniffer general interface statistics.

Don't leap to simple conclusions, though, when analyzing LAN performance, because the analysis isn't that simple. Consider these additional facts:

- The server in this case is a dual Pentium II processor machine with each processor running at 300MHz.

- The client is only a Pentium processor running at 166MHz.

- Transfers to a much faster client (a Pentium III at 600MHz) ran at a transfer rate of 4.5Mbps.

- Transfers to the faster client from another server, one on a 100Mbps LAN segment connected through a dual-speed hub to the 10Mbps segment, ran at an even faster 6.4Mbps.

- The hubs do not show significant collision activity until the transfers from the server on the 100Mbps LAN.

With this additional information, it's reasonable to conclude that the 10Mbps LAN itself is operating as effectively as it can for the transfer from the server to the slow client. Improvements in the performance of that transfer would require changes in the computer hardware or updates to the LAN to 100Mbps technology.

The default configuration for Ksniffer does not use promiscuous mode for the NIC to sample all LAN traffic independent of source or destination. You have to use the File, Options command to get the Preferences dialog box shown in Figure 15.5. The App Prefs tab on that dialog box has the setting you want; turn on the Promiscuous Mode check box to see all LAN traffic.

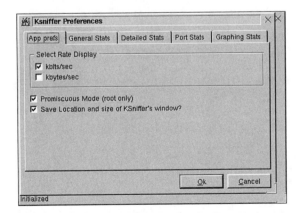

Figure 15.5: *Ksniffer Preferences dialog box.*

You saw in Figure 15.4 that Ksniffer reports both TCP/IP and non-TCP/IP packets. If you use the Network, Detailed Interface Stats command you'll see the display in Figure 15.6 showing a further breakdown of the traffic on the interface you select (we picked the first NIC, called eth0 in Linux, in the figure). Figure 15.6 shows not only a breakdown of the TCP/IP packets but also a count of IPX and other non-TCP/IP packets.

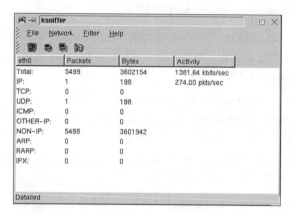

Figure 15.6: Ksniffer Detailed Interface Stats display.

You'd use the detailed statistics to verify tests you run are really loading the network the way you expect. For example, if you run a UDP-based performance test, such as in Example 15.1, you'd expect Ksniffer to be incrementing only the UDP traffic counters and not the TCP ones.

Improvement Strategies

Thinking about and measuring network performance in this chapter has shown that many factors can affect network performance:

- Network transmission rate, which is typically 10 or 100Mbps per second, but possibly 1Mbps on home telephone line networks

- Number of computers contending for access on the LAN segment

- Types of network traffic generated by each computer, such as UDP or TCP

- Speed of each computer

Each of these factors, with the possible exception of protocol, can be corrected in its own way to improve performance:

- **Network transmission rate.** If you had the foresight to install Category 5 cable and NICs capable of operation at either 10 or 100Mbps, you might be able to speed up your 10Base-T network simply by replacing a 10Mbps hub with one capable of operation at either 10 or 100Mbps. You don't have that option with telephone line or coaxial cable networks, which is one of the reasons why 10Base-T or 100Base-T technology is so widely favored.

- **Number of computers.** It's impractical to expect you to take computers out of service simply to improve the performance of the ones that remain, but it is true that fewer computers on a network segment generate less traffic and therefore attain higher performance. Instead of taking computers out of service, therefore, the answer is to create more network segments.

- **Computer speed.** Faster computers improve network performance to a point, but typically you'll have to either replace or upgrade the computers to make them faster. Keep in mind, though, that many computers lack the memory required to let them run at full speed in normal use; if your machines are at 16MB or 32MB, consider upgrading them to 64MB or 128MB.

The most interesting possibility for increasing network performance is increasing the number of segments, which reduces collisions on heavily loaded networks.

Partitioning Your Network with a Router

You can subdivide networks running TCP/IP or IPX/SPX using a router (see Figure 15.7). By connecting multiple LAN segments to the router and dividing the existing computers among those segments, you can isolate groups of computers from each other. Computers are most commonly grouped geographically using this approach; a segment on the router would typically connect to computers in a specific area, which might have the effect of separating traffic from computers on different floors of a building.

Figure 15.7 ignores the mechanics of how individual computers are connected to routers—a detail we've expanded in Figure 15.8, in which we've shown how you can use hubs to expand individual router ports to the many ports you're likely to want. Router ports are relatively expensive, far more expensive than ports on hubs. For that reason, people typically use a scheme like that in Figure 15.8.

Figure 15.8 makes clear the weakness of the router-based approach to partitioning your LAN segments: The partitioning does nothing to reduce contention among computers on the same hub. If you have a heavy traffic load among physically close computers, there may be no benefit to installing the router.

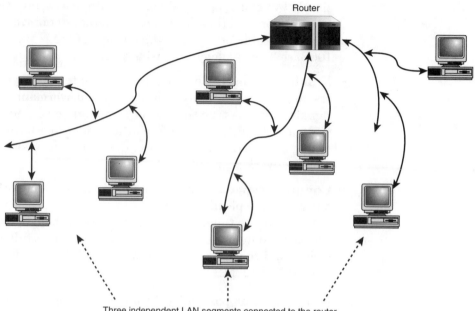

Three independent LAN segments connected to the router

Figure 15.7: Partitioning a LAN with a router.

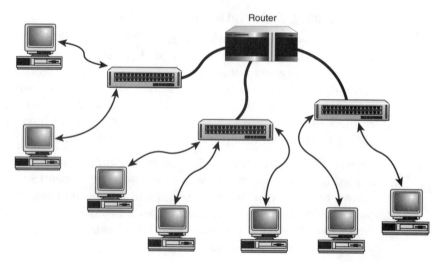

Figure 15.8: Connecting computers to a router.

Partitioning Your Network with an Ethernet Switch

There are other devices, called *switches*, you can use to partition your network. *Ethernet switches* replace hubs in your LAN. (There are also *Layer-2* and *Layer-3* switches, referring to the protocol stack layer at which switching occurs, that can replace routers and increase performance. See the next chapter for details.)

The key difference between a hub and an Ethernet switch is that the switch permits more than one packet to flow across the LAN segment at the same time. Figure 15.9 shows how a hub works; after we examine hub operation, you'll learn what's different in a switch.

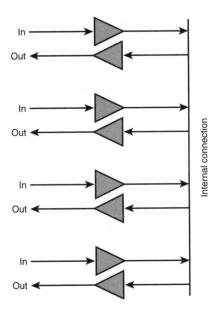

Figure 15.9: *Internal Ethernet hub structure.*

Recall from Figure 2.20 in Chapter 2, "Kinds of Networks," that 10/100Base-T Ethernet uses separate wires for the transmit and receive signal path. When a packet arrives on any of the input lines to the hub, the signal is transferred to an internal connection that in turn transmits the signal on the output lines of every port. You can see how collisions happen in a hub; if more than one input line is active, two signals are transferred to the internal connection, corrupting them both.

An Ethernet switch has a more complicated structure, as shown in Figure 15.10. Instead of a single internal connection, there's an entire array of connections. Intelligence in the switch tracks which physical NIC addresses the switch sees on each input port. When a packet arrives at some input port, the switch figures out which output port leads to the NIC having the correct destination physical address (broadcast packets go to all ports) and connects the input port only to the correct output port. Because the input port connects selectively to the output port, it's possible to make several input to output connections at the same time—up to four for the switch in Figure 15.10.

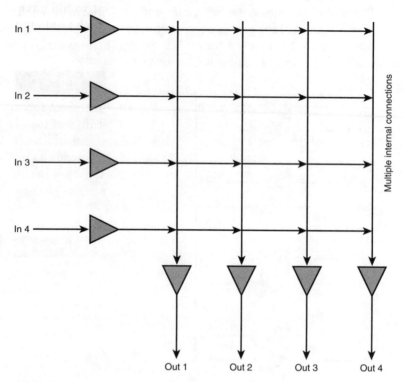

Figure 15.10: Internal Ethernet switch structure.

The ability to create multiple input to output paths simultaneously, and to alter those connections dynamically based on packet addresses, lets the switch effectively divide the LAN into as many segments as there are switch ports, even though the connections through the switch operate as if they were one segment for broadcast and routing purposes. Computers connected directly to switch ports see less contention on the LAN as a result and may be able to transmit and receive at the same time to further boost performance.

You can deploy switches as hub replacements or (if you don't need the other functions of a router) to replace more expensive routers in your LAN. In the latter case, the LAN would use the approach of Figure 15.8, but would cost less because Ethernet switches are far less expensive than routers.

You can also combine the two ideas, creating cascaded switch networks. Instead of the router and hubs in Figure 15.8, you'd have four Ethernet switches. Traffic that would have been local to a hub remains local but is switched to improve performance. Traffic that would have transited the router instead transits the central switch, which is likely to be faster than the routing operation would have been.

Summary

You learned in this chapter about the many different factors determining the performance of a LAN and discovered a range of tools—from indicator lights to sophisticated monitoring software—that can help you measure the performance of your LAN and diagnose why slowdowns occur. You then analyzed the steps you can take to improve network performance, ranging from computer and network hardware upgrades to changes in the LAN topology itself.

What's Next

Armed with the background knowledge of how to measure and analyze LAN performance, you're ready to explore specific products and approaches to enhancing the performance of your network.

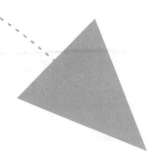

## 16

Enhancing Your Network

In this chapter you will learn

- What equipment to use to connect a cable or DSL modem to your LAN

- How to specify and choose servers for your network

- How to keep your network running and protect your work when the power fails

This chapter covers a number of products you can use to enhance your LAN, either by adding capabilities or by improving performance. Product categories you'll examine in this chapter include

- Routers

- Switches

- Servers

- Uninterruptible Power Supplies

As with the other product coverage in this book, this chapter is a look at good, useful products, not a comprehensive catalog.

Routers

You learned in Chapter 7, "Network Software—Protocol Stacks and Applications," that a router is a special-purpose computer operating at protocol layer 3 and dedicated to forwarding network messages to their ultimate destination. Refinements to the basic router functionality you learned about in Chapter 14, "Advanced Internet Access," include Network Address Translation (NAT) and firewalling for improved security.

Many of the cable and DSL modems being deployed for high-speed Internet access are external devices, using a 10Base-T Ethernet port for connection to a local computer. Figure 16.1 shows the usual installation: Even though there's an Ethernet connection, there's simply a two-device connection with a crossover cable (see Chapter 5, "Installing Your LAN Wiring"). You can get more complex units incorporating a router or NAT services, as you saw in Chapter 14, but the direct modem-to-PC configuration is very common.

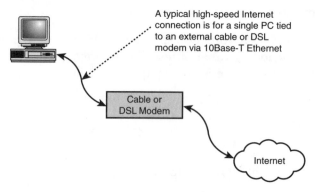

Figure 16.1: Single computer external cable or DSL modem installation.

You have two options for upgrading a basic setup such as the one in Figure 16.1 to support a LAN, add NAT, or add firewall capabilities:

- Replace the modem with a combined modem/router unit
- Add a router between the modem and computer

Replacing the existing modem with a combined modem/router isn't always an option. Your service provider might not offer an integrated modem/router product, the product they offer might not have the capabilities you want, or there might be a high price for the upgrade.

Instead, you should look into the option of keeping your existing modem and adding a separate router (and hub if necessary). If you choose this option, your setup will change from that in Figure 16.1 to the one in Figure 16.2.

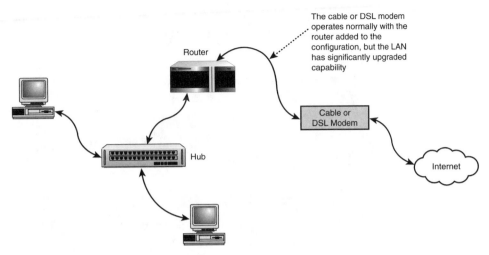

The cable or DSL modem operates normally with the router added to the configuration, but the LAN has significantly upgraded capability

Figure 16.2: *Using a router with an external cable or DSL modem installation.*

Macsense xRouter Internet Sharing Hub

What you need to implement Figure 16.2 is a router with two Ethernet ports, one for the LAN and one for the modem. Even routers with one Ethernet port and one serial port can be expensive (between $500 and $1000), whereas routers with two Ethernet ports can be prohibitive for homes or very small offices. Even the smallest two-port Cisco routers cost $1000–2000, largely because the market those routers address is for routers delivering Ethernet-class performance, handling 10 or 100Mbps data rates.

You're not going to get that kind of performance over a cable or DSL Internet connection, so all that performance goes to waste and you pay for excess capability with most Ethernet routers. What you want is a router that can handle about 1–3Mbps of traffic, offers NAT and (perhaps) firewall services, and is much lower in cost.

A product meeting just that description is the xRouter (Model MIH-120), manufactured by Macsense Connectivity, Incorporated. Don't be misled by the company's Macintosh orientation; the xRouter works with PCs and Linux machines as well as Macs. Figure 16.3 shows what the xRouter looks like; the package includes a 10Base-T Ethernet port for connection to the external modem and a four-port 10Base-T hub for connection to your computers and LAN. Hardware installation requires only that you plug in two 10Base-T cables and power.

The xRouter includes the key basic features, NAT and DHCP, with a Web-based configuration interface letting you set all the router parameters. Indicator lights on the front (see the close-up photograph in Figure 16.4)

give you visibility into link status and activity on the wide area and local area network ports, and show when collisions are occurring in the built-in hub.

Figure 16.3: Macsense xRouter.

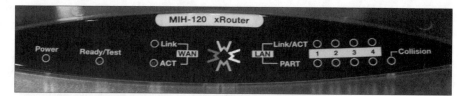

Figure 16.4: xRouter activity and status indicators.

The xRouter supports configuration through a Web browser, much as you saw in Chapter 14 with the 3Com LAN Modems. In most cases, you can complete basic xRouter configuration from a single screen. After you hook up the xRouter hardware (and check that your PC is configured to get a TCP/IP address automatically using DHCP), you simply direct your Web browser at the xRouter's default address, http://192.168.1.1. When you do, you'll see the Web page shown in Figure 16.5. The Private IP Address defines the addresses used on the LAN through the four port hub, whereas the Public IP Address defines the address used by the xRouter for communication with the Internet. If your cable or DSL modem supports DHCP, you can let the xRouter get its Internet address automatically, in which case no configuration might be necessary. If your modem requires you to assign a specific address to the computer it's connected to, change the setting to Specify an IP Address and fill in the usual parameters (address, netmask, gateway address, and DNS address).

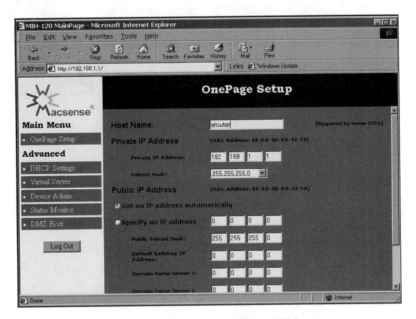

Figure 16.5: *xRouter basic configuration Web page.*

As soon as we configured the xRouter for the Internet address our setup required, we were immediately able to access the Web from the same computer we'd used for configuration. Figure 16.6 shows the results—access to the Intel Web site—along with the display from the Windows 98 `winipcfg` program showing that the computer has been assigned TCP/IP address 192.168.1.100.

Even though the xRouter provides only two Ethernet ports, so you can't create an electrical partition of your network into a demilitarized zone (DMZ) and a secure LAN, software capabilities in the router come close. Using what Macsense terms the Virtual Server capability, you can instruct the xRouter to transfer incoming connection request messages accessing specific TCP/IP ports to a specific computer on the secure LAN (see Figure 16.7). The remaining computers remain protected by the NAT service.

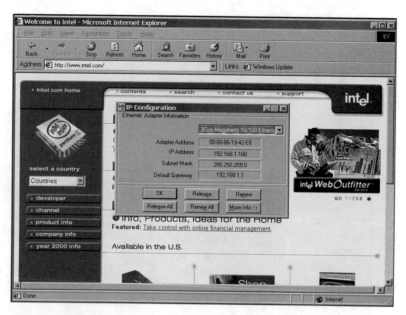

Figure 16.6: Web access through the xRouter.

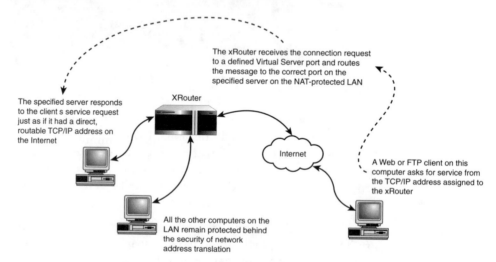

Figure 16.7: xRouter Virtual Server operation.

Figure 16.8 shows the Web page you use to configure virtual servers. You can identify different computers on your LAN to deliver individual services; in Figure 16.8, we've configured the xRouter to send incoming FTP requests to the computer at 192.168.1.100.

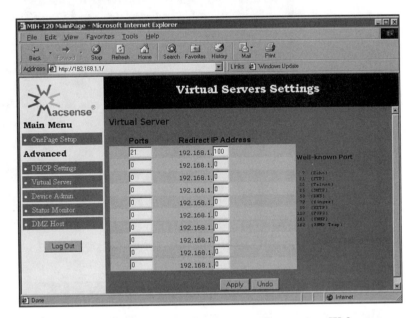

Figure 16.8: *xRouter virtual server configuration Web page.*

Rather than configure services individually, you can designate one computer as the target for all incoming Internet requests (this makes that computer the demilitarized zone in xRouter terminology; we prefer to use the term for a separate LAN segment). Figure 16.9 shows how you configure that capability; all that's required is that you identify the target computer and apply the setting.

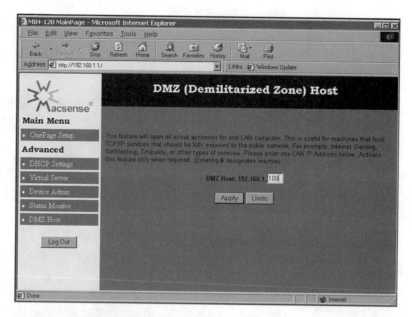

Figure 16.9: xRouter demilitarized zone host configuration Web page.

Switches

Most network switches, and all low-priced units, operate at layer 2 in the network protocol stack, meaning that the switch hardware examines the hardware Ethernet addresses in each packet to decide how to handle incoming messages. Example 16.1 describes what happens to a message passing through a layer 2 switch.

EXAMPLE

Example 16.1 Message Processing in a Layer 2 Network Switch

The processing in a switch is more complicated than simply handing off a packet from one switch port to another because before the switch can operate, it needs to know where each computer on the LAN is:

1. Computer A decides to send a message to computer B, and builds a packet with the Ethernet source address set to computer A and the Ethernet destination address set to computer B. Computer A then sends the packet out on the Ethernet.

2. The packet arrives at the incoming switch port, which logs the source Ethernet address as one accessible from that port. That information allows the switch to determine the output port for any messages addressed to computer A.

3. The switch searches its output ports to identify which port connects to computer B and outputs the message on that port. No activity occurs on the other output ports.

4. Computer B receives the packet, recognizes its Ethernet address in the destination address field, and accepts the message.

The key aspect of Example 16.1 is that all the processing occurs based on the hardware Ethernet addresses—layer 2 in the protocol stack. The switch works no matter what protocol is riding on the Ethernet packet. Broadcast messages are an exception to the processing in Example 16.1 and are output on all ports of the switch.

A layer 3 switch also looks at the source and destination addresses in the packet, but instead of interpreting the hardware Ethernet addresses, it looks at the source and destination addresses in the layer 3 protocol. Being able to do that requires the switch to know the design of the layer 3 protocols; most layer 3 switches are designed to process at least the TCP/IP and IPX/SPX protocols.

Ignoring broadcast messages for the moment, the Ethernet and TCP/IP addresses in packets going through a switch always match. Unless someone is changing TCP/IP addresses on the computers, a computer at a specific Ethernet address will always have the same TCP/IP address and vice versa.

Don't conclude, though, that a layer 3 switch has no more power than a layer 2 switch. Routers operate at layer 3 too, so the differences between Ethernet layer 2 switches and routers are the same as the differences between layer 2 and layer 3 switches. Viewed from that perspective, the key difference is that all the connections into an Ethernet switch are part of the same LAN segment, whereas connections into a router or layer 3 switch are different LAN segments with different TCP/IP subnet addresses.

Most routers require unique TCP/IP subnet addresses for each physical port, corresponding to a single LAN segment, and do not forward broadcast messages from one LAN segment to another. Many layer 3 switches enhance the router functionality to allow a LAN segment—a subnet—to be extended over several physical ports, forming what's commonly called a *virtual LAN* or *VLAN*. VLANs simplify the problem of readdressing computers when you move them from one LAN segment to another and aren't using DHCP, but (because they have to propagate broadcasts to all ports participating in the virtual LAN) they can create higher network traffic loads than do routers.

Intel InBusiness 8-Port 10/100 Switch

If you're running a relatively small network, you're likely to only need the capabilities of a layer 2 switch. The Intel InBusiness 8-Port 10/100 Switch is representative of many small, inexpensive layer 2 switches (see Figure 16.10). The device, except for the product name on the front, looks and connects the same as the Intel InBusiness 8-Port 10/100 Fast Hub (refer to Figure 15.1); indeed, you could remove a Fast Hub from your network and replace it with the switch and notice nothing but improved performance. There's no configuration to do.

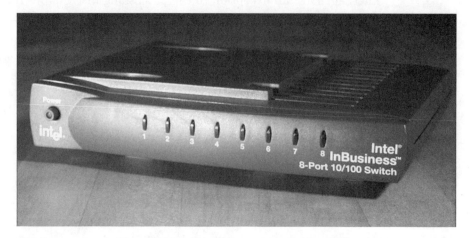

Figure 16.10: *Intel InBusiness 8-Port 10/100 Switch.*

Servers

As your LAN becomes more critical to what you do, you'll start to realize that having a server go down can be a real problem, and that having a slow server can slow down everyone on your LAN.

Your file server is likely your focus when you think about server reliability and performance, but Web and FTP servers can be performance bottlenecks, too. You can use a desktop-class computer as a server and do well, but if you decide to upgrade from a desktop computer there are several goals you might set:

- **Performance.** Network data rate, amount of installed memory, disk speed, and processor clock rate all affect the performance a server can deliver. You learned in the previous chapter that you have to do experiments and measurements to understand what factors limit performance. Random upgrades might work, but they might not.

- **Reliability.** People build PCs that are more reliable than the usual desktop computers. The three most common hardware failures are power supplies, disk drives, and memory; server computers built for reliability incorporate redundant power supplies and disk drives that can survive failures and use error correcting memory that can compensate for the most common memory errors.

- **Simple Setup and Administration.** Not everyone has highly skilled people available to set up and maintain computers, and many people simply don't want to invest any time in maintaining computers; they just want them to do their jobs. If that describes you, you might care most that the server be simple to deal with.

You can realize any or all of these goals in a server from any of several manufacturers, and you can achieve both performance and reliability in a computer you'd build yourself. (We ruled out simple setup and administration in computers you build yourself because knowing how to build a server implies you have very skilled people at hand with the time to invest!) The next two sections describe two servers from excellent companies. The Compaq server comes at a lower cost than many other servers, and stresses simplicity with good performance in its product characteristics. The Network Appliance server (and the larger versions in the same product line) stresses very high performance and reliability, but can have a price tag in the tens of thousands of dollars.

Compaq Internet Plus NeoServer 150

The Compaq Internet Plus NeoServer 150 packages many features used in small businesses—file sharing, automatic backup, local email, and a built-in hub—with Internet features including connectivity for a cable or DSL modem, shared Internet access, built-in preconfigured firewall, Internet email, and simple construction of stores for Internet electronic commerce. The computer comes as a sealed unit (you void the warranty if you open it) and runs a version of UNIX rather than Windows; you won't be loading and running applications on the system.

In return for limited expandability and fixed (but extensive) functionality, you get simple solutions to key server requirements:

- **File server.** The preconfigured setup of the server includes Windows-compatible file sharing for up to 100 users, including support for both a public file area and individual private file areas. The basic system configuration includes a 13GB disk drive, with support for an upgrade of another 13GB drive.

- **Automatic high-speed backup.** Backup is essential to protecting your data, but it's one of those things people ignore. Compaq has taken in interesting approach to backup in the NeoServer 150, using removable hard disk drives as backup storage. Because the removable disk is as fast as the online hard drive, backups are very fast. Software in the server is preconfigured to do backups once a week, but the setup is controllable through the user interface. You can get additional removable drives, letting you create a rotation so backed-up data remains available for some time.

- **Shared, secure, cached Internet access.** In addition to the shared Internet access, NAT, and firewall services common to a variety of software, the server comes configured with Web access caching software that stores copies of pages accessed by users. The cache software then makes commonly accessed pages available from the local copy, speeding access and reducing the load on the Internet connection.

You do give up more than some expansion capability and the ability to load your own applications; the NeoServer 150 does not incorporate redundant power supplies, processors, or disks and does not use error correcting memory. Because of that, most any hardware failure will make the server inoperative until repairs are finished. Compaq does simplify warranty or service plan repairs because no customer hardware modifications are possible; they simply ship a replacement computer. Customers keep their removable hard drive and insert it into the replacement computer.

Network Appliance NetApp Filers

Many companies—even very small ones—are completely dependent on their computers and networks for operation, and it doesn't take very many lost hours or lost orders to make a few thousand dollars saved on an inexpensive server a bad choice. If you're buying a server for a company like that, you should think about servers with redundant hardware. One such server is the Network Appliance NetApp F720 Filer, the low-end model of the F700 series (see Figure 16.11).

Hardware features in the F720 include the following:

- **RAID disk array.** RAID (Redundant Array of Inexpensive Disks) is a set of technologies using standard, widely available, high-performance disk drives in a way that preserves your data even if a disk drive fails. The most common RAID implementation for reliable operations is RAID 5, which spreads your data plus an error correction code across many drives. The error correction and user data are arranged across the drive array such that if any one drive fails the missing data can be reconstructed from the remaining information.

- **Redundant components.** Added hardware in the F720 compensates for failures until you can make repairs. Field operation data shows the F700 the servers have achieved very high reliability.

- **Hot swappable disks.** You can replace a failed disk in the F720 while the server runs, without turning off the server or suspending user access. When you do, the RAID array automatically starts reconstructing and writing the data belonging on the new disk.

Figure 16.11: *Network Appliance NetApp F720 Filer.*

The F720 is specifically designed to be a file server. It doesn't do anything else, but because it's tuned for that one job, it's much faster than comparable servers. We've seen significant performance gains replacing conventional file servers with Network Appliance servers at Internet service providers and in file-intensive software development environments.

Like the Compaq NeoServer 150, the F720 doesn't run Windows; it runs a unique operating system written by Network Appliance specifically for file servers. The server is more configurable and expandable than the Compaq, so the operating system configuration isn't preset and fixed as in the Compaq. That means you need to know somewhat more to operate the server, but because all the computer does is file serving, there aren't many commands to learn.

Uninterruptible Power Supplies

The most reliable computer in the world doesn't do much work when the power coming to it fails, something that seemingly happens with depressing regularity when you're trying to get work done. You can fix this problem using uninterruptible power supplies (UPS), devices that use batteries to provide backup power to bridge short failures and let you shut down your computers safely during longer ones.

Figure 16.12 shows how a UPS works. When the incoming utility power is normal, a switch in the UPS lets the power go directly to the computers, saving wear on the battery charger, battery, and power converter. If the utility power drops out or gets too high or low, the switch turns on the power converter and draws from the battery. That process continues either until normal power is restored, after which the battery charger starts recharging the battery, or until the battery runs out of power, in which case any computers still running shut down abruptly. All good UPS equipment includes a connection from the UPS to your computers and software that can shut down the computers automatically before power is exhausted.

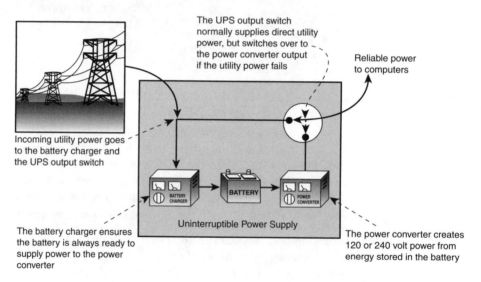

The UPS output switch normally supplies direct utility power, but switches over to the power converter output if the utility power fails

Reliable power to computers

Incoming utility power goes to the battery charger and the UPS output switch

BATTERY CHARGER

BATTERY

POWER CONVERTER

Uninterruptible Power Supply

The battery charger ensures the battery is always ready to supply power to the power converter

The power converter creates 120 or 240 volt power from energy stored in the battery

Figure 16.12: *UPS operation.*

Uninterruptible power supplies have two key characteristics: the amount of power they can supply (and for how long) and the quality of their design and construction. Don't take the quality issue lightly; we know of units that have literally burst into flames. We use uninterruptible power supplies from Belkin and American Power Conversion (APC) and have found them both to work well.

The first specification to check when you go to buy a UPS is the total power consumed by the equipment the UPS will serve. Power consumption is usually stated in watts for electronic equipment and generally indicated on a label outside the equipment. Add the wattage for each unit together to get a total; your UPS must be able to supply at least that much power, more if you want to add other equipment later. You shouldn't run a laser printer off a UPS because of its high power consumption; it's far cheaper to simply redo an interrupted print job than to protect the laser printer.

Picking a UPS is a little less direct than picking one that can handle enough watts, though, because UPS power handling capacity is stated in VA (volt-ampere) units, not watts. You can compute power in VA from power in watts by multiplying by 1.4—for example, a 100-watt unit consumes 140 VA.

After you figure out the minimum size UPS you need, you then pick a unit based on how long you want it to stay running after the power goes down. An APC SmartUPS 1400 UPS we use, for example, can support loads up to 1000 watts. The equipment we have connected to it loads it at 70%, or 700 watts, and under that load the UPS can maintain power for 13 minutes before exhausting the battery. A smaller load would extend the run time, whereas a larger load (staying under 1000 watts) would shorten it. Different capacity units also have different run times. For example, another UPS we use, an APC SmartUPS 700 (500 watt capacity) runs at 59% load (296 watts) and can keep its computers running for 14 minutes. When you go to buy a UPS, check the manufacturer's specifications for both capacity and run time.

Belkin Uninterruptible Power Supplies

The Belkin Regulator Pro Gold series of uninterruptible power supplies provides complete power protection for a desktop computer (see Figure 16.13). In addition to outlets on the top of the unit providing UPS protection for your computer and monitor, a second set of outlets on the top provide surge protected power for your printer, scanner, and other nonessential peripheral equipment. Surge-protected RJ-45 jacks can guard either your telephone line or 10Base-T network (the telephone line is probably more vulnerable), whereas a Universal Serial Bus (USB) connection keeps the UPS monitoring software up to date on the status of the unit and the incoming utility power.

The UPS shown in Figure 16.13 comes in three models, with capacity and run times as shown in Table 16.1. Belkin suggests that the 350VA unit has enough capacity to run a Pentium or Celeron desktop computer with a small (15-inch) monitor. The 500VA unit can run a Pentium or Celeron computer with a medium-sized (17-inch) or larger monitor, or a Pentium II or

III computer with a small monitor. The 650VA UPS can run a Pentium II or Pentium III computer with a 17-inch or larger monitor. (In practice, these estimates are conservative; you'll get a much more accurate picture of what you need by adding up the actual power consumption specifications for your equipment.)

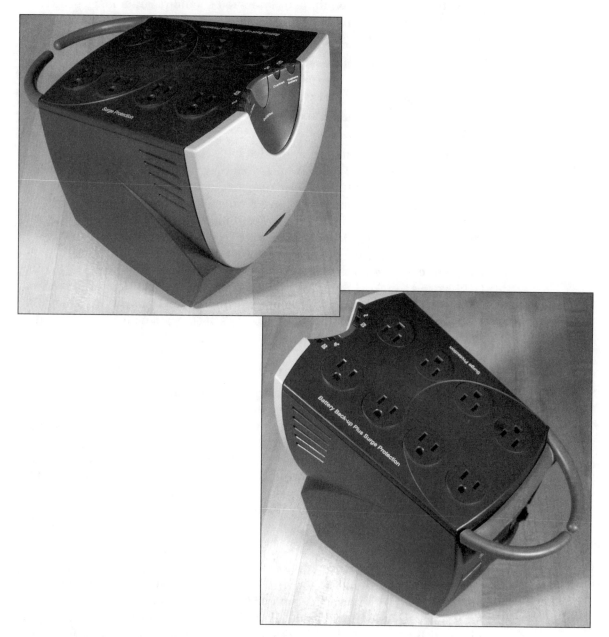

Figure 16.13: Belkin Regulator Pro Gold UPS.

Table 16.1: Belkin Regulator Pro Gold UPS Models and Capabilities

UPS Model	Capacity (VA)	Capacity (watts)	Run Time (min)
350VA	350	250	20
500VA	500	357	30
650VA	650	464	45

Don't forget your communications and network equipment—servers, modem, hub, switch, or router—when you're computing your power requirements, because you'll need all that equipment to work, not just your desktop computer. Depending on distances, you might want to split the load among multiple smaller UPSs rather than one enormous unit.

Summary

You've learned in this chapter that there's more to network equipment than stringing together cables and boxes; you can pick equipment that safeguards your work and keeps you working. You're going to have to think about the cost of having your network down and of losing work you've been doing to decide if the added protection is worth what it will cost. That can be hard to think through, but we promise it will become easier to understand the first time a server fails or the power goes out.

What's Next

The last chapter in this book covers what, to many, is the most unpleasant part of owning computers or networks: what to do when things stop working. You'll learn how to observe symptoms carefully, how to decide what to test, and how to make repairs.

## 17

Troubleshooting Network Problems

In this chapter you will learn

- How to approach analysis, diagnosis, and repair of a failed network
- What tools can help you when the network is broken

Having a network means eventually you'll have network problems. Troubleshooting and repairing your network is perhaps the most difficult topic in this book because being expert at any form of computer-related troubleshooting and repair requires an understanding of the technology, intuition about where and what to test, and discipline to work carefully and methodically. This book is your starting point for understanding the technology, whereas experience will help build your intuition. Discipline you'll need to bring with you.

The steps you should follow for network diagnosis and repair are the same as what we recommend for computer diagnosis and repair:

1. **Observe.** Diving right in to make changes when something goes wrong is absolutely the wrong thing to do. Much as a detective gathers all the information possible from a crime scene before allowing any changes, you'll want to observe carefully and gather all the information you can.

2. **Hypothesize.** Try to construct a model in your head of what could be wrong that accounts for what you observed. The more information you have, the easier that model should be to build.

3. **Examine and test.** Even if you can think of only one possibility for what's wrong, there could be others you've missed. It's equally likely that you'll have no ideas or can think of several options. For all these situations, you'll want to examine the computers and network to look for additional evidence and test for failures. Much of what you'll learn in this chapter covers how to do that examination and testing. You'll often want to try to simplify the test environment as much as possible

to cut your way down to the actual problem. Simplification can involve keeping extraneous software from running, isolating the problem equipment from the rest of the network, or other changes.

4. **Repair and test.** Eventually you'll be able to isolate the failed component, be it hardware or software. After you do, you'll make repairs and test to make sure the fixes worked.

In all cases, good troubleshooting discipline requires that you proceed from step to step methodically, recording what you see and what you do so you'll have accurate information and the ability to reverse any changes you make. Keep in mind that because your network is composed of both computers and network equipment, you might have both computer and network troubleshooting to do; you can't expect network operations to work properly if the underlying computer hardware or software is broken.

You should look at two key things when troubleshooting the computers themselves:

- **File version conflicts.** It's an unfortunate fact that a lot of computer problems are caused by incompatible versions of software installed on a computer. Under Windows, for example, programs can install updated versions of shared Dynamic Link Library (DLL) files that cause other installed programs to fail. Under Linux, version upgrades or shared library updates can cause similar problems. Sorting out what versions of what files work with what installed programs can be a nightmare, so much so that we know of companies that absolutely refuse to install new software unless they can get documentation of all modified files and the versions of those files with which the program has been tested.

  Most people can't afford the time required for that degree of control. Because the problem of incompatible DLL files can happen if there is more than one copy of the file on the computer as well as if the one copy is updated, you have a way to check: Reboot the machine and immediately run the failing program. Irritating as it can be to be told mindlessly to reboot your computer when you're on the telephone with some company's technical support line, that's the reasoning behind the request.

  Another trick we've used often with good results is to reinstall Windows on top of itself. You don't lose any of your existing software installations doing that, but the reinstallation helps ensure that the Windows file versions and configuration settings are what Windows expects and not modified versions set up by some application.

- **Hardware failures.** Don't fall into the trap of believing that the power-on self tests your computers run actually detect anything but the most blatant problems. If you're going to do your own trouble-shooting, you should have industrial strength hardware diagnostic software in your tool kit. We recommend the AMIDiag software from American Megatrends; it's relatively easy to use and quite comprehensive.

Another source of difficult, erratic problems is severe noise or dropouts on the incoming utility power line. You might not see any effects in the overhead lighting or on other equipment from disruptions severe enough to disrupt your computers or network equipment. As a general practice, you should use good-quality surge protectors on everything in your network, including all powered devices attached to the computers. Keep in mind that surge protectors have no effect on power line dropouts, though; only an uninterruptible power supply will solve those problems.

Don't overlook user error as a source of problems, either. Not everyone understands computers well, much less networks, so the solution to the problem might be training and not repair.

Assuming you've ruled out basic computer failures and user confusion, network problems fall into one of three groups:

- **Physical problems.** Cables can fail from being kicked, pulled on, or chewed by rats. Hubs, switches, and routers can break. Depending on how the building is wired, power to network equipment can go down without disturbing the computers themselves.

- **Connectivity problems.** Even if all your hardware is working perfectly, you might have the network software configured wrong; the wrong protocols or the wrong settings can raise havoc on a network. Misconfiguration of switches or routers can prevent computers from talking to each other.

- **Application software problems.** You might not face a complete network failure; instead, only one or a few applications might not be working. Assuming the client and server computers can talk to each other using the right protocols, you're likely facing a misconfiguration or a version incompatibility in the client or server software.

An exhaustive list of all that can go wrong in each of these categories wouldn't fit in a book you could hold in your hand. Rather than attempt that in the following sections, we've covered some of the most common problems and diagnostic approaches you'll want to know.

Physical Problems

After they're working properly, and as long as they're left alone and safe from errant reconfiguration, networks are surprisingly reliable. Much of the reason for that is that network equipment itself is reliable because it's relatively low power (unlike PCs, which consume hundreds of watts) and has no moving parts (also unlike PCs, which contain disk drives, CD-ROMs, and floppy drives).

Nevertheless, network hardware can break. The most common failures are caused by mechanical damage to the cabling, so watch out for these problems:

- **Broken 10Base-2 (thinnet) parts.** Internal damage to tees and terminators is very common in 10Base-2 networks. The damage can be invisible and still disrupt network operation. For example, we once repaired a failing 10Base-2 network by replacing a tee in the middle of the cable run. Later examination showed the tee was damaged internally; conversation with the computer's user later revealed the cause had been nothing more severe than pushing the computer back into a wall. We've also been told about hidden internal damage to terminators being used to protect 10Base-2 cable connectors while pulling cable through walls. Using a terminator that way isn't a bad idea, but be sure to mark the terminator so you can easily recognize it, and keep it in your tool box for just the one purpose; don't use it in an operational network.

  Connectors and terminators for 10Base-2 networks are really very inexpensive, so much so that a friend of ours stuck with a 10Base-2 network regularly replaces all the hardware in the cable system once a year, throwing out the parts he removes. His approach is a little extreme, but it has helped him minimize network problems.

- **Improperly constructed 10Base-2 cabling.** 10Base-2 cabling is designed to have the tee connector attached directly to the back of the network interface card (NIC). Although many people insert a cable between the NIC and the tee, that's bad practice and will introduce noise and reflections into the network. Your network might still work if you make several such connections, but make enough of them and the error rates will go up and the network will stop working.

- **Cracked 10/100Base-T RJ-45 connectors and poorly made cables.** Kicking or pulling on patch cables between the wall and your computers is almost guaranteed to create network problems, either by cracking connectors, pulling apart connections, or damaging the wires themselves. Knocking cables around is almost unavoidable if they're exposed, so it's worth keeping cables out of the way and protected if you can. It's also easy to keep a spare RJ-45 patch cable in your tool kit to use as a test replacement for a questionable in-service cable.

- **Corrosion in extreme environments.** Most network installations are in office buildings or homes, which are relatively benign environments. Networks near the ocean or on boats are subject to salt fog and to corrosion, which can attack network connectors and cause unreliable operation.

The link lights on 10/100Base-T network cards, hubs, and switches are your first diagnostic tools because they'll highlight the connections that aren't electrically sound. Until you have all the link lights for connected equipment on steadily, your network will have problems.

10Base-2 networks are much harder to troubleshoot for electrical problems because there's nothing corresponding to link lights, and because a problem anywhere on the cable can take the entire network down. Example 17.1 shows you how to troubleshoot electrical connection problems in a 10Base-2 network.

EXAMPLE

Example 17.1   Troubleshooting Electrical Connection Problems in a 10Base-2 Network

The key idea you'll use in this example, constantly dividing the network in two until you've isolated the failure, exploits the fact that a 10Base-2 cable is a single segment with no branches. This only works if there are a number of computers on the LAN because there's no good way to test a LAN segment with only one attached computer. Follow these steps:

1. **Divide the network in half.** Pick a connection near the physical middle of the network, and open the connection. Attach a tee and terminator to the open end of the cable; attach a terminator to the open end of the existing tee connector. You now have two independent LAN segments.

2. **Test the two networks.** Try different network operations on the computers on each LAN segment. One segment should work, whereas one should still exhibit problems.

3. **Repeat from step 1 on the failing segment.** Keep dividing down the failing segment until it can't be any smaller (that is, until it has only two computers) and examine the remaining cable and connector hardware for damage, replacing questionable items. If necessary, replace it all.

With the exception of connectors on LAN cables, which you can generally repair by cutting off the damaged connector and attaching a new one, you fix broken LAN hardware by replacing it; there's nothing you can repair inside a hub, switch, or NIC.

Connectivity Problems

After you've verified that the physical LAN hardware is in good shape, you'll move on up the stack in the seven-layer model to check the LAN protocols for proper installation and setup. There are three common protocol-level problems you should know about:

- **Incompatible protocol sets.** This is going to sound obvious, but it happens enough that it's worth checking: You have to have the same protocol running on both sides of a network connection for things to work. If one computer has only NetBEUI, while the other has only TCP/IP, the two won't be able to communicate.

- **Conflicting IP addresses.** It's possible to assign the same TCP/IP address to two computers on the same LAN segment, or to assign the same subnet address to two LAN segments, especially if you're manually assigning static TCP/IP addresses. If that happens, one or both of the computers won't be able to work on the LAN. Windows will usually detect this problem and disable the conflicting computer, giving you a warning message so you'll know what happened.

- **Misconfigured routing tables.** Some routing setups require you to enter routing tables by hand (the gateway address for each computer is a small example of a routing table). Incorrect routing tables cause messages to be sent to the wrong place, disrupting connectivity.

You'll learn about some common network troubleshooting software later in this chapter; the *ping* and *traceroute* programs are invaluable in diagnosing connectivity problems in TCP/IP networks.

Application Problems

Moving up the seven-layer model again, applications can fail to work even if the underlying hardware and protocols are working perfectly. Common application problems include misconfigured server addresses in the client software, incorrect passwords, faulty security access settings, and incompatible software versions on the client or server. There's no easy way to root out application-level problems. After you've shown the hardware and protocols are working, you'll just have to slog through the application settings looking for trouble.

Network Test Software

The inexpensive approach to network diagnosis continues the approach of Example 17.1, using your computers themselves as diagnostic tools.

ping and traceroute

Every TCP/IP-based computer you'll find today provides two powerful programs to help you troubleshoot TCP/IP protocol problems: ping and traceroute. Both are command-line programs under Windows and Linux. The Windows version of traceroute is called *tracert*; Linux's traceroute is in the /usr/sbin directory, so you might have to run the command as /usr/sbin/traceroute to access the program.

ping and traceroute both use the Internet Control Message Protocol (ICMP). ping is the simpler of the two, sending a message to the destination computer and waiting for a response. If a response arrives, ping reports the time taken for the round trip. If no response arrives, ping reports the request timed out. A typical Windows ping report on a working network looks like the following listing:

```
D:\>ping callisto

Pinging callisto [155.155.37.21] with 32 bytes of data:

Reply from 155.155.37.21: bytes=32 time=16ms TTL=128
Reply from 155.155.37.21: bytes=32 time=16ms TTL=128
Reply from 155.155.37.21: bytes=32 time=16ms TTL=128
Reply from 155.155.37.21: bytes=32 time=16ms TTL=128

D:\>
```

A failed ping report would look like this:

```
D:\>ping callisto

Pinging callisto [155.155.37.21] with 32 bytes of data:

Request timed out.
Request timed out.
Request timed out.
Request timed out.

D:\>
```

There's a lot of information in these reports. The first line of output shows that the computer name (callisto in these listings) can be translated on the network into a TCP/IP address (155.155.37.21), and that the ping message will include 32 bytes of message data in addition to the headers. If name resolution weren't working, you could use the computer's TCP/IP address directly, like this:

```
D:\>ping 155.155.37.21

Pinging 155.155.37.21 with 32 bytes of data:

Reply from 155.155.37.21: bytes=32 time<10ms TTL=128
Reply from 155.155.37.21: bytes=32 time=16ms TTL=128
Reply from 155.155.37.21: bytes=32 time=16ms TTL=128
Reply from 155.155.37.21: bytes=32 time=16ms TTL=128

D:\>
```

The replies include the round-trip time (typically a few milliseconds at most on a LAN, more if you're routing through a modem) and a field called TTL. TTL (Time To Live) is a counter that's decremented by 1 every time a TCP/IP message transits a computer or router, so it's a measure of how many hops the message makes. If the counter reaches 0, the message is returned to the originating computer as undeliverable.

Suppose you sent out a ping message with a very small TTL—for example, 0. The very next computer in line after the originator would receive the message, see the TTL has expired, and return the message, allowing you to discover the computer that's the first hop along the path to the destination. If you then sent out a message with a TTL of 1, the message would transit the first computer and be returned by the second one, letting you discover its identity and round-trip ping time.

If you continue the process of sending messages with ever higher TTL settings until the message response finally comes back from the destination computer, you'll discover the complete path from sender to receiver, including the identity of every computer and router along the way. That's what the traceroute program does; here's a traceroute to the Intel Web site:

```
D:\>tracert www.intel.com

Tracing route to www.intel.com [192.102.198.160]
over a maximum of 30 hops:

  1     *        *        *      Request timed out.
  2    32 ms    46 ms    47 ms  pm-7.press.net [155.155.17.79]
  3    47 ms    31 ms    63 ms  platinum.press.net [155.155.17.1]
  4    62 ms    63 ms    62 ms  Serial3-1-0.GW1.LNV1.ALTER.NET [155.130.107.33]
  5    62 ms    47 ms    62 ms  124.ATM3-0.XR1.LNV3.ALTER.NET [135.39.167.101]
  6    62 ms    47 ms    63 ms  295.ATM3-0.TR1.LNV3.ALTER.NET [246.188.224.14]
```

```
 7    63 ms    62 ms    78 ms   113.ATM6-0.TR1.SEA1.ALTER.NET [246.188.138.9]
 8    78 ms    94 ms    78 ms   299.ATM6-0.XR1.SEA4.ALTER.NET [246.188.200.201]
 9    78 ms    78 ms   110 ms   193.ATM9-0-0.GW1.POR2.ALTER.NET [246.188.200.177]
10    62 ms    63 ms   109 ms   intel-or-gw.customer.ALTER.NET [157.130.177.218]
11   192.102.197.19  reports: Destination net unreachable.

Trace complete.

D:\>tracert www.microsoft.com
```

The traceroute listing decodes both names and TCP/IP address at each hop and provides three sample round-trip times. What's interesting in the listing is the content of line numbers 1 and 11. In line 1, the router between our LAN and the ISP doesn't respond to the traceroute messages sent by Windows (although it *does* respond to the ones sent by Linux traceroute!), so the round-trip times aren't available. In line 11, traceroute reports that the destination is unreachable. In the case of the listing, that's because Intel doesn't respond to ping or traceroute requests for security reasons; if it happened on your LAN, it would mean the routing between the sender and receiver was broken at that hop.

WhatsUp

Although the versions of ping and traceroute included in Windows and Linux are capable and free, they're not as capable as other tools you can get for LAN monitoring and diagnosis. One of our favorites is WhatsUp, a product of Ipswitch Incorporated. Using WhatsUp, you can both monitor the status of your network and troubleshoot problems using a convenient graphical interface.

Figure 17.1 shows the basics of WhatsUp operation. The window displays a map of a small LAN; onscreen color coding indicates status. Green items are responding normally; other colors shading toward red indicate increasing numbers of packets have been lost or application servers are down. You can send alerts to pagers or other devices to warn you of problems.

Figure 17.2 shows what's possible for large networks with the enhanced version, WhatsUp Gold. The map in Figure 17.2, using extensions of the tools in Figure 17.1, shows both server computers (such as San Francisco, Los Angeles, and Tokyo) and subnets (London). Annotations on the map can provide information to users; links on the map show the communication links being used to interconnect sites. You can build submaps corresponding to subnets, providing the detail you'd want when you're looking for more information on a problem.

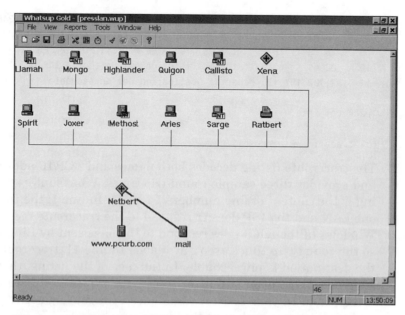

Figure 17.1: Simple WhatsUp LAN status map.

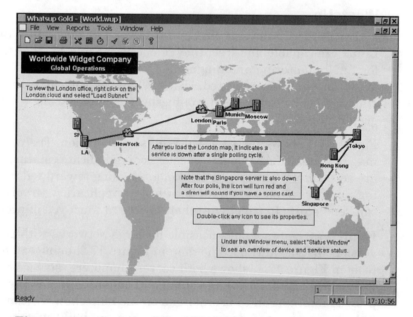

Figure 17.2: Complex WhatsUp Gold network status map with subnets and annotations.

In addition to map-based monitoring, WhatsUp includes an extensive set of analysis and troubleshooting tools in the Net Tools dialog box (access the dialog via the Tools, Net Tools command). The tabs shown in the Net Tools dialog box in Figure 17.3 illustrate the range of tools available; the window in the figure is the results of a ping to a host on the local network (you select the Ping tab, type in a host name or TCP/IP address, and then click Start to get the equivalent display). If you look carefully at the details of Figure 17.3, you'll see the ping tool gives you complete control over what protocol is used (ICMP, NetBEUI, or IPX) and the parameters of the ping packets. You'd use both ping and traceroute in the WhatsUp tool set much as you'd use the command-line tools provided with Windows and Linux; the only difference is that the WhatsUp versions are easier to use and more powerful.

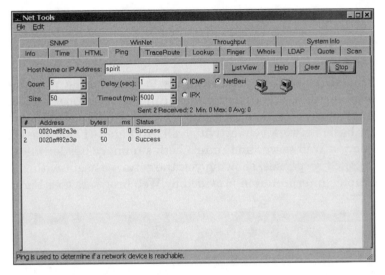

Figure 17.3: *WhatsUp ping tool.*

Figure 17.4 shows the throughput measurement tool in WhatsUp, an extension of what ping can do. The throughput tool measures the transfer rates possible between the computer running WhatsUp and a second computer you name by sending ever-larger packets and measuring the round-trip time. You can see from the results in Figure 17.4 that large packets generally result in greater performance on LANs, although that's not necessarily true on the Internet. By measuring the performance possible under known conditions when the LAN is working properly, you can both discover the performance capabilities of your equipment and establish a baseline for future testing. If you later discover significantly reduced throughput, you'll know to investigate to see what's changed or what isn't working properly.

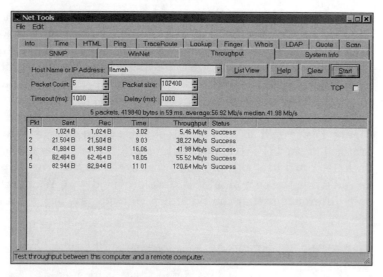

Figure 17.4: *WhatsUp throughput tool.*

WhatsUp also gives you the ability to examine the operation of application-level services. The basic map tool can check the operation of services including Web servers, domain name servers, or FTP servers as well as checking for basic network connectivity (refer to Figure 17.1). The HTML tool can query a Web server and return both summary header information and more detailed responses, showing you the return as sent without the additional graphic interpretation provided by Web browsers (see Figure 17.5).

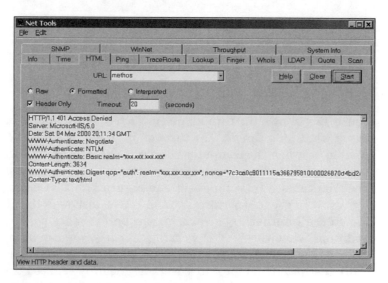

Figure 17.5: *WhatsUp HTML tool.*

Network Test Equipment

If your network grows to include a lot of computers, you're likely to find more and more of your time going to work on the network. If you're going to control your time investment, you need more powerful tools that can look more deeply into what's going on in the network.

Fluke OneTouch Series II Network Assistant

Looking more deeply into the network requires that you be able to see both faulty and correct transmissions on the wire. PCs are built to ignore faulty transmissions; what you'll need is a dedicated LAN analysis and test instrument such as the Fluke OneTouch Series II Network Assistant shown in Figure 17.6. The OneTouch implements a variety of tests and measurements on your 10/100Base-T LAN, all controlled from the touch-sensitive display.

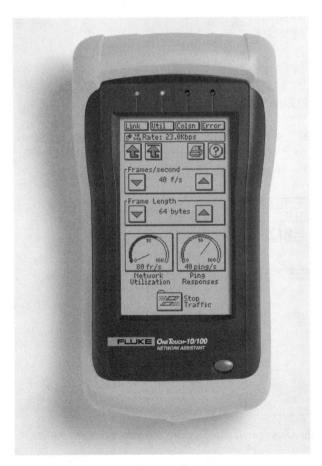

Figure 17.6: *Fluke OneTouch Series II Network Assistant.*

Figure 17.7 shows the NIC test display from the OneTouch. All that's required is to cable the tester directly to the NIC and start the test running. The display in Figure 17.7 shows that the NIC was running at 100Mbps, was capable of operation at either 10 or 100Mbps, was producing normal voltage levels as received by the tester, and (based on having decoded the NIC hardware Ethernet address) was manufactured by Cisco.

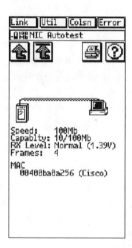

Figure 17.7: OneTouch NIC test.

The OneTouch can test your 10/100Base-T cables; measure cable length on open cable; and identify split pairs, opens, and shorts. (Figure 17.8 shows the result of a cable length test.)

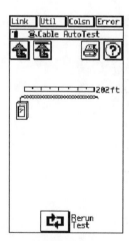

Figure 17.8: OneTouch open cable length measurement.

You can test a hub port with the OneTouch, analyzing the receive voltage level, signal polarity, receive signal pair, data rates supported by the hub port, and whether the port supports full-duplex operation. Figure 17.9 shows a hub connectivity test carried out by the OneTouch, indicating that one workstation was found to be accessible from the hub port connected to the OneTouch.

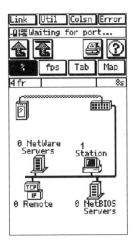

Figure 17.9: *OneTouch hub port connectivity test.*

Above the level of testing individual NICs, cables, and ports, the OneTouch can give you insight into the overall operational health of your LAN. Figure 17.10 shows the Network Health test display, on which the key indicators monitor LAN utilization, percent of packets with errors, and percent of packets subject to collisions. You can also see indicators for the percent of traffic using the IPX protocol, the number of network addresses detected, and the percent of packets using broadcast addresses. You want to watch for unusually heavy broadcast traffic loads because network performance can be degraded by "broadcast storms" resulting from computers or printers advertising their presence or searching for services.

Poor LAN performance is often caused by having more traffic than you expect or than your network can handle. If the utilization on your network, shown by the Network Health display, is too high, you can use the Top Senders analysis to find out the source of the traffic. In Figure 17.11, for example, over half the traffic is from a single computer using the IPX protocol.

Figure 17.10: OneTouch Network Health display.

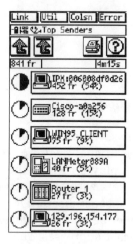

Figure 17.11: OneTouch Top Senders display.

Fluke Enterprise LANMeter

If you've used switches to boost performance on your LAN, you'll find the ability of the switch to route packets to just the intended destination limits the help most instruments can give you. Tools such as the Fluke Enterprise LANMeter solve that problem by including tests designed to discover the devices and services connected to each switch port (see Figure 17.12).

Figure 17.13 shows a typical switch performance display, in which the LANMeter has interrogated a 3Com LinkSwitch 1000 for its operating statistics.

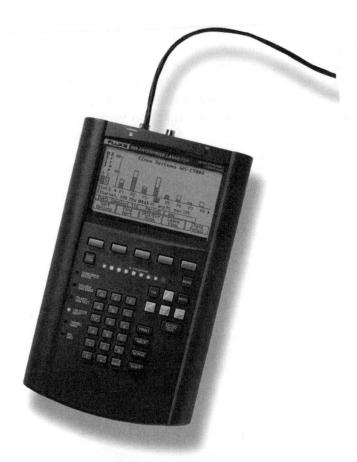

Figure 17.12: *Fluke Enterprise LANMeter.*

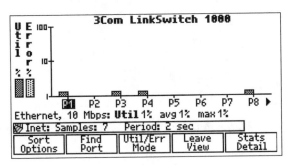

Figure 17.13: *LANMeter switch statistics display.*

Although the LANMeter's key capability is operation in a switched network, it offers convenience features too, including remote access to trigger tests and view displays via a Web browser. Figure 17.14 shows a display with information similar to that of the OneTouch Network Health display; Figure 17.15 shows the equivalent display through a Web browser, making the display accessible from anywhere on your net.

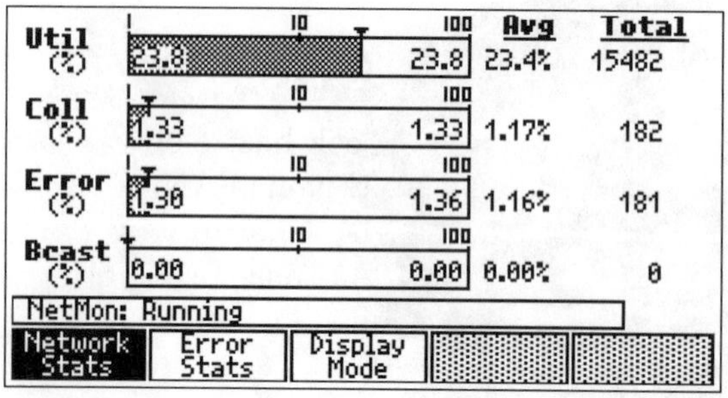

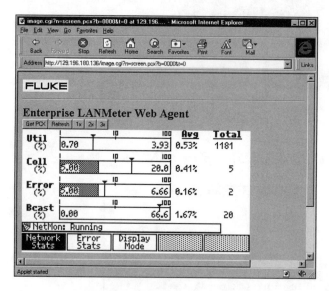

Figure 17.14: LANMeter network health display.

Figure 17.15: LANMeter network health display via Web browser.

Summary

You've seen in this chapter that troubleshooting your network requires a combination of knowledge, observation, discipline, and tools. You've learned techniques to help isolate and diagnose failures, what tools such as ping and traceroute can do for you, and what capabilities are available from instruments dedicated to networks.

What's Next

Now that you've learned what this book has to offer, your best teacher will be experience using and working with your LAN. Watch not only what works and what doesn't work, but also what in your work is clumsy, time consuming, or difficult. When you find those problems, think about them to see if your LAN can come to your aid.

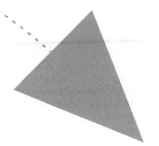

Index